The Pr[illegible]

Received on January 20th 2021

from a dear friend

Myra Holland

2021

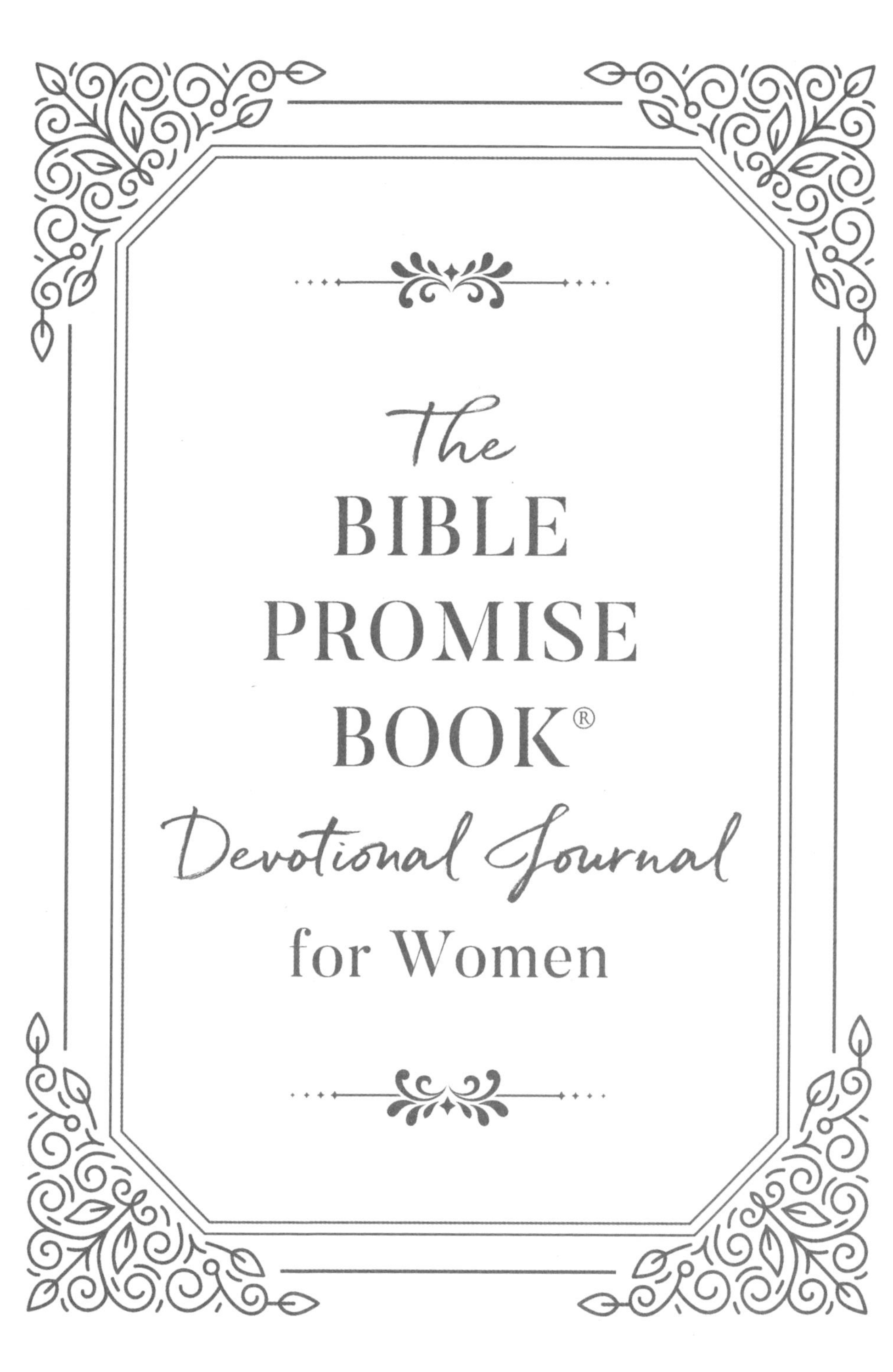

The BIBLE PROMISE BOOK® Devotional Journal for Women

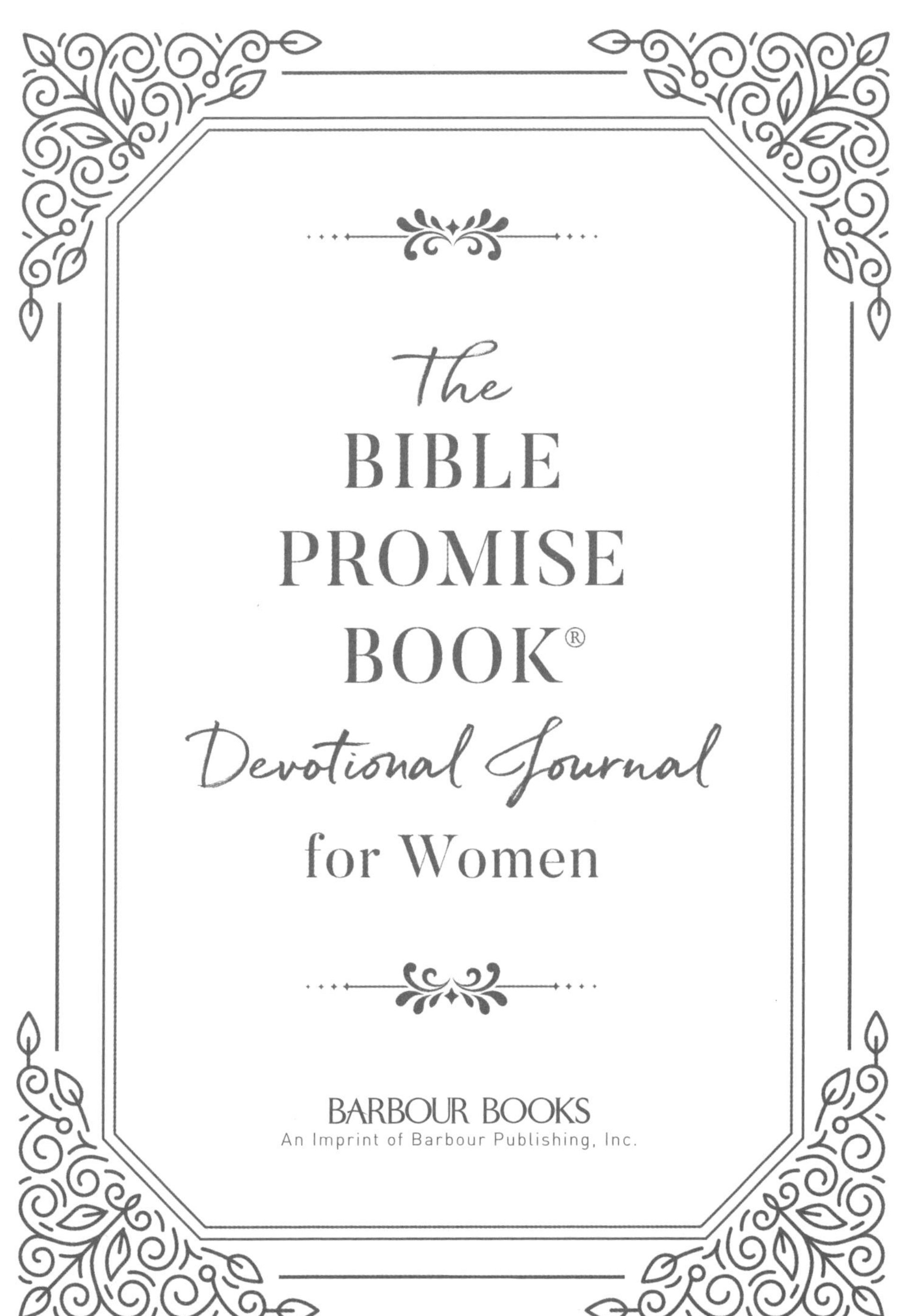

The BIBLE PROMISE BOOK®
Devotional Journal for Women

BARBOUR BOOKS
An Imprint of Barbour Publishing, Inc.

ISBN 978-1-64352-110-7

Prayers written by Marian Leslie.
Editorial assistance by Ed Strauss.

Published by Barbour Books, an imprint of Barbour Publishing, Inc., 1810 Barbour Drive, Uhrichsville, Ohio 44683, www.barbourbooks.com

Our mission is to inspire the world with the life-changing message of the Bible.

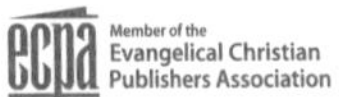

Printed in China.

Introduction

For more than three decades, *The Bible Promise Book* has blessed millions of lives by providing scriptural wisdom and encouragement for dozens of key life topics. This fantastic daily devotional is inspired by this bestselling book and is a rich source of assurance to ground you deeply in God's Word so that you won't be shaken by life's many troubles and storms.

How powerful are God's promises? He told the Israelites, "Set your hearts on all the words which I testify among you today. . . . For it is not a futile thing for you, because it is your life" (Deuteronomy 32:46–47 NKJV). Jesus said, "The words I have spoken to you—they are full of the Spirit and life" (John 6:63 NIV).

The verses in this book can unleash the grace and power of God's Spirit in your daily walk, and with great authority declare your new identity in Christ. You may be pressed and distracted by the troubles of life, constantly reminded of your sins and failures, but never forget—you are a daughter of God, washed and forgiven by the blood of Jesus Christ. So He's not giving up on you, no matter how often you fail or how discouraged you become with yourself.

Are you looking for guidance about a specific situation or topic? Check the table of contents for a breakdown of weekly themes. Or you may choose to start at the beginning and read all fifty-two weeks in order. Either way, you will be blessed by new insights into 365 of God's promises to His children.

May this devotional journal help you be daily encouraged and transformed by God's Holy Spirit. Remember, "His compassions fail not. They are new every morning: great is thy faithfulness" (Lamentations 3:22–23 KJV).

The Editors

WEEKLY THEMES

Day 1

IMPERISHABLE ETERNAL LIFE

The wages of sin is death; but the gift of God is eternal life through Jesus Christ our Lord.

ROMANS 6:23 KJV

Heaven is a place of wonder, breathtaking beauty, and boundless joy that you will enjoy forever. It consists of ever-unfolding panoramas of delight and astonishing vistas where you will enjoy everlasting life, together with your loved ones, the saints of all ages, and God Himself.

You were spiritually dead and destined for hell, but God has given you eternal life through Jesus Christ. What's more, you don't need to maintain possession of this inheritance through your own efforts. Jesus said, "I give them eternal life, and they shall never perish; neither shall anyone snatch them out of My hand" (John 10:28 NKJV).

No worry or fear or sorrow will ever mar your everlasting sojourn in this heavenly country. No sickness or infirmity will cause you to sigh. All the sorrows and pain you've known will be gone. "You will surely forget your trouble, recalling it only as waters gone by" (Job 11:16 NIV).

Heaven is not some stuffy landscape where bored saints dressed in starchy white robes make a discordant noise on harps day in and day out. Heaven is fascinating, interesting, and exciting. It will be far more beautiful than you ever hoped it could be.

Heavenly Father, I cannot imagine the glory of the home You have prepared for me! I long for the day when I can see Your face. Amen.

Day 2

WE SHALL BE CHANGED

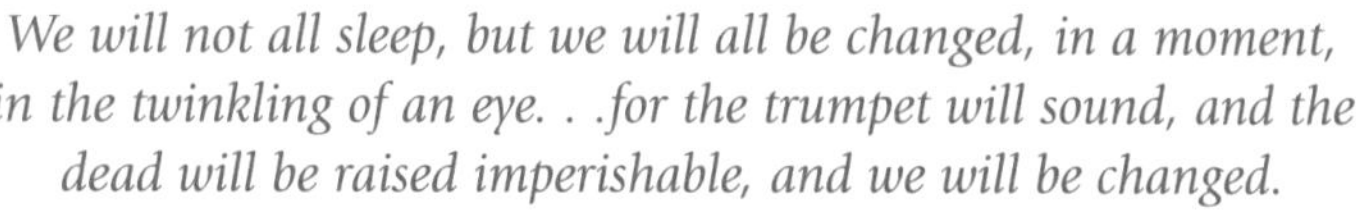

We will not all sleep, but we will all be changed, in a moment, in the twinkling of an eye. . .for the trumpet will sound, and the dead will be raised imperishable, and we will be changed.

1 Corinthians 15:51–52 NASB

When you pass from this life, your spirit is separated from your mortal body and goes into the presence of God. But you won't be a disembodied spirit for all eternity. When Jesus returns in the Rapture, if you're still living, your physical body will be instantly transformed.

If you're no longer alive on that day, your body—though it's scattered dust and ashes—will be resurrected and reunited with your spirit.

Your new body will be physical and solid. Though once weak and aging, it will be gloriously transformed and made eternally youthful. It will have powers that you never dreamed of. Your body is now perishable, but it will be raised imperishable; it's full of imperfections, but it will be raised in glory; it is weak, but it will be raised in power (see 1 Corinthians 15:42–44).

You can get along fine in heaven as just a spirit, but you will *need* an amazing new body to live on the wonderful new earth and all the many other worlds you will go to.

Lord, some days I wish I could be rid of this weary body of mine. Thank You for preparing a new one for me! Amen.

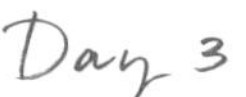

HOLY NEW JERUSALEM

And I John saw the holy city, new Jerusalem, coming down from God out of heaven, prepared as a bride adorned for her husband.

REVELATION 21:2 KJV

God said of the Old Testament saints, "But now they desire. . .a heavenly country. Therefore God. . .has prepared a city for them" (Hebrews 11:16 NKJV). And *what* a city! Just as a bride goes to great pains to make herself lovely, so God will spare no effort to make the new Jerusalem beautiful beyond compare.

The heavenly Jerusalem is an enormous city complex, fashioned out of unearthly, crystalline gold, vaster than any earthly city. The Bible states that it's over 1,400 miles high, wide, and long. This doesn't necessarily mean that it's a giant cube. Likely it's a towering, many-spired structure.

Believers have been desiring just such a fantastic city for thousands of years. It's therefore the true home of every longing soul, because "the Jerusalem above is free, which is the mother of us all" (Galatians 4:26 NKJV). Right now this amazing city is in the heavens, but in the future it will descend to Earth.

This city is where God dwells, where His throne is, and where millions of palaces, boulevards, and parks glow with the glory of the Almighty. It's a real place, and you'll be there soon.

Oh how beautiful Your works are, God! Help me to get ready to be a good citizen in Your heavenly city. Amen.

ETERNAL HEAVENLY DWELLINGS

"There is more than enough room in my Father's home. If this were not so, would I have told you that I am going to prepare a place for you? When everything is ready, I will come and get you, so that you will always be with me where I am."

JOHN 14:2–3 NLT

Jesus has gone ahead into the highest heavens, where He sits enthroned at the right hand of the Eternal Father, robed in splendor and magnificent light. He said that He wanted His disciples to be with Him where He was so that you could see Him in all the glory that His Father gave Him (see John 17:5, 24).

But Jesus' presence and light fill the *entire* city, not just the throne room (see Revelation 21:23). There are many places in this fabulous city where you can "always be with Him where He is." Jesus will also visit you in your heavenly palace—a spacious, mansion-like dwelling. He went ahead to personally prepare your eternal abode. Every detail of your reward will reveal His intricate care and love for you.

The Son of God wants you to always be with Him, forever. That's why He makes this beautiful promise: He's coming back to get you, to take you to His astonishing city, where you will dwell joyfully forevermore.

I love to bask in the rays of Your sun. But living in the light of Your glory will be a million times better. Come, Lord Jesus! Amen.

Day 5

TREASURE IN HEAVEN

Lay up for yourselves treasures in heaven,
where neither moth nor rust doth corrupt,
and where thieves do not break through nor steal.

MATTHEW 6:20 KJV

Jesus urged believers to diligently store up treasure in heaven, but many Christians don't take it literally. They think it's a metaphor for some transcendent reality. They envision heaven as an enormous cloud bank where believers perpetually drift around, strumming harps and singing hymns. They therefore think that the "treasure" Jesus was referring to must refer to abstract qualities like joy and peace.

But the truth is, God has promised you treasure in the afterlife. He said, "Behold, I come quickly; and my reward is with me, to give every man according as his work shall be" (Revelation 22:12 KJV). Consider the heavenly mansion you will live in, the crown you will wear, and the streets of gold you will walk on.

The Bible repeatedly tells you about heavenly rewards to motivate you to do good deeds, and whatever form these rewards take, they're well worth striving for.

You obey Jesus simply because it's the right thing to do, regardless of whether He ever rewards you. Just the privilege of living in the heavenly city would be enough. But be assured, it's God's good pleasure to bless you beyond measure.

Lord, do You ever stop thinking of good gifts to give us? Help me to remember I have treasure in heaven, waiting for me to claim it. Amen.

A CROWN OF RIGHTEOUSNESS

In the future there is laid up for me the crown of righteousness, which the Lord, the righteous Judge, will award to me on that day; and not only to me, but also to all who have loved His appearing.

2 Timothy 4:8 NASB

God has promised to abundantly reward those who love Him, who believe and follow Him. These heavenly rewards will take myriad forms, for God will delight in surprising you with His goodness for all eternity. "In Your presence is fullness of joy; at Your right hand are pleasures forevermore" (Psalm 16:11 NKJV).

One of these rewards is the crown of righteousness—also called the "crown of life." These crowns will be unique for each believer and will likely reflect your virtues and the righteous deeds you've done for the Lord—a permanent glorious declaration of your accomplishments.

Some people think it odd that believers in heaven will always wear a crown, but bear in mind that the Greek word doesn't refer to a heavyset European-type crown, but a light tiara. Since it will glow with radiant light, it's probably what many people refer to as a halo.

All you need to do is love and obey Jesus. He says, "Be faithful until death, and I will give you the crown of life" (Revelation 2:10 NKJV).

My King, I am so honored to be Your daughter. I cannot wait to live as a princess in Your beautiful kingdom. Amen!

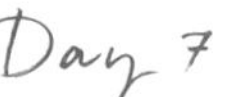

Day 7

EXALTED THRONES

"I grant you that you may eat and drink at My table in My kingdom, and you will sit on thrones judging the twelve tribes of Israel."
LUKE 22:29–30 NASB

God has promised that faithful believers will rule with Him in paradise, as well as reign over the nations of the earth. John promised that "they will be priests of God and of Christ and will reign with Him" (Revelation 20:6 NASB).

But bear in mind that not all believers will sit on thrones governing the nations—only the most faithful. When they stand before God, if they have rendered extraordinary service, He will say, "Well done, good and faithful servant; you were faithful over a few things, I will make you ruler over many things. Enter into the joy of your lord" (Matthew 25:21 NKJV).

Those who have served well will be set over cities; those who have given exemplary service will be made rulers of districts; those who have served most faithfully will rule over entire nations.

Are you serving Christ now so that He can trust you with great responsibility? You may be of little account, unrecognized by the powerful of this world, and passed over by the ambitious, but God knows the qualities that make a true ruler—humility, compassion, and integrity.

Servant King, help me to care for others with the gentleness, humility, and kindness that You had when You served so many here on earth. Amen.

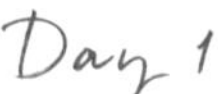

BEARING THE WEIGHT OF SIN

But he was pierced for our rebellion, crushed for our sins. He was beaten so we could be whole. He was whipped so we could be healed. All of us, like sheep, have strayed away. We have left God's paths to follow our own. Yet the Lord *laid on him the sins of us all.*

Isaiah 53:5–6 nlt

Sin, by its nature, is heavy. When your spouse or best friend betrays you, or when someone robs or assaults you, or when somebody lies to you and offends you, you feel the full weight of the other person's sin. It damages your trust, wounds your heart, and leaves lasting effects—sometimes even physically.

Imagine the weight Jesus felt when He was pierced for the sins of the world. He was beaten and whipped for every sin. God laid on Him the sins of the world, and yet He bore it willingly. You groan over the sins of one person because you feel its effects. Jesus spread His arms and endured crucifixion, even stopping to pray for His executioners because they were ignorant (see Luke 23:34).

How might visualizing the way Jesus mercifully handled your sin change your attitude about the reality and heaviness of your sin and the sin of others?

Lord Jesus, the thought of You bearing the crushing ache of my sin makes my eyes fill with tears. I'm so sorry You had to do that, Lord. Amen.

REMEMBER NO MORE

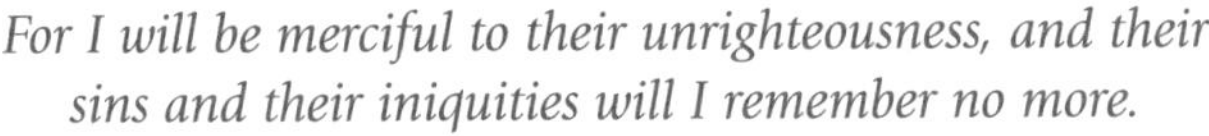

For I will be merciful to their unrighteousness, and their sins and their iniquities will I remember no more.

HEBREWS 8:12 KJV

Think about the last person who wronged you. Is that person's name firmly in your mind? Who did you talk to about the circumstances that led up to this offending party's infraction? Your best friend? A coworker? Your spouse? Whoever it was, how much time did you spend in that conversation going over every detail?

Was it worth it? No doubt, you probably felt better—at least temporarily. But did it bring you any closer to offering the offending party forgiveness? Or did it drive an even bigger wedge between you?

Praise God, He is merciful to your unrighteousness, and He even forgets your sins—even though He has every reason and every right to remember every single one. Yet, He doesn't hold your sins against you. Nor does He talk to others about them. Instead, His love covers a multitude of sins. As far as the east is from the west, so far has He removed your transgressions from you.

How can you do anything other than imitate His actions? Forgive the offender. Cast their sins so far from your mind that you're unable to retrieve them.

God, I want to learn to forgive like You do, with infinite patience and unfathomable love. Amen.

Day 3

CHRIST'S RIGHTEOUSNESS

Here is a trustworthy saying that deserves full acceptance: Christ Jesus came into the world to save sinners—of whom I am the worst.

1 Timothy 1:15 niv

A person who is trusting in his own righteousness seeks to be great in the kingdom of God. This is the very thing the disciples did in Matthew 18 when they approached Jesus to ask who was the greatest in the kingdom.

His answer? Only those who take the lowly position of a child. And whoever welcomes such a child in His name. For only children are completely dependent on their parents.

Paul had more reason than most to trust in his own righteousness. He spelled out his reasons in Philippians 3:4–6 (niv): "If someone else thinks they have reasons to put confidence in the flesh, I have more: circumcised on the eighth day, of the people of Israel, of the tribe of Benjamin, a Hebrew of Hebrews; in regard to the law, a Pharisee; as for zeal, persecuting the church; as for righteousness based on the law, faultless."

And yet, in today's verse, he referred to himself as the worst of sinners. He knew that his righteousness was only filthy rags. How about you? What are you trusting in? Nothing but Christ's righteousness will suffice.

Lord, help me to remember that I am nothing without You. Amen.

Day 4

FREED FROM SIN

Knowing this, that our old man is crucified with him, that the body of sin might be destroyed, that henceforth we should not serve sin. For he that is dead is freed from sin.

ROMANS 6:6–7 KJV

Your old sinful nature was crucified with Christ for two reasons, according to the apostle Paul in today's verses: so your body of sin (in its totality) might be destroyed, and so you would no longer serve your sinful desires.

You have power from on high living inside you that allows you to overcome the old man who is still exerting his influence. That's not to say you will never sin or that the old, sinful habits have no allure, but you no longer have to give in to them. Christ has freed you.

Practically speaking, how does your life look different since you've become a Christian? What sins that you engaged in before you were redeemed has Christ enabled you to overcome? Has He calmed your rage? Tamed your tongue? Stopped your gossip? However, what sins have you carried over to your new life in Christ? What has prevented you from obeying Christ, rather than the old man?

Take heart. If you belong to Christ, He is still working in you to destroy your sinful nature.

God, You know the sins that return to plague me again and again. Replace my sinful desires with Your goodness, Lord. Amen.

THE DELIVERER

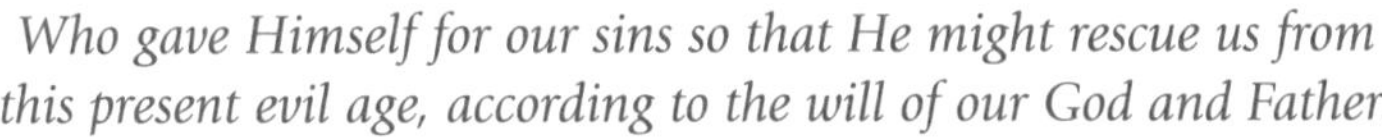

Who gave Himself for our sins so that He might rescue us from this present evil age, according to the will of our God and Father.

GALATIANS 1:4 NASB

When you attended a worship service last Sunday, did your mind drift at any point to what you were having for lunch or maybe what you had planned for later in the day? When you last attended a Bible study, did you glance at your watch more than once, wondering when it would be over because you had other things you needed to do?

If so, you aren't alone. The world pulls you away from Christ—even when you are in sanctuaries. The demands of this world and the lusts of your heart are strong, no doubt. But Christ came to rescue you from this present evil age, and He did so according to the will of God the Father.

"Jesus Christ has died to deliver us from this present evil world, not presently to remove his people out of it, but to rescue them from the power of it, to keep them from the evil of it, and in due time to possess them of another and better world." So writes Bible commentator Matthew Henry.

This is God's promise to you: He rescues and delivers.

God, so many things distract me from Your Word and Your will. Help me to focus on You alone. Amen.

WALK IN THE LIGHT

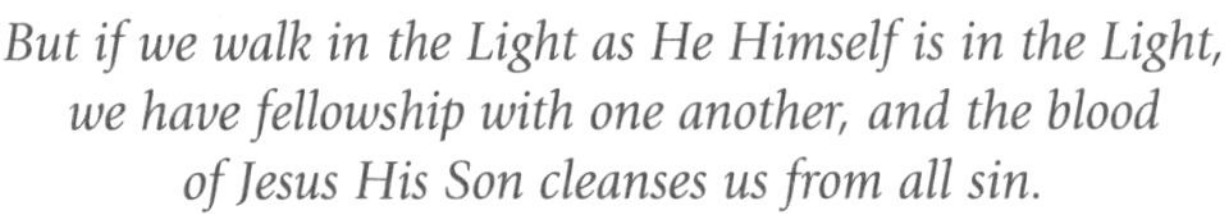

But if we walk in the Light as He Himself is in the Light, we have fellowship with one another, and the blood of Jesus His Son cleanses us from all sin.

1 John 1:7 NASB

When you're walking in darkness, it's easy to fall for Satan's lie that walking in the light isn't really possible. Nobody's perfect, right? How can engaging in sin really be harmful, given that everybody else is doing it?

The truth is, you *can* walk in the light, as long as you aren't trying to do it in your own strength. And you already know and feel the full effects of your sin, and the sin of those around you, so you know how harmful it is.

Today's verse gives you a hint of what walking in the light entails. When you're doing it, you're in fellowship with other believers. Fellowship involves much more than sitting next to another Christian on Sunday mornings. The Greek word for "fellowship" here means "partnership" and "participation."

Does this sort of spiritual intimacy describe your current relationships with other believers? If not, then step into the light. Join a Bible study. Volunteer for a church mission trip. Begin meeting with the men's or women's church group you've been avoiding.

Lord, please surround me with those good souls who will help me keep following Your light. Amen.

Day 7

REASONING WITH THE LORD

"Come now, let us settle the matter," says the LORD.
"Though your sins are like scarlet, they shall be as white as snow; though they are red as crimson, they shall be like wool."
ISAIAH 1:18 NIV

In the old covenant, God's people purposely separated themselves from Him—fearing the repercussions of their sin. They knew what happened to Nadab and Abihu when they were struck dead after offering unholy fire (see Leviticus 10), and what happened to Uzzah when he was struck dead after touching the ark of the covenant (see 2 Samuel 6).

While sin certainly has its repercussions, today's verse paints a picture of a merciful God—One who asks His people to come to Him so they can reason together regarding their sins. In a sense, He is calling them to a courtroom and asking them to confess their guilt. As long as they do so, He will pardon their sin and make them white as snow.

Have you been hiding from God, fearing how He will react to your sin? You know He can find you anywhere, but maybe you've concluded that if you give up the battle, He'll leave you alone. Today, this very moment, He calls to you and says, "Come now, let us reason together."

Lord, I confess my sins before You. I lay down my life and offer it to You. Renew my spirit, Lord. Amen.

Day 1

WHERE IT ALL BEGINS

Faith shows the reality of what we hope for;
it is the evidence of things we cannot see.

Hebrews 11:1 NLT

Faith is a term used by many, but is often misunderstood. *Faith* isn't a term applied to people who believe God has a *cool factor*. It doesn't apply to the personal motivation to pray to an undetermined deity. It's not wishfully thinking that everything will work out.

For the Christian, faith is a decision about whether you really believe God can do what He's promised. Faith is confidence in God's perfect plan. Faith is knowing that you need rescue and accepting it. Faith is believing God's truth even without proof. Faith is the assurance that God directs your everyday steps and has your best interests in mind.

Faith is more than a "God" acknowledgment in an acceptance speech. It's more than working hard for a spiritual cause. Faith is substantially more than you may give it credit for.

Over the next few days we'll learn that faith believes the impossible and then sees the impossible become possible. Faith leans into God's plan and is supported by God's hand. Faith introduces you to a forever friendship with the Father and delivers the benefits of a sold-out belief in a truth the world needs to discover.

God, help me to believe without seeing. I trust You, Lord.
Help me to keep trusting You every day. Amen.

STAND FIRM

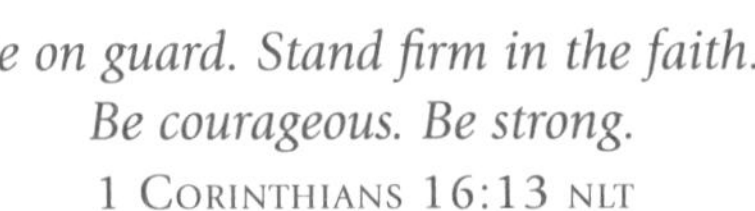

Be on guard. Stand firm in the faith.
Be courageous. Be strong.
1 Corinthians 16:13 nlt

For every decision you make there will be someone who questions your choice. A decision made by faith withstands these challenges. God knew your worst adversary would try to confuse you and make you think good decisions are bad and bad decisions are best.

The Bible says this adversary comes to "steal and kill and destroy" (John 10:10 nlt). No wonder you're told to "be on guard, be courageous, and be strong." You need all the encouragement you can get, because your adversary works overtime to move you from the narrow path God created to a road leading to destruction. He challenges your faith. He questions whether God can be trusted, if He really cares for you, or even whether God loves you at all.

Because faith is an absolute trust in the God of all gods, you can discover that entertaining the challenges of the adversary increases the chance that you will falter in your faith.

The armor of God is supplied to help you stand firm (see Ephesians 6:10–18). Each piece of armor is designed to help you remember who you are in Christ and then to remind your adversary that you never stand alone. Be courageous. Stand firm.

Lord Jesus, I know how important it is to be ready for spiritual battles.
Help me to be strong and firm and to stand for You. Amen.

HAVING GOD TRUST

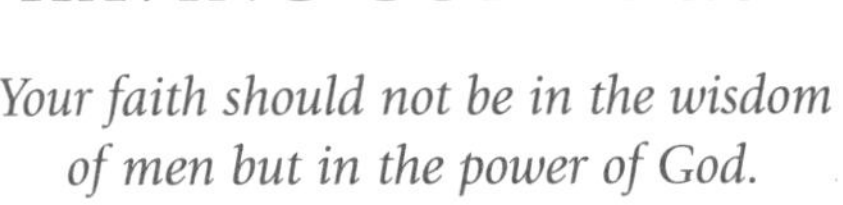

Your faith should not be in the wisdom of men but in the power of God.
1 CORINTHIANS 2:5 NKJV

Friends disappoint you. Coworkers say things that are untrue. Strangers gossip. Your sense of trust and self-worth are battered with each betrayal. Yet this shouldn't come as a surprise.

Think about it. You place your trust in people who sin (see Romans 3:23) and aren't even sure what they think about God (see Romans 1:25), and in your own deceitful heart (see Jeremiah 17:9). God calls you to love imperfect people, but your *faith* should be placed in the power of God. He doesn't disappoint, He speaks truth, and He never gossips.

The wisest of men can't measure up to the wisdom of God, but you may treat the opinion of other humans as more valuable than God's instructions for living. Faith is a trust that rests on the certainty that God is the same "yesterday, today, and forever" (Hebrews 13:8 NKJV).

You need friendship with others, so you shouldn't eliminate their companionship. However, there will be moments when someone lets you down, or you disappoint them. No human can save you, restore your past, or ensure your future. This is God's domain. This is God's promise. This is God's gift.

You should accept by faith what only *He* can provide.

God, sometimes I forget that humans will always let me down. Help me to remember that You never do. Amen.

A GIFT ONLY GOD COULD GIVE

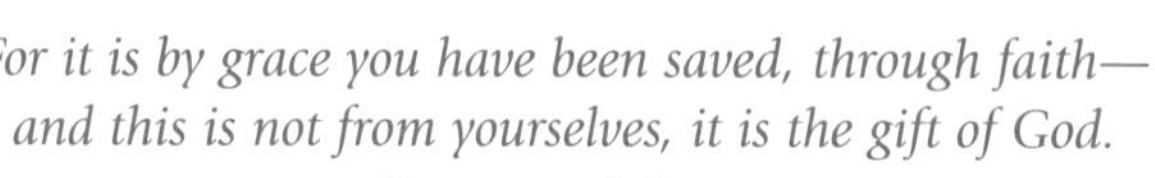
For it is by grace you have been saved, through faith—
and this is not from yourselves, it is the gift of God.

EPHESIANS 2:8 NIV

Consider a paraphrase of today's verse: "God offers to rescue you and make you part of His family. You have to believe you can't rescue yourself and need His help. When you act on that belief you receive a gift only God can give."

It may sound peculiar, but you have to have faith (believe) that you can't rescue yourself. You may agree that you need faith and need God, but you must be wholeheartedly convinced that on your own you can't do enough good, make up for bad decisions, or rely on your ability to make perfect decisions in the future. You will fail yourself, others, and God.

God's gift is important for two reasons. (1) It takes the pressure off because you accept the perfection of God's Son, Jesus, on your behalf and, (2) it ensures that if you accept His gift you're completely accepted by God.

If you believe you have the ability to live up to God's standard you also indicate that you don't believe you need to be rescued. Without rescue you can't be part of God's family.

God, my Rescuer, thank You for saving me.
I know I'd be lost without You, Lord. Amen.

THE FAITH SENSE

For we walk by faith, not by sight.
2 Corinthians 5:7 KJV

If you couldn't see, you'd use other senses to compensate. You'd feel for obstacles, listen for echoes, or smell for the familiar or dangerous. You learn to trust different senses when they're the only way to engage life.

Faith is the primary sense of your spiritual life, so when you come to new life in Christ your sight is less useful in determining where you go. But faith can be a difficult sense to understand.

You'll try to assign faith to secondary roles in your journey. You might attempt to make faith a feeling, or a statement (I have faith), or a physical place of union with Christians (church). While faith can interact with emotion, conversation, and partnership with other followers, it trusts in the One who leads, is certain of the future He's prepared, and is confident in God's plan even when you can't see beyond your next step (see Psalm 119:105).

Faith assures you that each *next step* with God is infinitely better than any steps you take on your own. It's not easy to trust what you can't see, but faith isn't just walking forward, it's walking with God. Each new step leads closer to home.

Lord, help me to step out in confidence, knowing You are my guide. Amen.

IT COMES STANDARD

It is impossible to please God without faith. Anyone who wants to come to him must believe that God exists and that he rewards those who sincerely seek him.
HEBREWS 11:6 NLT

When you buy a car you have certain options to consider. It could be things like heated seats and GPS or something like remote start and rear camera. You could purchase the basic model and it would provide the transportation you need, but the options are what make it feel more like the car was made for you.

When you try to customize your spiritual life you'll discover that certain things that come standard aren't options to be removed from your new life in Christ. It's impossible to follow Him from a distance. You can't view Christianity like a documentary of what others have experienced. You can't even say you're associated with those who follow and still expect to please God.

If you're going to come to God for life rescue and restoration you have to be convinced that He exists and He provides spiritual rewards to those who ask for help, seek His wisdom, and knock on doors of spiritual opportunity (see Matthew 7:7–12).

You can't remake God in your image. His new life for you requires the transformation of your mind, heart, and soul.

Lord, I believe in You. Help me to share my beliefs with others so they can learn to believe in You too. Amen.

Day 7

GROW DEEP

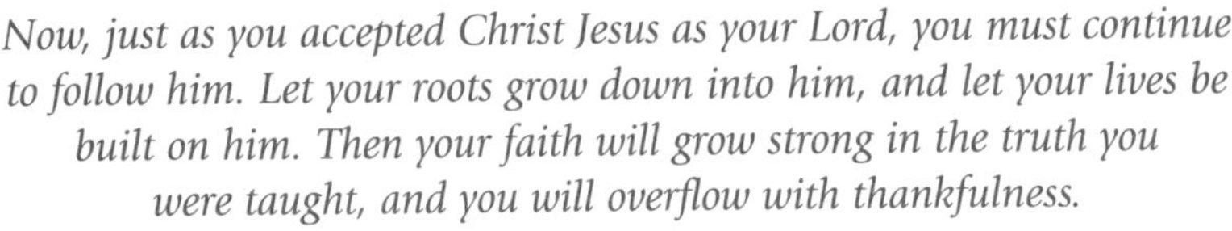

Now, just as you accepted Christ Jesus as your Lord, you must continue to follow him. Let your roots grow down into him, and let your lives be built on him. Then your faith will grow strong in the truth you were taught, and you will overflow with thankfulness.

COLOSSIANS 2:6–7 NLT

God's Word contains word pictures that help you to understand spiritual truth. In today's verse your journey with Jesus is explained through an illustration of seeds and soil inviting you to the garden, field, or flowerpot. These images encourage you to consider that something within a seed reacts with nutrient-rich soil to create new life. The roots grow deep into the soil and the seed is transformed into something more (see John 12:24).

You also have a front-row refresher to a story of how you choose to build your life. Do you trust your own strength and build on the sands of personal preference or do you trust God and build your life on the solid rock foundation of One who has all knowledge, power, and wisdom? (See Matthew 7:24–27.)

True faith provides that "Aha!" moment when you realize there's no other answer to life's purpose than trust (faith) in the God who asks you to love, forgive, share, and overflow with thankfulness.

Plant my roots deep into Your life-giving foundation, Lord.
I want to grow and be supported by You. Amen.

Day 1

HOW TO LOVE GOD

But whoever loves God is known by God.
1 Corinthians 8:3 niv

It's a simple thing to say you love God, but harder to reflect that love in the way you live. And there's a big difference between loving God in the best way you know how and loving Him the way He tells you to. You show your love for God two ways: obeying His commands and loving the way He loves. Paul observed that "knowledge puffs up while love builds up. Those who think they know something do not yet know as they ought to know" (1 Corinthians 8:1–2 niv). In other words, if you think you know everything about love, you've got a lot to learn.

What is it that we're supposed to know? How to love.

You show God you love Him as you love others the way He loves you. God loves you sacrificially, knowing who you are completely, all your pros and cons, and investing His absolute best in your highest good. Something happens when you try to love others like that: you also love God.

As it turns out, you may not know the first thing about love, but God does. When you love Him enough to love others the way He loves you, He will teach you all you need to know.

Lord, be my teacher. Show me how to love others the way that You do. And help me to obey You always. Amen.

....

....

....

....

....

....

....

....

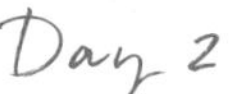

Day 2

INCREASING YOUR APPETITE

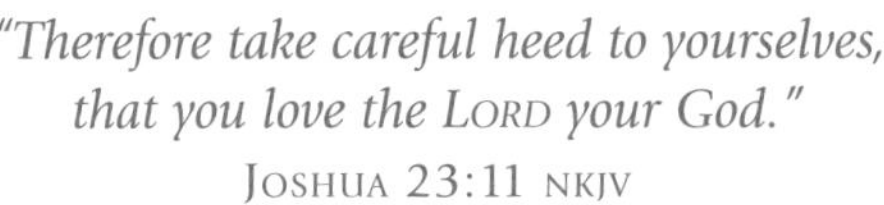

"Therefore take careful heed to yourselves,
that you love the Lord *your God."*
Joshua 23:11 nkjv

You can't really love someone you don't know. Until you move beyond your idea of who that person is and see who they really are—in all their complex, imperfect ways—you can't truly love them. The same goes for loving God. The best way to learn to love Him is to get to know Him, and one of the best ways to know Him better is through His Word.

Joshua advised God's people to "meditate in [God's Word] day and night, that you may observe to do according to all that is written in it. For then you will make your way prosperous, and then you will have good success" (Joshua 1:8 nkjv). What you're doing right now—reading a devotional—is a great icebreaker in getting to know God, but you'll whet your appetite even more by spending time reading His Word each day.

Ask Him to show you something about Him as you read, and He will give you wisdom and righteousness (see Psalm 119:98, 101), and His words will be "sweeter than honey" (Psalm 119:103 niv). God's Word is His love letter to you, and you show your love for Him when you read it, think about it, and apply it.

Lord God, I want to know You more and more every day.
Remind me to seek You through prayer and
through studying Your Word. Amen.

ALL IN

"You shall love the Lord *your God with all your heart and with all your soul and with all your might."*
Deuteronomy 6:5 nasb

Going all in to love God means learning to love like He does—no holding back. Jesus said, "If you love Me, keep My commandments" (John 14:15 nkjv). That boils down to putting God first and foremost in all you do, and loving others like you do yourself (see Mark 12:29–31). Loving God wholeheartedly will transform your life—your relationships, your work, your leisure time, your life goals.

Learning to love God as the first and highest priority in your life is part of the ongoing process of the Christian life, your sanctification. Because He is faithful, you'll get better at it as you go, digging into His Word to know Him better and acting on what you uncover there by loving others.

One way to check your love quotient is to ask yourself what you love more, God or _____? Fill in the blank: spouse, work, kids, recognition, accomplishment—because chances are good that you're still learning to love God more than whatever fills that line. Have faith that He is worth the effort. Above all else, avoid loving Him in half-measures; God took your worst and gave you His very best in Jesus.

Lord, examine my heart. Help me to know where I am lacking in love, and show me how to do a better job. Amen.

OPEN EYES, FULL HEART, CAN'T LOSE

Give me your heart, my son,
and let your eyes delight in my ways.
PROVERBS 23:26 NASB

Solomon's words to his son mirror what God would say to you as His child. You show Him a great deal of love when you submit to His will for you—trusting that He knows best and wants the best for you. You have faith that His warnings are for your protection and His chastening for your growth. Whether or not you had an earthly father whom you could trust in those ways, God will not let you down.

God's track record is impeccable: He has never broken a promise, never forsaken or forgotten His children, never gone back on His word, never left unfinished anything that He started.

Love God with all the freedom of a child running into loving arms. Enjoy getting to know Him in His Word, and relish the blessings He gives you each day. Let yourself be vulnerable before Him; He knows you better than anyone else ever could, and He cherishes you. The better you know Him, the more you'll love Him, and the more you love Him, the better you'll know Him. That sounds circular, but think of it instead as a spiral, lifting you to a higher and deeper relationship with your heavenly Father.

God, You know how I have sinned against You. Forgive me, Father,
and help me to have a better understanding of Your will. Amen.

Day 5

THE IMAGE OF LOVE

"I have made you known to them, and will continue to make you known in order that the love you have for me may be in them and that I myself may be in them."
John 17:26 NIV

If you've ever wondered what God looks like, just look at Jesus. The Bible avoids any physical descriptions of this carpenter from Nazareth, except in the prophecy that there was "nothing beautiful or majestic about his appearance, nothing to attract us to him" (Isaiah 53:2 NLT).

When Jesus was here the first time, He was just another book judged by its cover: "Can anything good come out of Nazareth?" (John 1:46 NKJV). So His looks matter less than His words, no doubt by design, so you wouldn't get lost in the woods wondering what color His eyes or hair were. So, how did Jesus make God known to you? By His love.

Nowhere is God's love for you clearer than in the person and work of Jesus Christ. Jesus is the image of the invisible God (Colossians 1:15), His promise never to leave you or forsake you (Deuteronomy 31:6) made flesh. This amazing revelation of God's heart makes it possible for you to truly love God, since, as John said, "We love Him because He first loved us" (1 John 4:19 NKJV).

God, I have so often wondered what it would be like to look on Your face. Help me to see Your face in the faces of those You love. Amen.

OPEN ARMS

The Lord *says, "I will rescue those who love me. I will protect those who trust in my name. When they call on me, I will answer; I will be with them in trouble."*
Psalm 91:14–15 nlt

The comfort of God's presence and protection in times of trouble can't be overstated. The peace you have when you have no business being peaceful not only impacts you but also others who are left wondering why you're not totally freaking out.

While it's God's pleasure as your heavenly Father to protect and provide for you, especially in the clutch, there are things you can do to show that you appreciate His love and to love Him back.

Many assign Psalm 91 to Moses, who was deeply acquainted with God. God even called him a friend (Exodus 33:11)—not because he was perfect but because he poured his heart into everything he did, seeking God's glory.

Moses established conditions for having God as your 911: "If you make the Lord your refuge, if you make the Most High your shelter, no evil will conquer you" (Psalm 91:9–10 nlt). God will send angels to protect you and give you strength to handle danger in your path (vv. 11–13). You show your love for God by running to Him in hard times, trusting Him with your trouble.

Father God, I want to feel Your loving arms around me. Comfort me with Your presence, Lord. Amen.

Day 7

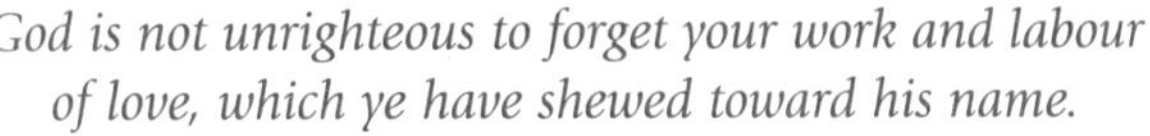

DON'T LOSE HEART

God is not unrighteous to forget your work and labour of love, which ye have shewed toward his name.
HEBREWS 6:10 KJV

You sometimes hit rough patches in your walk with God where the way is rocky, slippery, and isolated. It's especially hard when you're clicking on all cylinders spiritually—God is regularly showing you new things in His Word, your prayers seem aligned with His will, and you discern His hand at work in and through you—but then, suddenly, it's not clicking. Your prayers seem to bounce off the ceiling, and when you beg God to show Himself to you, you see nothing.

After a few panicky moments, it slowly dawns on you: you're being tested, something you're told to patiently endure (James 1:12) without losing your confidence in God (Hebrews 10:35–38). When you shift from asking "Why, Lord?" to "What are You trying to accomplish, Lord?" you're on the right track.

Because you have His promise that He will remember the love you've shown in your time of closeness to Him and your hard work for Him, you can, without understanding the specific details of your desert experience, trust that God hasn't forgotten you. You will be able to sense His presence again in due time "if [you] do not lose heart" (Galatians 6:9 NKJV).

Lord, I know sometimes You are testing me. Help me to be grateful for those tests. Amen.

AN INCOMPLETE REPENTANCE

Rend your heart and not your garments. Return to the LORD your God, for he is gracious and compassionate, slow to anger and abounding in love, and he relents from sending calamity.

JOEL 2:13 NIV

It was the custom of the day to rip apart one's garments to express deep grief or sorrow. The prophet Joel wasn't telling God's people to discontinue that practice as much as he was telling them to go beyond an external expression of sorrow for sin, all the way to the heart.

Today, Christians no longer tear their clothes in grief, but it's common to pay lip service to sins—often referring to them as mistakes or struggles, but stopping short of doing the difficult work of "rending the heart" (ripping the urges from the heart). This makes for an incomplete repentance.

In Psalm 51:17, King David properly acknowledged that God would not despise a broken and contrite heart. Such a heart stops making excuses and looking for loopholes and instead, with God's empowerment, seeks to change from the inside out.

Don't stop short in your repentance. God is slow to anger, and He will be gracious and compassionate when you have done the difficult work of naming your sin and then turning from it to walk in His mercy.

God, I am so sorry for the sins I have committed against You. My heart breaks at the thought of hurting You, Lord. Forgive me. Amen.

Day 2

CAUSE FOR CELEBRATION

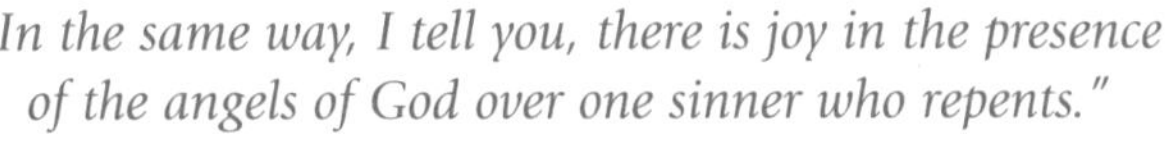

"In the same way, I tell you, there is joy in the presence of the angels of God over one sinner who repents."
LUKE 15:10 NASB

Twenty years ago, Kansas City police officer Sgt. Jeff Colvin went above and beyond the call of duty for a nine-year-old girl on his beat who grew up in a home filled with drugs and violence.

A television station in Memphis recently reported that Colvin stopped by her house every day to check on her and her two brothers, telling her he was there for them if they needed him. She says he was the only person she trusted as a child, referring to him now as a hero. She tracked her hero down recently and was reunited with him, thanking him for everything he did and surprising him by saying that she is on the road to becoming a police officer because of him.

Reunions are cause for celebration. Luke says every time a sinner repents and is reunited with the Father through the finished work of Christ, there is joy in the presence of the angels.

All of heaven is waiting for your friends and coworkers to turn to Christ. Are you like a Sgt. Colvin to them? Can they turn to you, no matter what, for spiritual truth?

*Lord, I want to celebrate with You when a sinner comes home.
Help me to reach out to my friends who don't know You yet. Amen.*

YOU CANNOT HIDE FROM GOD

Come near to God and he will come near to you. Wash your hands, you sinners, and purify your hearts, you double-minded.

James 4:8 NIV

Man's natural inclination is to run from God after sinning. Adam and Eve did it in the garden of Eden. Isaiah 2:6–10 describes the propensity of God's people to hide in caves, fearing His judgment for their idolatry. Apparently, even King David considered running from God but concluded that he couldn't see the point.

"Where can I go from your Spirit?" he asks in Psalm 139:7–10 (NIV). "Where can I flee from your presence? If I go up to the heavens, you are there; if I make my bed in the depths, you are there. If I rise on the wings of the dawn, if I settle on the far side of the sea, even there your hand will guide me, your right hand will hold me fast."

James wants you to stop running *from* God and start running *toward* Him. This is the way of biblical repentance. As David pointed out, there's no use in trying to hide from God, anyway. He's omnipresent and He sees everything. The good news is, He's quick to settle accounts with those who are quick to confess.

God, I don't want to run away. I want to stay with You. Help me not to be afraid of standing in Your presence, Lord. Amen.

WAKE UP!

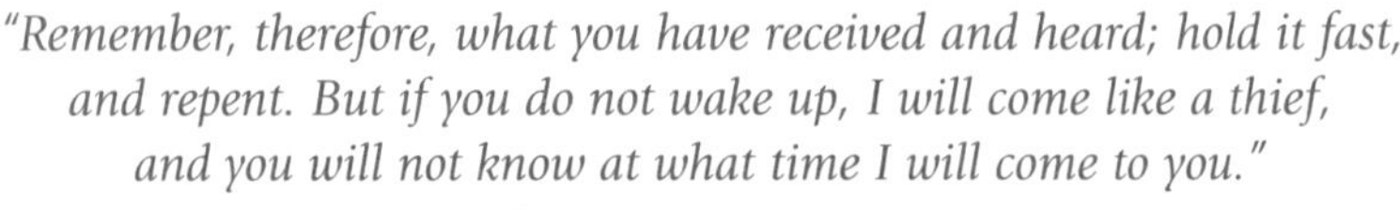

"Remember, therefore, what you have received and heard; hold it fast, and repent. But if you do not wake up, I will come like a thief, and you will not know at what time I will come to you."
REVELATION 3:3 NIV

Sin dulls the conscience, making it easier to indulge the flesh in ways previously unexplored, with fewer internal warning bells sounding the alarm. If you can get through a day without a warning from the Holy Spirit, then you're already sleeping.

For a time is coming, writes Bible commentator Matthew Henry about this verse, when Christ will come as a thief to strip those who are asleep "of their remaining enjoyments and mercies, not by fraud, but in justice and righteousness." What a dreadful time that will be.

The antidote is your memory. Remember how it used to feel when you heard a sermon that spoke directly to a spiritual need, and you responded? Remember how eager you used to be to rise up early every morning to meet with God in His Word because He felt so near? Remember the sweet fellowship you used to share with other believers? Remember what you have received and heard; obey it and repent, says the apostle John. Turn back to the God who loves you.

Lord, help me to be alert so that I can hear You speaking to me. Pierce my spirit, Lord. Make my heart tender toward You. Amen.

....

....

....

....

....

....

....

....

TAKE HEART

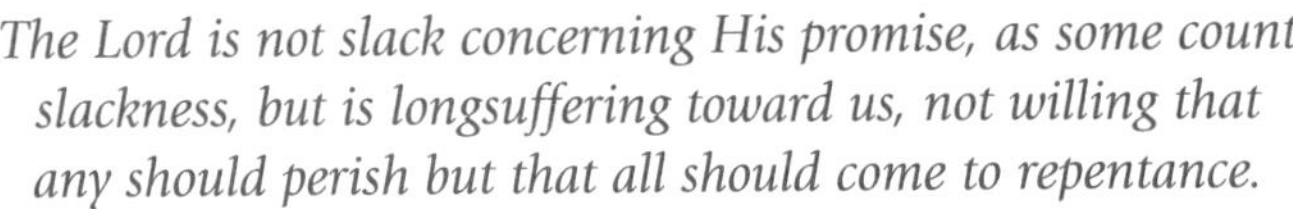

The Lord is not slack concerning His promise, as some count slackness, but is longsuffering toward us, not willing that any should perish but that all should come to repentance.

2 Peter 3:9 NKJV

If you're a parent, teacher, coach, aunt, or uncle, your patience has been tried by children who are under your authority. They throw temper tantrums. They say selfish things. And they make the same mistakes over and over again, no matter how many times you correct them.

Then, finally, one day they begin to understand the danger they pose to themselves and others, and their practices begin to change. They still make poor choices at times and they still put themselves first on occasion, but you see progress, and it makes it all worth it. You never even considered giving up on them because you cared deeply about seeing their character shaped for the better.

God feels the same way about you. He sends correction your way, and sometimes you view it as a negative—as if He doesn't love you. But nothing could be further from the truth. In fact, if you aren't feeling His loving discipline on occasion, be concerned, because God disciplines those He loves (Hebrews 12:5–6). Take heart! God isn't done with you yet.

Lord, some days I pray hard for You to come back soon. But I want everyone to get to know You. Thank You for not giving up on us. Amen.

Day 6

THE LORD IS NIGH

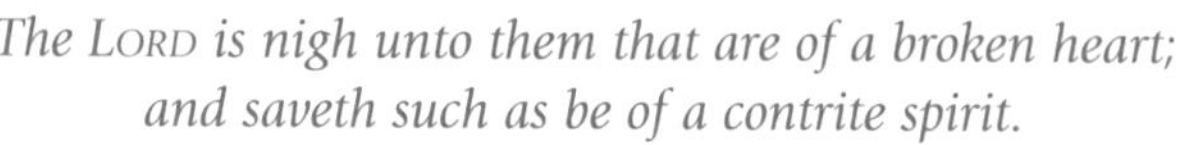

The Lord is nigh unto them that are of a broken heart; and saveth such as be of a contrite spirit.

Psalm 34:18 KJV

In modern culture, it's difficult to imagine a person having a broken heart over anything other than a relationship that has gone bad or the death of a loved one. But in today's verse, the psalmist promises that God is close—in a special way—to those who are brokenhearted over their sin.

What's the first emotion you typically feel after committing a sin? Is it shame? Remorse? Fear? Nominal conviction? The psalmist's words in today's verse indicate that you ought to feel the effects on a much deeper level. When is the last time your sin wore on you so heavily that the people around you would have said you appeared to be brokenhearted? Have you *ever* felt that way?

God cannot comfort a man who is cavalier about his sin. Therefore, He doesn't draw near to the sinner who is never brokenhearted. Take inventory of your heart today. What ongoing sin is just part of your routine? Consider your sin in light of the cross and the awful penalty that Jesus paid for it. Allow His Spirit to convict you and break your heart.

God, break my heart with the hurts that break Yours. Help me to feel the weight of sin deeply, like You do. Amen.

REPENTANCE IS A COMMAND

"God overlooked people's ignorance about these things in earlier times, but now he commands everyone everywhere to repent of their sins and turn to him."
ACTS 17:30 NLT

The prevailing thought in the West in the twenty-first century is that all religions are created equal and all paths lead to God. There was a time in Israel's history when God overlooked such theological ignorance—a time when priests stood in the gap and made ritualistic sacrifices to atone for the sins of God's people without fully understanding the call to repentance.

But when God came in the flesh, the old covenant came to an end and such ignorance was no longer acceptable in His sight.

In the new covenant, He commands all men everywhere to repent and turn to Him. Inherent in that command is to not turn to any other god. Your call, as a member of His church, is to take that message everywhere you go, even though it's not popular. You'll certainly need to be as wise as a serpent and as gentle as a dove as you do, but you must not fall prey to the misconception that all belief systems are correct. They can't be, for Christ claimed to be the only way to the Father (John 14:6).

Lord, I know You are the only way to salvation.
Help me to teach others this truth. Amen.

Day 1

FREE GIFT OF ETERNAL LIFE

For the wages of sin is death, but the free gift of God is eternal life through Christ Jesus our Lord.
ROMANS 6:23 NLT

If you knew that moving ahead with something would lead to certain death, would you still do it? Odds are you didn't even need to think about that for one-tenth of a second before responding with a firm, "No!" You'd look for a way to avoid death at all costs, right?

The Bible says that "the wages of sin is death." Every human being is born into sin, and there's nothing you, or anyone else, can do to change that. Sin leads to death 100 percent of the time. However, because of Jesus, there's a promise of hope. Through the sacrifice of His Son on the cross, God provided a way for all people to be free from sin. . .free from death *forever*!

All you need to do is believe. Choose to become a Christ-follower. Choose to accept God's gift of salvation. Choose eternal life! If you haven't already done so, pray this prayer: "Father God, I know I'm a sinner. I believe that Jesus died on the cross for my sins. Please forgive me. Send the Spirit of Jesus into my heart today. Lead me, and I will follow. Amen."

Lord, every day I need to ask for Your forgiveness. Every day I sin. Please Lord, help me to break free from sin forever! Amen.

Day 2

NEW AND IMPROVED

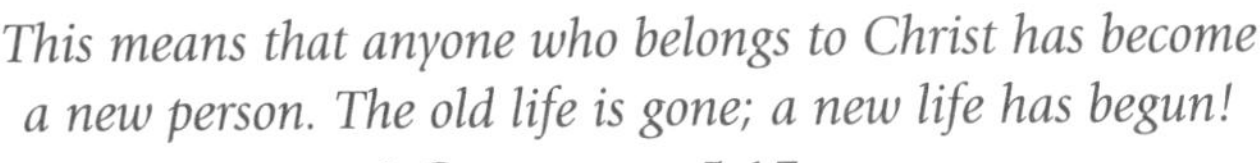

This means that anyone who belongs to Christ has become a new person. The old life is gone; a new life has begun!
2 Corinthians 5:17 NLT

The idea of a do-over, a fresh, new beginning, is quite appealing, isn't it?

With God's promise of salvation, a do-over isn't a far-fetched dream. The wonderful reality for those who make the decision to follow Christ is this: your past may be one giant mess. . .but just ask—just *believe*—and God will wipe the slate clean. He will present you with an opportunity to leave your old self behind and become a brand-new version of yourself!

In your sin, you were dead, separated from God. When you acknowledged your sin and asked God to forgive—and as you trusted Him to come into your life and lead, accepting His gift of eternal life—you became His beautiful child! He looks at you through the clear lens of His matchless grace.

As His child, your life will never again look the same. "Since you have heard about Jesus and have learned the truth. . .throw off your old sinful nature and your former way of life. . . . Put on your new nature, created to be like God—truly righteous and holy" (Ephesians 4:21–22, 24 NLT).

God, sometimes I go around acting like my old self—like the person I was before I knew You. Help me to live in this new life, Lord! Amen.

Day 3

HEAVENLY HERITAGE

Yet to all who did receive him, to those who believed in his name, he gave the right to become children of God—children born not of natural descent, nor of human decision or a husband's will, but born of God.

JOHN 1:12–13 NIV

Imagine the perfect earthly father. What kind of characteristics would he exude? For starters, he'd be loving, rich in wisdom, kind, fair, humble, and full of joy . . . He'd be a provider. A source of protection. A calm and steady presence. But even in all of this "perfection," human nature is destined to kick in at some point, and he will let his kids down—in things both large and small.

No matter who your earthly father may be, if you've accepted Christ into your life, God is your heavenly Father. On the day you believed and asked Him to become Lord of your life, you were immediately adopted into His kingdom and became His child.

He is the *only* perfect father. He will always love you *perfectly*. He will always provide for you *perfectly*. He will always protect you *perfectly*. "See what great love the Father has lavished on us, that we should be called children of God! And that is what we are!" (1 John 3:1 NIV).

Praise Him! Thank God today for your heavenly heritage!

Father God, there is no one like You. You are perfect in every way. And You love me perfectly. Thank You! Amen.

ONE WAY

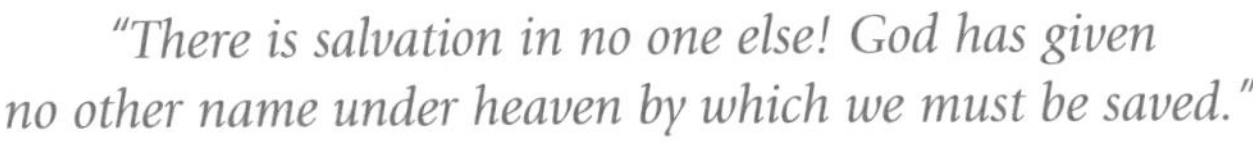

"There is salvation in no one else! God has given no other name under heaven by which we must be saved."
ACTS 4:12 NLT

When you're traveling, there are often several different roads that will lead you to your final destination. Just Google directions to a place you'd like to visit. Be it the beach or a private mountain getaway, chances are you could take a direct route or a more scenic route, if you'd rather enjoy the sights along the way.

But know this: if your final destination is heaven, there are no two ways to get there. Just *one* way. . .just *one* path. . .leads to eternity with the heavenly Father. In John 14:6 (NLT), Jesus said, "I am the way, the truth, and the life. No one can come to the Father except through me."

God gives the promise of eternal life through the sacrifice of His Son on the cross. "He has given us eternal life, and this life is in his Son. Whoever has the Son has life; whoever does not have God's Son does not have life" (1 John 5:11–12 NLT).

"Believe in the Lord Jesus and you will be saved" (Acts 16:31 NLT). If you have faith in the one and only Savior of humankind, your future—your eternal destination—is secure.

Lord, I believe You when You say there is no way to the Father except through You. Help me not to lose sight of that way! Amen.

FREEDOM!

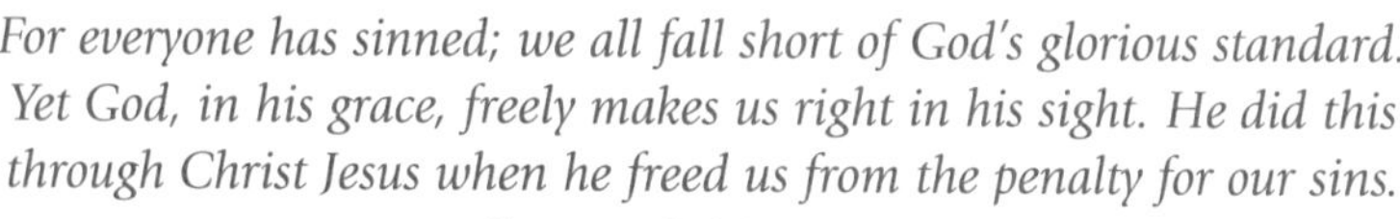

For everyone has sinned; we all fall short of God's glorious standard. Yet God, in his grace, freely makes us right in his sight. He did this through Christ Jesus when he freed us from the penalty for our sins.
ROMANS 3:23–24 NLT

"I'm a good person. I volunteer my time to help others less fortunate than myself. I treat others the way I want to be treated. Love others? Sure, I do! And of course, I pray too!"

No matter how "good" you are, there's *nothing* you can do to earn a place in heaven. There's no way for you to earn your salvation.

Everyone born into this world—every child, mother, father, brother, sister, grandparent, cousin, aunt, and uncle—is sinful. But there's hope. Because of God's amazing love for you and for *all* humankind, He provided a way for your eternal freedom through His amazing grace. The price of your sins was paid in full by Jesus alone.

If you ever feel less than worthy of God's love, or doubt His love for you, remember this: His love for you is perfect. When you talk to Him, when you tell Him you're sorry, He wraps His arms around you and whispers, "I forgive you, child. I love you." Every. Single. Time. That's a promise you can count on.

Lord Jesus, I'm so glad You love me so. I'm glad I can tell You what's on my heart, and You always listen, even though I don't deserve it. Amen.

LOVE'S GREATEST GIFT

"For God so loved the world that he gave his one and only Son, that whoever believes in him shall not perish but have eternal life."

JOHN 3:16 NIV

Do you ever struggle with feelings of being not quite "enough"? The world carelessly communicates so many hurtful messages. Messages like. . .

You're not smart enough. You're not rich enough. You're not talented enough. You're not handsome or beautiful enough. You're not good enough. You're simply not. . .*enough*.

God wants you to quit believing the world's lies, because for Him, you *are* enough. He loves you so much that He forgives your every sin. He loves you so much that He listens to your every prayer. He loves you so much that He sent His only Son, Jesus, to die for you so you can spend eternity with Him. And the best thing? Love's greatest gift doesn't cost a thing: the only requirement is that you believe.

Believe. Place all of your hope, all of your trust, in the One who loves you more than your mind could ever fathom. *Believe.* Know there's nothing you could do to make God love you more and nothing you could do to make Him love you less. *Believe.* You are enough!

God, I feel complete and whole when I am following You and living in Your will. Remind me of that every day, please. Amen.

BY GRACE

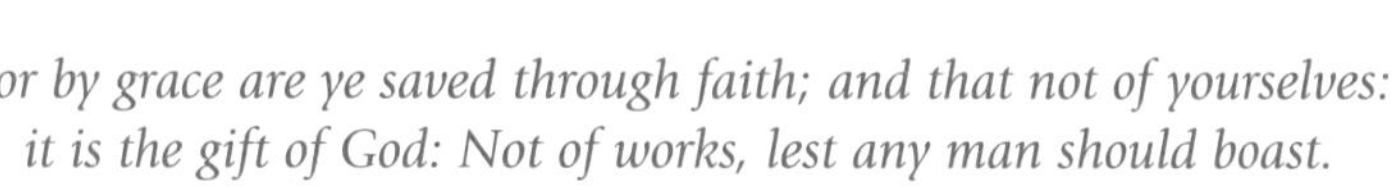

For by grace are ye saved through faith; and that not of yourselves: it is the gift of God: Not of works, lest any man should boast.

Ephesians 2:8–9 kjv

When it comes to salvation, do you ever feel like you must complete a checklist to secure your spot in Christ's heavenly kingdom?

Do you volunteer at church? Check! Do you tithe 10 percent of your income? Check! Do you spend time in prayer every day? Check! Do you show up for church every time the doors are open? Check!

But the Christian life doesn't consist of an exhausting, never-ending to-do list. Jesus said in Matthew 11:28–30 (nlt), "Come to me, all of you who are weary and carry heavy burdens, and I will give you rest. Take my yoke upon you. Let me teach you, because I am humble and gentle at heart, and you will find rest for your souls. For my yoke is easy to bear, and the burden I give you is light." A personal relationship with Christ leads to a fulfilling life, not a burdensome task list.

Know this: the heavenly Father always lavishes His abundant grace on you. Good works are the *result* of, not the reason for, your salvation. You provide the faith, and God will do the rest. His grace is all you need.

Lord, I know I could never ever do enough good deeds to make up for my sins. I'm so glad I don't have to. Thank You for Your grace. Amen.

Day 1

NO MORE FOREVER WOUNDS

"Forgive us our debts, as we also have forgiven our debtors."
MATTHEW 6:12 NIV

Unforgiveness is like acid to the soul. It's an inhuman IV that drips, burns, and damages the core of who you were meant to be. God never wanted you to endure this pain.

When you refuse to forgive you're inviting the acid of past offenses to affect your mood, decision-making, and relationships. . .every day. You can wrongly think that withholding forgiveness is your right and that you have the power to make others whole or damaged based entirely on whether you forgive them. *You don't.*

However, you do have the ability to free *yourself* from pain by releasing the offender through forgiveness. That may seem counterintuitive, but the choice is to live with the same wound for the rest of your life *or* discover healing.

You receive forgiveness from God when you accept salvation and restoration from His Son, Jesus. The restoration God offers, however, necessitates you setting aside the anger you may feel for past offenses. Why? That's exactly what He's done for you. You owed God a debt for the things you'd done that offended Him. You couldn't pay, so He paid the price. If you're offended by the actions of others, know that God has a remedy: forgiveness.

Father, someone has hurt me. I don't want bitterness to poison my soul, Lord. Help me to know how to forgive. Amen.

FORGIVEN AND FREE

O Lord, you are so good, so ready to forgive,
so full of unfailing love for all who ask for your help.
Psalm 86:5 NLT

God promised forgiveness. That's good! You *need* to be forgiven. The part where you forgive others? That's a little harder.

The concept of forgiveness isn't exactly foreign. When you were a child your parents insisted you apologize for something done to a sibling. The sibling was then encouraged to forgive. These early responses weren't always genuine. You didn't want to apologize and you didn't want to forgive. If you forgive, how do you fuel your anger? How do you blackmail the offender? How do you justify withholding love?

God knew forgiveness would make no sense to you, but He forgave you. When He forgives, nothing comes between you and God. He won't even bring up the past.

It's unnatural to forgive. People want war. They secretly find pleasure in being angry with others. Why? Maybe if they're the *offended* instead of the *offender* they feel superior. To keep their focus on the sins of others makes them feel better about their personal sin count.

Blaming others has never been part of God's promise. Forgiveness came at a cost, and when Jesus paid the price you were set free.

God, I know I have to wake up every day and choose to forgive.
Some days that is hard. Help me, Lord! Amen.

Day 3

THAT THING WE DO

Sensible people control their temper;
they earn respect by overlooking wrongs.
PROVERBS 19:11 NLT

"I wouldn't have to forgive if other people would just do the right thing." If that sounds like a logical argument, then you should probably clear some things up first. God's Word says in Romans 3:23 (NLT), "Everyone has sinned; we all fall short of God's glorious standard."

To discover a perfect response in every situation *everyone* would need to live up to God's standard. *They can't.* You wouldn't need to offer forgiveness if no one sinned. *They will.*

Overlooking wrongs is an important concept. It doesn't mean the offense wasn't painful. It doesn't mean you have to immediately offer the same level of trust to that person. It doesn't ignore the offense. Forgiveness simply removes the power of the offense to hurt you.

As long as you live, and because you're human, you *will* make mistakes. Since you make mistakes then you should remember that every other human will do the same. Everyone sins. All people fail to live up to God's perfect standard. That's why Proverbs 19 says controlling anger is something sensible people do.

If someone's offended you, you must remember that you've offended others too. That's what humans do. To forgive? That's what Christ-followers do. That's what God did for you.

God, whenever I get caught up in trivial grievances,
shake some sense into me! I don't want to let my
pride stop me from loving people. Help! Amen.

Day 4

A WORLD WITHOUT COMPASSION

Be kind and compassionate to one another,
forgiving each other, just as in Christ God forgave you.
EPHESIANS 4:32 NIV

Imagine a world without forgiveness. The ancient feud between the Hatfields and McCoys seems tame by comparison. Wars would be the norm, not the exception. Everyone would push for a vendetta against others. There would be no kindness. There would be no compassion. There would be no trust.

In this alternate world you would exist without empathy for others, without meaningful relationships, and without hope for something better tomorrow.

Followed to its natural conclusion, payback would be required for every offense, hatred for every slight, and revenge for each infraction. Yet, there's a wise God who instructed you to do something unnatural—forgive. This forgiveness is to be marked by kindness, compassion, and relationship. This forgiveness gives the world hope, urges peace, and inspires friendship.

Your motivation for offering the gift of forgiveness to others is your gratitude for the gift of forgiveness you've received from your great God.

People who forgive tend to be the ones you remember most fondly. Why? They care about you. That compassion shows up in their willingness to follow God's example—forgive when forgiveness is needed, show compassion when help's needed, and offer kindness when friendship's simply a dream.

Lord, my capacity for compassion could use some expansion.
Help me to feel for others when they are hurting. Amen.

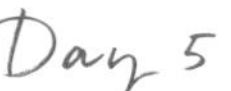

NOT YOUR ENEMY

Don't repay evil for evil. Don't retaliate with insults when people insult you. Instead, pay them back with a blessing. That is what God has called you to do, and he will grant you his blessing.
1 PETER 3:9 NLT

Laws determine a punishment for every offense. There are consequences for every choice to sin. Galatians 6:7 (NKJV) says, "Whatever a man sows, that he will also reap."

Forgiveness isn't a free pass. It doesn't excuse bad behavior. It doesn't act as if the offense didn't matter. Forgiveness allows the offended party to acknowledge the pain, set aside revenge, and reengage life without the baggage of bitterness.

The Bible urges you to repay evil with a blessing. This is another difficult concept within the role of forgiveness. You offended God with your sin and the *Offended* (God) forgives and extends blessings to the *offender* (you).

Think about it this way: how do you argue with someone who refuses to argue? You try to make them mad, but they refuse to fight. At some point you move on. It's hard to fight with someone who won't play the part of an enemy.

Adding a blessing to forgiveness suggests you don't plan on being an enemy. God's blessings in the midst of forgiveness assures you *He* is not your enemy.

Lord, I'll admit it. I have a hard time biting my tongue when some people say mean things or are disrespectful. Help me to bless others more. Amen.

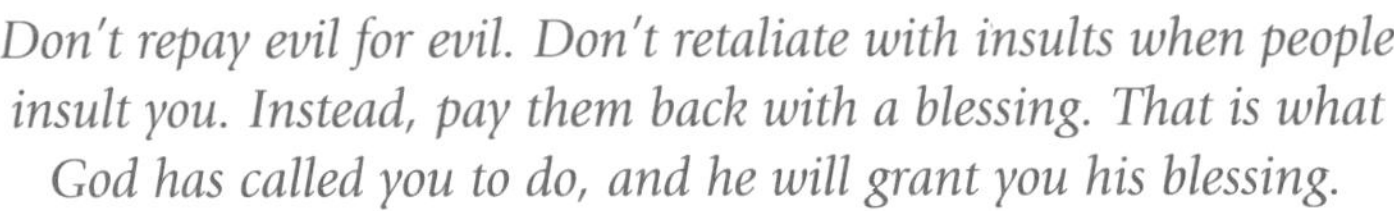

THE FORGIVENESS CARD

Then Peter came and said to Him, "Lord, how often shall my brother sin against me and I forgive him? Up to seven times?" Jesus said to him, "I do not say to you, up to seven times, but up to seventy times seven."

MATTHEW 18:21–22 NASB

God never asks you to do something He wouldn't do Himself. If He asks you to love it's because He loves. If He asks you to forgive it's because He forgives.

Humans tend to think there's a limit to things like patience, kindness, and forgiveness. Maybe that's why Peter wanted a defined ending point to the responsibility to forgive. Whatever *forgiveness limit* Peter had in mind was probably lower than seven, but that was the number he suggested.

Jesus had other ideas. He came up with the figure of 490 times. Most scholars believe the number was simply high enough that people would stop counting each offense and understand forgiveness should have no limit.

Did God restrict Himself to the number of times He'd forgive you? He's the God of second chances, and He asks *you* to give second chances. You don't get to tell other people, "Looks like you just got your last punch on the forgiveness card. Congratulations, you blew it."

God has promised forgiveness, and He commands you to forgive.

I know there is no limit to Your love for us, Lord. You forgive and forgive, again and again. Help me to be like You. Amen.

DO WHAT HE DOES

"And whenever you stand praying, if you have anything against anyone, forgive him, that your Father in heaven may also forgive you your trespasses. But if you do not forgive, neither will your Father in heaven forgive your trespasses."

Mark 11:25–26 NKJV

The message of today's verses is pretty straightforward: It's hard to expect forgiveness when you refuse to forgive. To be clear, God is able to offer forgiveness because His Son, Jesus, paid the price for your sin. To accept Jesus' payment is to embrace forgiveness, not just as something you receive, but something you give.

To follow Jesus means to do what He does. Sure, you'll forgive imperfectly, but it should be the goal of your life to reflect His character in how you deal with others. Forgiveness is an act of love, and Jesus said the greatest commandments were to love God and then love everyone else (see Matthew 22:36–40).

You might marvel at God's promised gifts and want to receive them for yourself, but the same gifts you receive are the very gifts God wants you to share with others. When you don't share it's as if you're saying you want preferential treatment and would like to play by a different set of rules.

God said, "Forgive." What's your response?

Lord, I've got this burden of unforgiveness that I've been carrying for a while now. Could you please take it from me? Thank You, Lord. Amen.

THE GIFT OF MERCY

Be ye therefore merciful,
as your Father also is merciful.
Luke 6:36 kjv

Did you ever play Mercy as a kid? It's a rather silly and painful game, locking hands and fingers with your opponent and testing strength and endurance by bending until one person gives up in pain, crying, "Mercy!"—or maybe "Uncle!"

Thankfully, God's mercy is nothing like this foolish children's game. You can find examples and descriptions of it all throughout His Word. Only Jesus can offer the mercy that saves people from sin, as described in 1 Peter 1:3 (niv): "Praise be to the God and Father of our Lord Jesus Christ! In his great mercy he has given us new birth into a living hope through the resurrection of Jesus Christ from the dead." And in Ephesians 2:4–5 (nkjv): "But God, who is rich in mercy, because of His great love with which He loved us, even when we were dead in trespasses, made us alive together with Christ (by grace you have been saved)."

Christians are called to be grateful for mercy and to offer it to others, mimicking the way God expresses it and grants it so freely. This week, may you discover more about mercy and what a gift it is to both receive and give it.

My King, I want to be "rich in mercy," just like You.
Help me to stretch my mercy muscles whenever I can. Amen.

MERCY FOR ALL

Even though I was once a blasphemer and a persecutor and a violent man, I was shown mercy because I acted in ignorance and unbelief. The grace of our Lord was poured out on me abundantly, along with the faith and love that are in Christ Jesus. Here is a trustworthy saying that deserves full acceptance: Christ Jesus came into the world to save sinners—of whom I am the worst.

1 Timothy 1:13–15 NIV

As the apostle Paul so clearly communicates in this scripture passage, God's mercy is available to *all* people, even the very worst of sinners—even the kind who kill and persecute others and blaspheme God Himself. That was Paul once upon a time. But he was shown mercy by a merciful God, "so that in [him], the worst of sinners, Christ Jesus might display his immense patience as an example for those who would believe in him and receive eternal life" (1 Timothy 1:16 NIV).

Oh what hope is in that scripture! Such confident assurance for absolutely anyone, no matter what kind of sin they might be entrenched in! No darkness is black enough to blot out the saving light of God's mercy through Jesus Christ, a beacon calling sinners to repentance and full acceptance by God.

God, it's amazing to me that no one is beyond Your mercy.
Help me to see everyone as You see them, Lord. Amen.

Day 3

PLENTEOUS MERCY

For thou, Lord, art good, and ready to forgive; and plenteous in mercy unto all them that call upon thee.

Psalm 86:5 KJV

"*Plenteous* in mercy," the psalmist in the King James Version says. What a good thought! To mimic the Lord's mercy, believers must be ready to forgive and have an abundance of mercy to share.

Are you quick to forgive and offer mercy? It's difficult at times, for sure, especially if the offense is serious. But your heavenly Father never weighs the offense to decide whether to give or withhold His mercy from you. No, He's constantly ready, wanting you to come to Him at any and all times to make things right in your relationship with Him.

Because He so mercifully and readily forgives, you are called to do the same. And the more you give mercy, the more you receive. Matthew 5:7 (NKJV) says, "Blessed are the merciful, for they shall obtain mercy."

Those who don't offer mercy and forgiveness, however, are in grave danger, for if "you forgive those who sin against you, your heavenly Father will forgive you. But if you refuse to forgive others, your Father will not forgive your sins" (Matthew 6:14–15 NLT).

Lord, it's hard for me to understand mercy in some cases. Help me to love like You, so that I can forgive my enemies. Amen.

SLOW TO ANGER

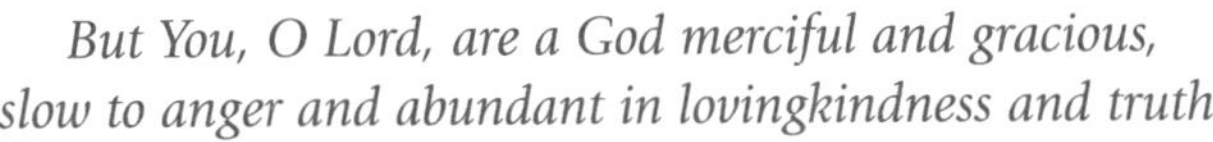

But You, O Lord, are a God merciful and gracious,
slow to anger and abundant in lovingkindness and truth.
Psalm 86:15 NASB

God's character reveals that being slow to anger goes hand in hand with being merciful. What a blessing that He's not quick to get mad, but is abundant in lovingkindness. If God were easily angered, imagine how upset He would constantly be with you and your sins.

When a difficult situation arises or someone frustrates or wrongs you, take a deep breath (literally), count to ten, or do whatever you need to do to hinder the anger rising in you. Ecclesiastes 7:9 (NIV) says, "Do not be quickly provoked in your spirit, for anger resides in the lap of fools." And James 1:19–20 (NIV) says, "My dear brothers and sisters, take note of this: everyone should be quick to listen, slow to speak and slow to become angry, because human anger does not produce the righteousness that God desires."

As you work to control anger, think about mistakes you have made and be grateful that God has been slow to anger with you. Pray and thank God, and then extend that same kind of mercy to others, remembering that Proverbs 19:11 (NASB) says, "A man's discretion makes him slow to anger, and it is his glory to overlook a transgression."

Lord, my temper is usually controlled. But I know I've snapped and lashed out at others at times. Help me to understand why and learn how to control that. Amen.

Day 5

TENDER MERCIES

The LORD is good to all: and his tender mercies are over all his works.
PSALM 145:9 KJV

Everything God does is full of His tender mercy and goodness. That might seem hard to understand in a world so broken and painful. Yes, it's impossible to fully figure out on this side of heaven, but it's a promise from God's Word, and it's worthy of your trust.

Evil is hard at work here on the earth, but that never means God is unseeing or uncaring. His tender mercies will prevail over all things in the long run, and you must keep on trusting Him to sustain you through the good and bad. Lamentations 3:19–23 (NLT) says, "The thought of my suffering and homelessness is bitter beyond words. I will never forget this awful time, as I grieve over my loss. Yet I still dare to hope when I remember this: The faithful love of the LORD never ends! His mercies never cease. Great is his faithfulness; his mercies begin afresh each morning."

Your hope is in heaven. There you'll find perfect eternal life with your Savior, where He'll wipe away every tear (Revelation 21:4). There's nothing more merciful than the God who has prepared such an eternal home for you. And in the meantime, He offers fresh new mercies with each new dawn. Praise Him!

Lord God, You meet me in the middle of my sorrows and offer peace I cannot comprehend. Thank You for being there for me. Amen.

BECAUSE OF HIS MERCY

He saved us, not because of the righteous things we had done, but because of his mercy. He washed away our sins, giving us a new birth and new life through the Holy Spirit. He generously poured out the Spirit upon us through Jesus Christ our Savior. Because of his grace he made us right in his sight and gave us confidence that we will inherit eternal life.

TITUS 3:5–7 NLT

No one can earn God's mercy. No amount of good deeds can make up for the fact that your sin separates you from Him. Only because of God's character and His great love and mercy for you does He provide a way to make things right, through the blood of the Lamb, Jesus Christ. And there are no works required to *keep* mercy either.

True believers will do good works and share love and offer mercy to others, but not because they feel obligated; such works are a spontaneous result of sincere faith and the Holy Spirit's work in their lives. Works are never required to gain the great mercy of salvation. "For it is by grace you have been saved, through faith—and this is not from yourselves, it is the gift of God—not by works, so that no one can boast" (Ephesians 2:8–9 NIV).

Father, let my works pour out of my love for You.
Help me not to think too much about what I'm doing.
Help me to focus on who I'm serving. Amen.

LIMITLESS MERCY

Surely goodness and mercy shall follow me all the days of my life: and I will dwell in the house of the LORD for ever.

PSALM 23:6 KJV

God's mercy is limitless; it follows those who fear Him all the days of their lives and it spreads to their children and grandchildren and generations more. Luke 1:50 (NIV) says, "His mercy extends to those who fear him, from generation to generation."

What are you doing to teach the children in your life about God's love and mercy? Are you encouraging them to be authentic and sincere in their faith, receiving and giving mercy and growing more mature each day in their walk with Jesus? It matters, not only for their current lives and relationships but for their long-term future and their children's and grandchildren's futures as well.

Deuteronomy 6:4–7 (NLT) urges, "Listen, O Israel! The LORD is our God, the LORD alone. And you must love the LORD your God with all your heart, all your soul, and all your strength. And you must commit yourselves wholeheartedly to these commands that I am giving you today. Repeat them again and again to your children. Talk about them when you are at home and when you are on the road, when you are going to bed and when you are getting up."

God, thank You for Your goodness and mercy. Help me to tell my children about the beauty of Your blessings in my life. Amen.

FEAR GOD

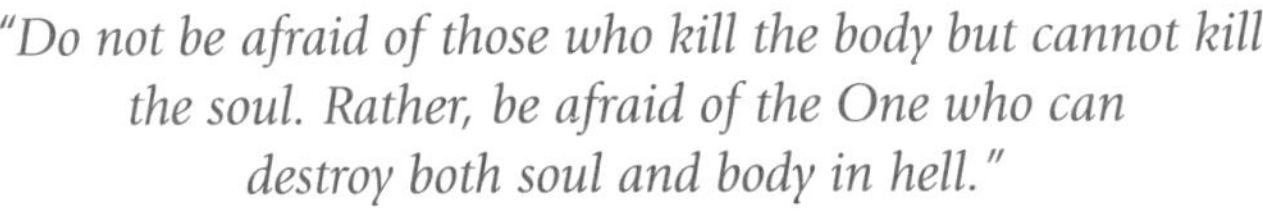

"Do not be afraid of those who kill the body but cannot kill the soul. Rather, be afraid of the One who can destroy both soul and body in hell."

Matthew 10:28 niv

Many people believe that since "God is love" and "there is no fear in love" (1 John 4:8, 18 kjv), that the Bible's admonitions to "fear God" must be somehow wrong. Statements like, "God is greatly to be feared" (Psalm 89:7 kjv) are, at the very least, considered outdated.

People have problems with Jesus' command to fear God "who can destroy both soul and body in hell" because they believe that a loving God would never punish people in the afterlife. But the God of love is also the God of justice and righteousness, and He must judge evil.

Part of the confusion over the word *fear* is resolved by Bible versions such as the niv which frequently translates "fear" as "revere." When it states that you are to fear God, the Bible means you are to greatly honor and respect God.

Fearing God is not a negative thing. The Bible says, "The fear of the Lord is pure" (Psalm 19:9 niv). Revering and fearing God motivates you to do good, knowing that "we will all stand before God's judgment seat" (Romans 14:10 niv) to account for our deeds.

Lord, may I never get so comfortable with my version of You that I forget who You really are. I honor You, Lord! Amen.

Day 2

THE FOUNDATION OF KNOWLEDGE

Fear of the Lord is the foundation of true knowledge,
but fools despise wisdom and discipline.
Proverbs 1:7 NLT

Many people are very learned in a worldly way and have a reputation for being wise and knowledgeable, but this isn't true knowledge. It's often mere head-stuffing with facts and figures.

You also have to consider the *effect* of such vaunted knowledge. Paul declared, "We know that 'We all possess knowledge.' But knowledge puffs up while love builds up" (1 Corinthians 8:1 NIV). Worldly knowledge is like a bullfrog, vainly puffed up beyond its true size, boasting that it's greater than it really is. It's proud and showing off.

But knowledge founded on the fear of God actually does something constructive and helps others. The "fear of the Lord is the foundation of true knowledge." If you fear God, the most immediate effect is that you obey Him, and His greatest commands are for you to love God and the people He created. This kind of knowledge will move you to do good to others.

Something else: "The fear of the Lord is to hate evil" (Proverbs 8:13 NASB). Love what is good and hate what is evil, and you'll be motivated to do good with the knowledge you possess. Now, that's *true* knowledge!

Lord, I don't want to be puffed up with ideas that
don't matter. I want to know all I can about You. Amen.

Day 3

BENEFITS OF FEARING GOD

The angel of the LORD *encamps around those who fear him, and he delivers them.*

PSALM 34:7 NIV

There are distinct benefits to fearing God. One is that if you fear God, you won't need to fear the devil. The reason is that if you have a healthy fear of God, you'll draw near to Him and will focus on obeying Him. These things bring you close to His all-powerful presence and cause Him to bless and protect you.

"The angel of the LORD encamps around those who fear him, and he delivers them." The Angel of the Lord isn't just one of the many angels of God. This title refers to the very presence and person of God Himself.

"He who dwells in the secret place of the Most High shall abide under the shadow of the Almighty. I will say of the LORD, 'He is my refuge' " (Psalm 91:1–2 NKJV). Fearing God causes you to dwell under His protective shadow.

There is a similar promise elsewhere in Psalms: "He will fulfil the desire of them that fear him: he also will hear their cry, and will save them" (Psalm 145:19 KJV). God will not only protect you, but will also hear your prayers and give you the things you truly need. It pays to fear God!

Lord of all, I love to envision Your angel watching over me and the ones I love. Thank You for protecting us so well. Amen.

HAVING THINGS GO WELL

"Oh that they had such a heart in them, that they would fear Me and keep all My commandments always, that it may be well with them and with their sons forever!"

DEUTERONOMY 5:29 NASB

God wants things to go well for you. He promises that if you're faithful to Him, revere Him, and keep His commands, things *will* go well with you. In the verse above, you can hear God yearning for His people to love Him. Know that God longs to bless you. He has promised, "Draw near to God and He will draw near to you" (James 4:8 NASB).

When you realize that God is all-powerful and that you're immeasurably weaker than He is, it causes you to experience a godly fear. This kind of fear is healthy. Realizing that God is eternal and that you, by comparison, are mere dust in the wind, gives you a humble attitude. Such humility is the beginning of true worship and brings you many blessings.

The prophet Samuel told the Israelites, "Be sure to fear the LORD and faithfully serve him. Think of all the wonderful things he has done for you" (1 Samuel 12:24 NLT). Sit down and count your blessings. God has been good to you. And He isn't done yet! He wishes to bless you even more.

Lord, I know Your blessings are already too numerous for me to count. I'm so glad I have an eternity to thank You. Amen.

MOTIVATED BY GODLY FEAR

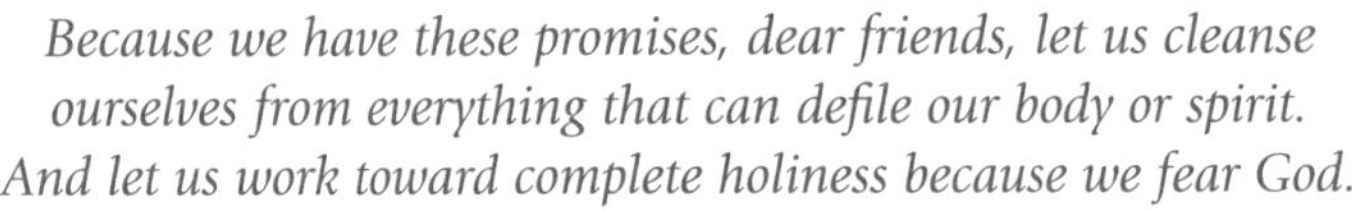

Because we have these promises, dear friends, let us cleanse ourselves from everything that can defile our body or spirit. And let us work toward complete holiness because we fear God.

2 CORINTHIANS 7:1 NLT

God has given many promises in His Word which, empowered by His Spirit, can transform you into the image of His Son (2 Corinthians 3:18). But being changed from your present imperfect state into the image of Jesus Christ means letting go of your faults and habits, and this often isn't easy to do.

You have to be highly motivated to change. Only if you sincerely fear God will you be compelled to cleanse yourself from everything that displeases Him, that defiles your body or your spirit.

The Bible urges you to "work out your own salvation with fear and trembling" (Philippians 2:12 NKJV), but it's also clear that you can't do good works to *earn* your salvation (see Ephesians 2:8–9). So what does this command mean? It means to continually implore God to change you, and though you're already saved, to complete the process of renewal.

Jesus described this ongoing work of transformation when He stated that the kingdom of God was like yeast being worked through an entire lump of dough until it was all leavened (Matthew 13:33).

Lord of lords, I want to be holy, as You are holy. Cleanse me from even the hint of wickedness. Amen.

Day 6

BEYOND FEARING GOD

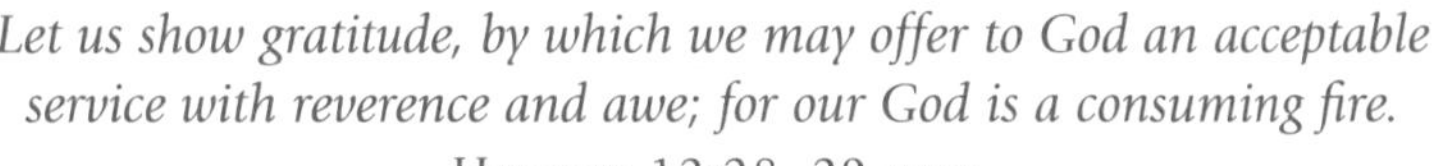
Let us show gratitude, by which we may offer to God an acceptable service with reverence and awe; for our God is a consuming fire.
HEBREWS 12:28–29 NASB

As important as it is to fear God, fear and awe in themselves aren't enough. After all, even the demons believe in the existence of one supreme, all-powerful Being of absolute good, and shudder with terror (James 2:19). They know that He's a consuming fire. Their problem is that they're set in rebellion against God, hate Him, and have no intention of repenting.

Hebrews 11:6 (NIV) says about God, "Anyone who comes to him must believe that he exists." That's the first step. The second step is to be aware of your sinful nature and believe that God will one day judge you. This causes you to revere and fear Him (see Acts 24:25).

The third step is to "love the LORD your God with all your heart and with all your soul and with all your strength" (Deuteronomy 6:5 NIV). As Jesus said, if you love Him you will automatically obey Him. "Whoever has my commands and keeps them is the one who loves me" (John 14:21 NIV). Only then will you offer to God an acceptable service with reverence and awe.

The fear of God should motivate you to love Him and obey Him.

Lord, I want to love You with everything that is in me. Amen.

Day 7

IN CONCLUSION

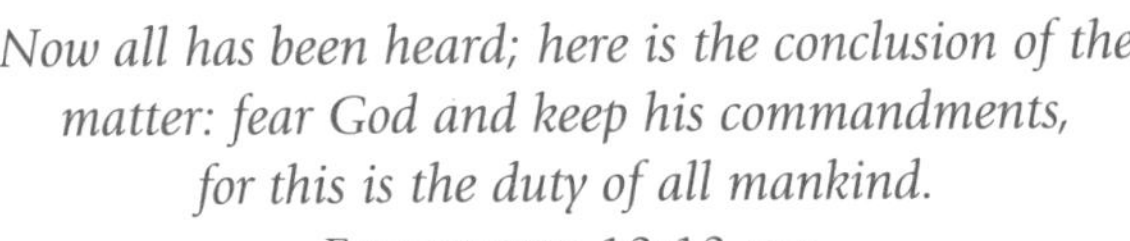

Now all has been heard; here is the conclusion of the matter: fear God and keep his commandments, for this is the duty of all mankind.

ECCLESIASTES 12:13 NIV

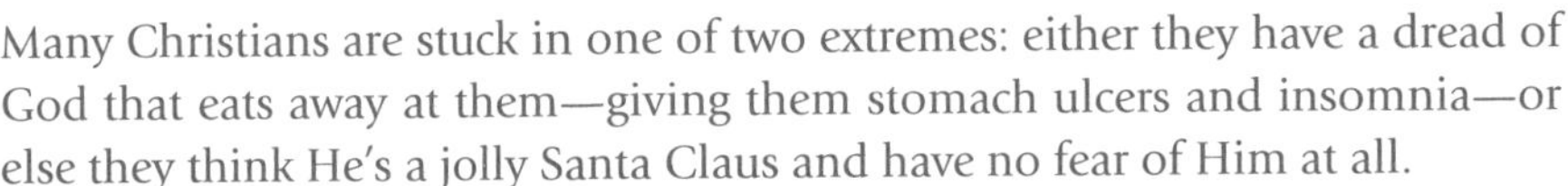

Many Christians are stuck in one of two extremes: either they have a dread of God that eats away at them—giving them stomach ulcers and insomnia—or else they think He's a jolly Santa Claus and have no fear of Him at all.

In the first camp, people have "a certain fearful looking for of judgment and fiery indignation" (Hebrews 10:27 KJV) that destroys them from the inside. They're consumed by the negative image of a judgmental God. In the second camp, they've latched onto an unrealistic image of a God of endless grace who never judges sin.

God is not defined by human doctrines. He lives in eternity, complete and perfect, and is both a God of infinite love (1 John 4:8) and a God who sits in judgment of sin. While His mighty hand graciously upholds your weak spirit (Psalm 37:24; 63:8), for the disobedient it is "a fearful thing to fall into the hands of the living God" (Hebrews 10:31 KJV).

Learn to have a balanced view of God. Fear and love Him, and you'll keep His commandments—and all will be well with your soul.

Lord, help me to be careful with how I speak and think about You. I want to respect and honor You as my King, and love You as my Father. Amen.

Day 1

THE RIGHTEOUS ARE SATISFIED

"Blessed are those who hunger and thirst for righteousness, for they shall be satisfied."
MATTHEW 5:6 NASB

Righteousness has a bad name today. Those who aren't pursuing it often criticize those who are—falsely believing that Christians think they are better than everybody else. This is simply not the case for the true Christ-follower. In reality, those who are truly seeking the narrow path have a real understanding of how sinful they are. As a result, they constantly exchange their sin for Christ's righteousness.

If you're seeking righteousness through your own merits, rather than through the finished work of Christ, you'll never achieve it. *Beatitudes* means "a state of supreme happiness," and in them, Jesus says that those who hunger and thirst for righteousness are blessed and satisfied. Notice the need for the *pursuit* of righteousness—for this brings blessings and satisfaction.

Pursuing righteousness doesn't come naturally, though, even for Christians. Your hunger and thirst must be stirred up regularly by attending worship services, reading your Bible, fellowshipping with other believers, and praying. If you neglect these, you'll seek your own righteousness by default, thinking more highly of yourself than you ought, and your spiritual life will become dry.

God, I want to be hungry for Your Word and thirsty for Your Spirit. Let me burn with the need to be righteous before You. Amen.

SURRENDER YOUR KINGDOM

"Seek the Kingdom of God above all else, and live righteously, and he will give you everything you need."
MATTHEW 6:33 NLT

Near the end of Jesus' temptation, Satan made one final attempt to get Him to stumble. He took Jesus to the peak of a high mountain and showed him all the kingdoms of the world. " 'I will give it all to you,' [Satan] said, 'if you will kneel down and worship me' " (Matthew 4:9 NLT).

But Jesus didn't buy it. Instead he told Satan to flee.

That doesn't stop Satan from trying to get you to focus on ruling your own little kingdom in search of your perceived needs, though, rather than seeking the kingdom of God. How do you know if you've fallen for his ploy?

Earthly kings are authoritarian, refusing to bow the knee to anyone or anything, short of being conquered. They are the final authority on all matters—the top of the appeals chain. Does this resemble your life? Are you unwilling to submit to authority? If so, be careful, because you're on shaky ground.

The paradox of the Christian life is that you lay down your life to live. You stop pursuing your kingdom in favor of a superior one—one that ultimately will provide everything you need.

Jesus, keep me from being so wrapped up in my own world that I don't see those who need You. Amen.

THE DIVINE NATURE

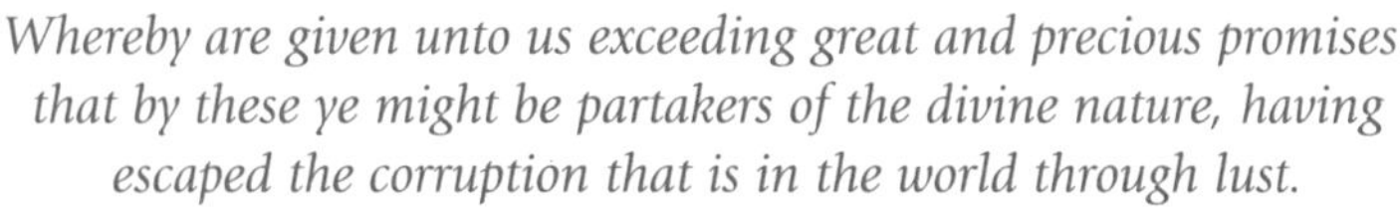

Whereby are given unto us exceeding great and precious promises: that by these ye might be partakers of the divine nature, having escaped the corruption that is in the world through lust.

2 PETER 1:4 KJV

Peter wrote his two epistles to persecuted Christians who were scattered across Asia Minor. As difficult as it would have been for them, Peter wanted them to remember to be partakers of the divine nature, rather than giving in to the lusts of the world. But he didn't leave them wondering how.

He reminded them that they had been given the great and precious promises of God. Those promises were the means to the divine nature. In Matthew Henry's *Commentary on the Whole Bible*, he states: "Those who receive the promises of the gospel partake of the divine nature. They are renewed in the spirit of their mind, after the image of God, in knowledge, righteousness, and holiness; their hearts are set for God and his service; they have a divine temper and disposition of soul."

How are the promises of the Gospel shaping you today? Are you jotting them on index cards and referencing them? Are you talking about them in Bible studies? Are you texting them to your friends?

God, I'm so thankful for Your promises. I find in them the consistent, everlasting message of Your love. Amen.

IT'S NEVER TOO LATE

Do you not know that the unrighteous will not inherit the kingdom of God? Do not be deceived. Neither fornicators, nor idolaters, nor adulterers, nor homosexuals, nor sodomites.

1 Corinthians 6:9 NKJV

Have you ever looked at a list of sins such as this in scripture and wondered how you could possibly inherit the kingdom of God? In one sense or another, you're guilty of one or more of these evils. At the very least, it's hard to deny what John Calvin said about the human heart: "Man's nature, so to speak, is a perpetual factory of idols."

So what's a Christian to do with such a promise?

Note that this list of sins contains no mention of repentance. A person who openly embraces one of these lifestyles with no struggle or regard for God and His ways is already condemned. This isn't to say a Christian can't fall, but he will always get back up if he is regenerate.

Consider your behaviors in light of the list in 1 Corinthians 6:9. Have you given yourself over to any of these sins? Have you given up the fight? It's never too late to repent. Seek the strong support of a believer who is in the habit of mortifying the flesh.

Lord, I don't know my own heart. But I know it can't be trusted. Help me to keep from worshipping other things besides You, Lord. Amen.

Day 5

ABIDING WITH GOD

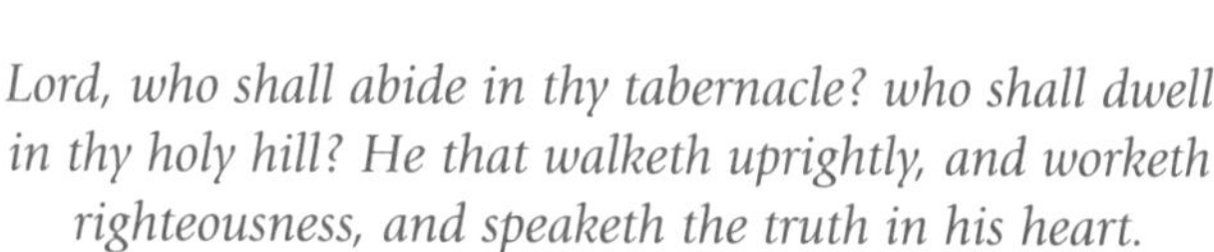

Lord, who shall abide in thy tabernacle? who shall dwell in thy holy hill? He that walketh uprightly, and worketh righteousness, and speaketh the truth in his heart.

PSALM 15:1–2 KJV

The psalmist here asks a twofold question, and it's the most important question any person can ask himself: Who can dwell in God's tabernacle (meaning an earthly dwelling place where God's presence is represented, such as the church)? And who can dwell in His holy hill (heaven)?

The answer to both questions is the same: those who walk (live) uprightly, work righteousness (perform deeds of righteousness), and speak the truth to themselves.

If you're living uprightly, working righteousness, and speaking truth to yourself, you'll have much less time to dabble or immerse yourself in sin and falsehoods. But this sort of lifestyle doesn't happen on its own. It can only be lived intentionally, with your heart and mind firmly fixed on truth. How are you doing in all three areas? If you see some deficiencies, don't ignore them.

Instead, look at the list and work backward. Speak truth to yourself by making God's Word a bigger priority. From there, you'll want to perform righteous deeds. And then, as God's Spirit flows through you, He will empower you to live righteously.

God, help me to fill my mind with Your Word, instead of listening to so many other influences. Amen.

HOLD THE LINE

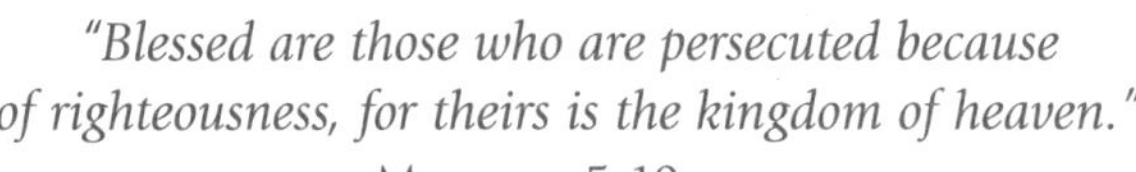

"Blessed are those who are persecuted because of righteousness, for theirs is the kingdom of heaven."
Matthew 5:10 NIV

Pressure reveals what you truly believe. Nobody knows that more than Christians who are persecuted around the world because of their righteousness—their unwavering refusal to bow the knee to false doctrines or false messiahs. Jesus says they are blessed, though, because theirs is the kingdom of heaven.

For the first time, the West is becoming intolerant toward Christianity and those who embrace it as truth. The unregenerate see it as an archaic system driven by hate. Societal laws that were once rooted in biblical truth are being overturned. And if you're vocal about certain Christian beliefs, you can expect to pay a price. It might cost you your job, your reputation, and one day, maybe even your freedom.

Working to maintain religious freedom is a must, but if the day comes when that battle is lost, are you prepared to face the pressure cooker of persecution? Will you stand strong, while still speaking about the love of Christ for sinners? Will you accept the consequences? Will you keep the big picture (heaven) in mind?

Jesus will call you one of the blessed if you just hold the line.

Jesus, give me the courage and strength that I need to stand up and speak out for You. Amen.

TELL THE TRUTH

A righteous man hateth lying: but a wicked man is loathsome, and cometh to shame.
PROVERBS 13:5 KJV

You don't hear the phrase "little white lies" much anymore, but a generation ago, people used it to justify one action or another, or simply to be polite. Today, people—including Christians—are quicker to simply lie without even trying to justify it. But a man who is walking in the truth, a righteous man, hates lying.

Lying is a grievous sin with alarming consequences. Revelation 21:27 (KJV) says, "And there shall in no wise enter into [heaven] any thing that defileth, neither whatsoever worketh abomination, or maketh a lie: but they which are written in the Lamb's book of life."

How quick are you to lie to your boss, your spouse, or your friends when one of them asks you a question you'd rather not answer because you know they wouldn't like what you have to say? How quick are you to embellish your accomplishments to make yourself seem more qualified?

When you read a scripture verse such as Proverbs 13:5, does it prick your conscience? If so, take heart. Deep down, the Holy Spirit is telling you that something is off. Repent and resolve to tell the truth.

Lord, I confess that I am deceitful in many ways. Point those ways out to me and help me to strive to be truthful in speech and action. Amen.

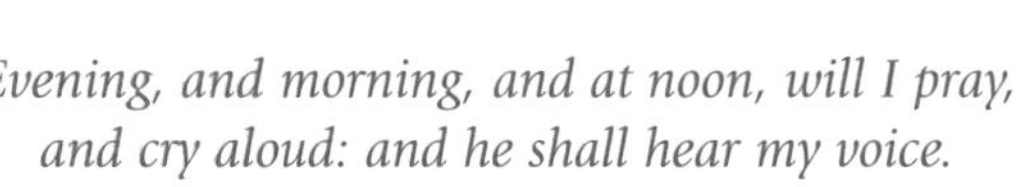

THE RIGHT FIT

Evening, and morning, and at noon, will I pray,
and cry aloud: and he shall hear my voice.
PSALM 55:17 KJV

The psalmist David prayed to God three times a day. Think about the last time you talked to God. Was it this morning? . . . Last night? . . . Last week? . . . Last month? . . . Do you even remember when you last prayed? Many of you would be ashamed to admit that it was much too long ago.

Life gets in the way. Every day seems like a repeat of the same drudgery: rush to work, rush home, rush through supper, rush through laundry, bills, homework . . .rush to bed. It's difficult managing life as is, without adding more to your to-do list. So where does your one-on-one time with the heavenly Creator fit into your daily routine?

The good news is that prayer can fit in anywhere, any time. Morning. Noon. Night. God will hear you. He will give you His undivided attention. "This is the confidence we have in approaching God: that if we ask anything according to his will, he hears us" (1 John 5:14 NIV).

You too can pray as David prayed. God never tires of hearing your voice. Whatever is on your heart, share it with Him today.

I'm so thankful I can come to You any time of the day
or night, Lord. Help me to remember to come to
You first when I need help. Amen.

PERSEVERE IN PRAYER

Rejoice in our confident hope.
Be patient in trouble, and keep on praying.
ROMANS 12:12 NLT

One peek at the daily news and it's difficult to remain hopeful. Troubling events take place every day in every corner of the world, and it seems there's no end in sight.

But God promises that, amidst the world's turmoil, you can remain confident as you keep an eye toward heaven. Whether you're inundated with news of terrorist attacks, natural disasters, or crime in your hometown, you can rejoice in the hope that you have through Jesus Christ.

Rather than throwing your hands up in defeat, God's Word tells you to patiently endure tough times and to persevere in prayer. While the state of the world is in decline, and it seems as though your prayers for peace aren't being answered, you can have complete assurance—the hope!—of eternal life: "For the wages of sin is death; but the gift of God is eternal life through Jesus Christ our Lord" (Romans 6:23 KJV).

You can *know* with 100 percent assurance that perfect peace is the ultimate hope for your future: "He will wipe every tear from their eyes, and there will be no more death or sorrow or crying or pain. All these things are gone forever" (Revelation 21:4 NLT). You need only wait on God.

Lord, sometimes I feel so anxious. There is so much trouble in the world! Help me to feel Your peace deep within me. Amen.

Day 3

WITH BOLDNESS!

Let us therefore come boldly unto the throne of grace, that we may obtain mercy, and find grace to help in time of need.
HEBREWS 4:16 KJV

When you enter the Lord's presence, do you go boldly? Or do you make a tip-toe-like entrance?

Your heavenly Father wants you to approach Him with confidence. Unafraid, you may reveal your heart—your fears, your flaws, your frustrations—to Him. Whatever it is you're feeling, share it *boldly*. He is a mighty God. He can take it!

Nothing in this life depends on you, but rather on Him. God is merciful. A sufficient sacrifice was made on your behalf when He sent His Son, Jesus, to die on the cross. "If we confess our sins, he is faithful and just to forgive us our sins, and to cleanse us from all unrighteousness" (1 John 1:9 KJV). He is faithful. He is just. He is a forgiver of sins.

And your loving heavenly Father always has your best interests in mind. " 'For I know the plans I have for you,' declares the LORD, 'plans to prosper you and not to harm you, plans to give you hope and a future' " (Jeremiah 29:11 NIV). He looks on you with holy favor because you belong to Him. You are His beloved child! Go boldly!

Jesus, I know You understand me and my struggles. Let me come to You without hesitation, and with the assurance of Your love. Amen.

A WORD OF HOPE

Then you will call upon Me and go and pray to Me, and I will listen to you. And you will seek Me and find Me, when you search for Me with all your heart.

JEREMIAH 29:12–13 NKJV

Have you ever felt like God is so very far away? That every time you call on His name, your prayer falls on deaf ears? That your mistakes, your imperfections, your unlovable qualities have put miles and miles of distance between your heart and His?

Here's a word of hope: *nothing* can change the fact that you are His beloved child. He loves you in all of your imperfection. Because of His boundless love, you can call on Him any time, day or night, and He will hear you. There are no miles of separation. No difficult travels are required to gain His ear.

What can separate you from His love? *Nothing!* "Neither death nor life, neither angels nor demons, neither our fears for today nor our worries about tomorrow—not even the powers of hell can separate us from God's love. No power in the sky above or in the earth below—indeed, nothing in all creation will ever be able to separate us from the love of God that is revealed in Christ Jesus our Lord" (Romans 8:38–39 NLT).

Nothing can keep me from You, Lord! Even when I feel so far away from You, I'm so thankful that You keep pursuing me. Amen.

IN ALL CIRCUMSTANCES

Is any among you afflicted? let him pray. Is any merry?
let him sing psalms. Is any sick among you? let him call for
the elders of the church; and let them pray over him, anointing
him with oil in the name of the Lord: And the prayer of faith
shall save the sick, and the Lord shall raise him up;
and if he have committed sins, they shall be forgiven him.

JAMES 5:13–15 KJV

When life is going as planned and you're healthy, happy, content, and energized, pray!

When life is handing you one difficulty after another and you're sick, sad, dissatisfied, and weary, pray!

In *all* circumstances, where should you go but to God? He wants you to approach Him first—before your spouse, before your best friend, before your parents (see Proverbs 3:6). Every. Single. Time.

God's Word says that the prayers of the righteous are powerful: "The earnest prayer of a righteous person has great power and produces wonderful results" (James 5:16 NLT). Don't you want powerful, wonderful results from your conversations with the Almighty?

The expression that is always fitting for both sorrow and joy is worship, and prayer is an important element of worship. In the words of hymn writer Joseph M. Scriven, "What a privilege to carry everything to God in prayer!"

All day long, Lord, I am reminded that I need You. Help me to take the time to stop and spend time with You every day. Amen.

Day 6

BECAUSE HE IS GOOD

Oh, that men would give thanks to the Lord for His goodness, and for His wonderful works to the children of men!
Psalm 107:15 NKJV

When you last sent a prayer heavenward, did your words include thanks to your heavenly Creator? Or were they laden with requests for Him to fulfill your every want and need?

There's certainly nothing wrong with asking God to meet your needs. In fact, you *should* ask Him for those things. "If you. . .know how to give good gifts to your children, how much more will your Father in heaven give the Holy Spirit to those who ask Him!" (Luke 11:13 NKJV).

There's nothing wrong with asking Him for your wants either. "Take delight in the Lord, and he will give you the desires of your heart" (Psalm 37:4 NIV). If you're in need of a new job, include that request in your prayers. If you'd like a new car, by all means mention that too. However, don't forget to pray with a thankful heart.

God is gracious and merciful. He forgives. He delivers. He loves. Reflect on His goodness, and you'll be certain to include a "Thank You, Father!" in your daily prayers. "Give thanks to the Lord, for he is good; his love endures forever" (Psalm 107:1 NIV). Pray today. . .and give thanks!

For Your love and mercy, I thank You. For the beauty of mountains and seas and tall trees, I thank You. For Your justice and truth, I honor You. Amen.

Day 7

THE PRAYERS OF YOUR HEART

Because he bends down to listen,
I will pray as long as I have breath!
PSALM 116:2 NLT

Need some motivation to help jump-start your prayer life? This verse from Psalm 116 is it. The psalmist says, "Because he bends down to listen. . ." Imagine your loving heavenly Father bending low to better hear your voice. He's listening intently to every word coming out of your mouth. No smartphone distracts Him. Because He's omnipotent, no other voices drown you out. He listens intently to the prayers of your heart.

Now think about that one friend who listens to you best. Does that certain someone always give you her undivided attention? Or do distractions sometimes creep up in the middle of your conversations? A text that can't be ignored? . . . A phone call that has to be taken *right this very minute*? . . . No matter how loyal the listener, human minds are often preoccupied, and therefore, ears are missing out on what you're trying to communicate.

Your heavenly Creator misses *not one single word*. What better reason to continue praying to Him each and every day of your life?

Do as the psalmist says, and pray as long as you have breath. Talk to the One who listens to you best.

Lord, I whisper my innermost secrets to You, knowing You carefully listen to every word. Help me to find Your answers. Help me to hear Your voice. Amen.

Day 1

NO LONGER ORPHANS

Behold, what manner of love the Father hath bestowed upon us, that we should be called the sons of God.

1 John 3:1 KJV

Ask people if God exists and some will say that *if* He exists He's cold and uncaring. Some picture Him as an old man who strikes fear into the hearts of humanity. He's often viewed as cruel. Yet today's verse tells something different.

The writer wanted you to stop and pay attention to a profound love sent from God to humankind. The gift of love was paired with the gift of grace. How do you know this? God's Word says the love of God was so profound that you became something more than a follower, adherent, disciple, or student. You became a *child* of God who is loved by your Father and given all the rights of a family member. You aren't an acquaintance, part of His extended network, or an employee. You're family. By God's love you were offered the grace to become a son or daughter.

God's love didn't just provide rescue. It moved you from an orphan without a home to a family member with *anytime* access to God.

This is a big deal! Many have never accepted the lavish love God has for them. Maybe they can see it in you.

God, I am unbelievably humbled at the idea that I am Your child— that You have added me to Your family. Thank You, Father! Amen.

Day 2

WITHOUT GOD'S LOVE

God commendeth his love toward us, in that, while we were yet sinners, Christ died for us.
ROMANS 5:8 KJV

Mankind broke God's law repeatedly. God's commands were ignored daily. His plans went unrecognized globally. And in the midst of man's disregard, God developed a plan that defied all expectations. When you distanced yourself from His wisdom, rejected His claim on your life, and acted as if He didn't matter, and when your sin defined your choices, God sent His Son to pay the full price for your rebellion.

Why did He do this? He loved you. How did He demonstrate His love? By removing every barrier to relationship with Him. If it weren't for God's greatest sacrifice you'd be perpetually separated from Him.

God's love is as much a choice for Him as it is for you. Without God's choice to love, you'd be expected to personally accept the wages of sin—death (see Romans 6:23). God hates sin, but loves the people He created. In the midst of humanity's rebellion, Christ died so you could live, forgiven and free.

God's love provides the example you need to love others and return His love. A catastrophic future was radically altered because God loves you. Discover this most incredible reason for joy. Share it.

Lord, I want to be able to love unconditionally. I can't understand why You keep loving me, even when I mess up so many times, but I thank You for it. Amen.

Day 3

RETURNING GOD'S LOVE

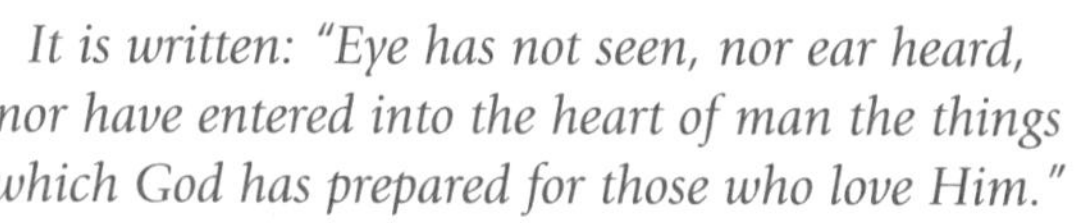

It is written: "Eye has not seen, nor ear heard,
nor have entered into the heart of man the things
which God has prepared for those who love Him."
1 Corinthians 2:9 NKJV

God's love is promised and available to all who trust (have faith) in the perfect sacrifice of the sinless Jesus Christ. Your sins can only be removed through an act of faith. The greatest ideas you have of what God's love is like will always be too small. How do you know this? Stop for a moment and read the verse again. Take your time.

Welcome back. Let's share the verse another way: "No story has fully expressed it, no song has adequately conveyed it, and our minds can only begin to imagine the planned blessings God lavishes on those who love Him."

God loves you intensely, and richly blesses you if you love Him in return. His blessings always outshine money because while you can buy a house, God can bless you with a home (there's a difference). Money is useful when you need things that don't last. However, when you want things that are everlasting look first to your relationship with God.

He's better than your best dream and greater than your greatest hope. Accept His blessings by offering your love to the God who loved you first.

God, I pour out my heart to You. I offer my hands to Your
service, my mind to Your will, and my spirit to
Your worship. I love You! Amen.

Day 4

NOTHING

I am convinced that nothing can ever separate us from God's love. Neither death nor life, neither angels nor demons, neither our fears for today nor our worries about tomorrow—not even the powers of hell can separate us from God's love. No power in the sky above or in the earth below—indeed, nothing in all creation will ever be able to separate us from the love of God that is revealed in Christ Jesus our Lord.

ROMANS 8:38–39 NLT

God's love is real. No one can match it, take it away, or make God stop loving you.

You can reject Him. You can stiff-arm God. You can try to run away from Him. In the end, God isn't moved in His opinion of you. He has, does, and always will love you. Only you have the power to separate yourself from Him by *never* accepting His love. Even that won't stop Him from offering His love.

As a believer you can be sure that nothing can ever separate (remove) you from His love—when you die, while you live, the meddling of spiritual beings, fear, worry, or physical objects. Nothing separates God's children from the love of God. Let that sink in and then look at the verse again. *Nothing* can *ever* separate you from God's love.

Lord, even the strongest love I have here on earth is no comparison to the love You have for me. That amazes me. I love Your love! Amen.

Day 5

COMPLETELY DRENCHED

Hope does not put us to shame, because God's love has been poured out into our hearts through the Holy Spirit, who has been given to us.

ROMANS 5:5 NIV

We're told that hope anchors the soul (see Hebrews 6:19). Hope holds your spiritual life in place in a societal stream bent on the mad rush, the latest trend, and the mocking insistence that God is dead.

Like most things, shame is a choice. When your hope is in the love of God there's no shame in embracing it. It should be a primary source of joy.

Like a cloudburst in a drought, a blanket on a cold night, or snow on Christmas morning, God's love completely envelopes the core of what makes you "you." There's no part left out of His loving touch, and God's living water saturates. . .daily.

For the first time in this look at God's love, please discover your Helper, Guide, and Counselor, the Holy Spirit. It's His job to drench you in the love of God.

God is rich in love, and He shares the source of that richness with you. It's a promise, a gift, and the perfect environment for life change. Bring it on, accept its fullness, and let it spill over into your life. You need it. He gives it. Accept it.

God, shame has made me feel bad about who I am.
Please lift that feeling off me. Please wrap me in Your love. Amen.

Day 6

RETURN ON INVESTMENT

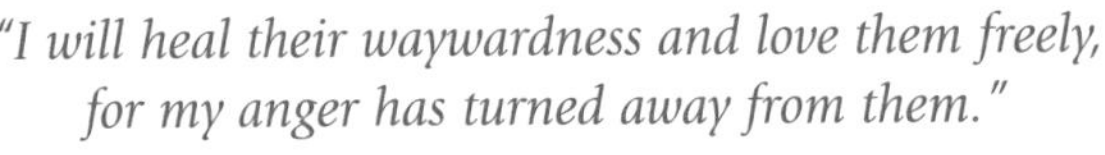

"I will heal their waywardness and love them freely, for my anger has turned away from them."
HOSEA 14:4 NIV

You've probably heard the term, *Return on Investment* (ROI). Most people use the term when talking about financial investments. If applied to your spiritual life two very different outcomes to investment strategies emerge.

One strategy occurs when *you* invest love in the God who designed you and gave you life. The return on your investment is forgiveness, eternal life, the guidance of His Spirit, and His ability to work all things together for the good "of those who love him, who have been called according to his purpose" (Romans 8:28 NIV).

A second strategy occurs when *God* invests love in you. His ROI is less assured. You could choose to follow, be transformed through obedience, and become close to God; or you could ignore His love, turn from His rescue plan for your life, and act as if you never knew about His plans.

God always invests love in others. Do you? He cares for all people. Do you play favorites? He has a plan for each life. Can you help someone follow it?

When you invest in love, it's returned. You make investments. Some investments don't seem like much, but God offers you incredible investment opportunities. Choose wisely.

God, I want to spread Your love around. Help me to see those who need You. Help me to reach out and make a difference—even a small one—today. Amen.

Day 7

TAKE HIS HAND

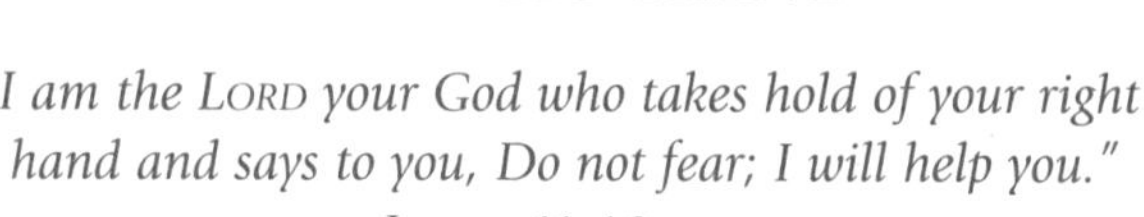

"I am the LORD your God who takes hold of your right hand and says to you, Do not fear; I will help you."
ISAIAH 41:13 NIV

Visit any mall or shopping center. If a child is walking with her parents, there's a good chance she's holding hands. Kids instinctively reach for Mom's hand when they're nervous or just want assurance that everything is going to be all right.

This gesture that delivers confidence to a child and delight to parents is how God deals with you. He uses that word-picture to describe His care and promise to be present during life's most stressful moments.

If you think of the worst life issue you've ever experienced, you should add the word-picture of God holding your hand through it. Imagine His words, "Do not fear; I will help you." When you deal with others who are going through similar pain and need assurance, remember today's verse and share this reassuring picture.

There's no truth to the statement, "God helps those who help themselves." It's not in the Bible. You should work hard, do your best, and complete tasks. However, He Himself holds your right hand, so your future is never left to blind chance. He's with you in every moment of joy and instance of sorrow. Take His hand. Feel accepted.

Lord, when I am lost in fear and crushed by stress,
help me to feel Your hand reaching for mine. Amen.

Day 1

THE UNBREAKABLE TETHER

"The LORD is my portion," says my soul, "Therefore I have hope in Him." The LORD is good to those who wait for Him, to the person who seeks Him.
LAMENTATIONS 3:24–25 NASB

For the child of God, hope is a rich inheritance, a priceless, limitless resource that lights the darkest night and kindles the dullest ember. To belong to God is to have hope on speed dial, a prayer or scripture away, a ready connection with your sovereign Savior who purchased hope for you on the cross.

Sometimes, though, the only way to appreciate what you've been given is to think of what life would be like without it. To lose hope, then, is to pull anchor in a storm, to be untethered from the very idea that tomorrow might be better than today. Hopeless people give up on relationships because they've gotten stuck in fight-or-flight mode. They give up on getting help because how could anything ever be good again?

As a Christian, though, God tenderly holds you in the palm of His hand: "The LORD directs the steps of the godly. . . . Though they stumble, they will never fall, for the LORD holds them by the hand" (Psalm 37:23–24 NLT). Nothing can separate you from His love (Romans 8:38–39) or the hope you have in Christ.

God, my Rock, my Anchor, thank You for being a solid place for me to land, no matter how much life tosses me around. Amen.

Day 2

A DIFFERENT GRIEF

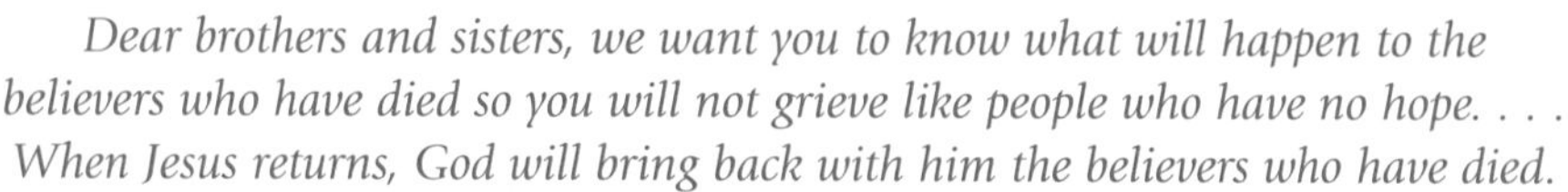

Dear brothers and sisters, we want you to know what will happen to the believers who have died so you will not grieve like people who have no hope. . . . When Jesus returns, God will bring back with him the believers who have died.

1 THESSALONIANS 4:13–14 NLT

It's hard to keep an eternal perspective when you're waist deep in grief. Sometimes the sorrow barely covers your toes, and other times it's up your nose and stinging your eyes. Forget heaven, you just want to get to the next moment. But here's the thing: you *will* get to the next moment, and the next. The world should have stopped spinning, but it just keeps on keeping on.

As annoying as that is, it's also pretty astonishing, because while grief or sickness or getting fired has put a pin in your life, God is holding your place. He will comfort you when your thoughts have all gone black, and when you're ready to take a next step, He will be right there on the path ahead of you.

And in the end, your Father is holding your place in heaven, the place He made specifically for you, a place of reunion and rejoicing. Death stinks, but it really has lost its sting because of the wonder of Jesus' resurrection.

Lord, when grief overwhelms me and steals my joy,
protect my heart. Help me to see Your light.
Help me to know the hope I have. Amen.

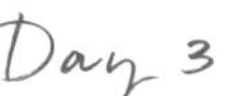

PROGRESSION AND PROCESS

We glory in tribulations also: knowing that tribulation worketh patience; and patience, experience; and experience, hope: and hope maketh not ashamed.

Romans 5:3–5 KJV

The Christian life starts in the most hopeful way, riding the crest of a wave of joyful expectation. You thought that shifting your eternal destination from hell to heaven surely meant sunny skies and smooth sailing from here on out. Not quite. While the glory that awaits you is worth celebrating, you have just begun a process that will consume the rest of your time on earth—sanctification.

Your response to everything you go through from then on will either make you more like Jesus or less like Him. And you'll be doing it with a target painted on your back, a mark for Satan's wiles and society's scorn, even as you fight the battle of the flesh. Would it be easier if you hadn't responded to Christ's call on your heart? Maybe—but only in this life. Eternity is a lot longer than the seventy or so years you might get here, so it's worth the preparation.

That preparation, though, will come through tribulation, patience, and experience. Take encouragement from the progress and the process, because the hope that results is ironclad, unassailable by the very gates of hell. You are Christ's, and the ultimate victory is yours.

Lord, let me see what I can learn through the trials I am going through. Help me to come out wiser and stronger. Amen.

HOPE'S SPOKESPERSON

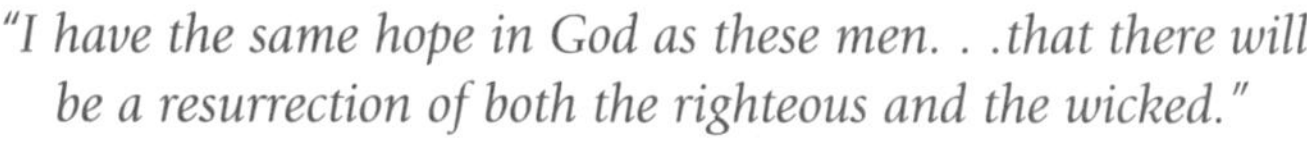

"I have the same hope in God as these men. . .that there will be a resurrection of both the righteous and the wicked."
ACTS 24:15 NIV

The world's evil knows few bounds, and it can be a satisfying thought to know that God will righteously judge each unrepentant terrorist and child molester. But hell is only an appeasing thought if you think you could never possibly feel its flames—that your goodness and decency are enough to keep you in the clear. A redeemed soul recognizes each evil act for what it truly represents: an assault on the hope of knowing God's love and grace through Christ. Never forget who the real enemy is.

Evil should be a stench to you the way it is to God, but will you breathe through it and remember a lost and dying world? Jesus broke through death and hell to build a bridge back to God, and He calls you to show the way, to be this world's salt and light—its preservative against decay and its hope in the darkness.

You are truth's ambassador and hope's spokesperson. The stakes are eternal, and you know the only way out of this mess. You know God's heart: John 3:16. Focus your prayers today on as many being covered by the blood of Christ as possible.

Lord, I am grateful that I know Your grace. Help me to tell others about this gift so they can be freed from the bondage of sin too. Amen.

Day 5

RECONNECT AND REJOICE

For in this hope we were saved. But hope that is seen is no hope at all. Who hopes for what they already have? But if we hope for what we do not yet have, we wait for it patiently.
Romans 8:24–25 niv

Sometimes, hope seems to slip away so secretly that you don't even know it's gone. Nothing disastrous has struck; everything's cruising along, but you look around and feel like you took a wrong turn somewhere. Maybe you thought you'd be further along in your career or in a relationship, or that you would have done more with your life—traveling, maybe, or even ministering.

The fact that you can't be fully satisfied in this life suggests that this life isn't meant to fully satisfy you. Life's importance isn't the end products of your work or relationships but what you learn about God, others, and yourself along the way. Only God can grasp the full scope of every little thing you think, say, and do, but you have His promise that He is working it all together for your good (Romans 8:28).

When you lose sight of God's path, reconnect with Him—through prayer, His Word, and Christian fellowship. Be reassured that all the things you can't see are clear as day to the One who directs your steps.

God, I am restless in this world. Help me to be able to focus on what I need to do. And remind me that You are working with me and in me. Amen.

....

....

....

....

....

....

....

....

Day 6

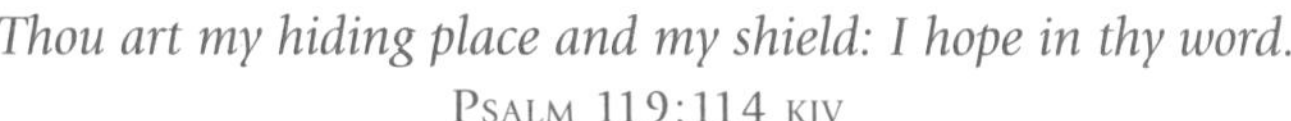

A DAILY GETAWAY PLAN

Thou art my hiding place and my shield: I hope in thy word.
Psalm 119:114 KJV

If you've recently had the chance for a quick getaway, you know what a blessing it can be to take in a new setting, to get a break from the busyness of the everyday hustle and bustle. Sometimes, the refreshment can last you quite a while; other times it evaporates on the drive home.

Most times, even getting away for a weekend just can't be done. The question becomes, *How can I be refreshed in the middle of all that I have to do today?* David offered a solution: God's Word. You may not be able to go out of town or even go camping, but scripture can be your hiding place, a refuge of hope and rejuvenation when life is spinning madly around you.

Reading the Bible enables you to look beyond your circumstances and rest. "Blessed is the man who trusts in the Lord, and whose hope is the Lord" (Jeremiah 17:7 NKJV). After all, no matter where you are, your "soul finds rest in God" (Psalm 62:1 NIV), and "those who hope in the Lord will renew their strength" (Isaiah 40:31 NIV). A spa day or fishing trip is great, but God's Word gives deep refreshing no matter where you are.

Lord, I need help remembering to carve out space in my schedule just to be with You and to study Your Word. Help me, Lord. Amen.

Day 7

THE WONDER OF HOPE

Who, contrary to hope, in hope believed, so that he became the father of many nations, according to what was spoken, "So shall your descendants be."
Romans 4:18 NKJV

Hope is a contrary thing. It flies in the face of common sense. What Abraham did, for example, makes no sense—uprooting his family, taking them from their ancestral homeland to some place he'd never heard of or seen, all on the say-so of an unknown Deity who came and told him to get going, that He had big plans for him. And yet, something about God gave Abraham hope that all His promises would come true.

The power of hope lies in belief, or, more specifically, the one in whom belief is placed. To hope in God is to believe in Someone you can't see now but will someday. And when you do, everything you hoped would be true about Him will be dwarfed by His reality. Everything about Him—His love, His warmth, His wonder—will be more than you could ever imagine.

After all, if Paul said all the troubles of this life, which overwhelm you, are but momentary things compared with heaven's glories (2 Corinthians 4:17), how great must heaven be? And how much greater the One who makes it *heaven*—God Himself? Hope in Him is well placed.

God, I want to be the kind of person who can just go where You send me, with no reservations. Help me to stand firm in the knowledge of You. Amen.

WHY LOVE?

We love, because He first loved us.
1 John 4:19 NASB

It's interesting that God created some animals to be mostly loners. Examples are bears, koalas, and sea turtles. Sometimes a solitary life seems appealing doesn't it? Wouldn't it be a peaceful existence to just do your own thing without answering to or dealing with anyone? No cooperation or communication required. Yet what a lonely life too—void of relationships, connection, and love.

God created solitary animals in their unique ways, but He created humans entirely different. He created people in His image, to be more like Him. And that's exactly why people *do* have love for others. "We love, because He first loved us." It's as simple and profound and beautiful as that.

God is love itself, as the whole chapter of 1 John 4 explains. Apart from Him, it's impossible to know what real love is. And because He created you and showed His love for you—especially through the sacrifice of His Son, Jesus Christ—people are consequently wired to want to imitate Him in sharing love and being part of loving relationships with others.

You taught me about love, Lord, and now I need to share what I know with others. Give me the courage to love others boldly. Amen.

Day 2

NO GREATER GOAL

And now these three remain: faith, hope and love.
But the greatest of these is love.
1 Corinthians 13:13 NIV

Faith, hope, and love are vitally important virtues for Christians. Without them, there is no Christian life. They're fundamental to your walk with God through your Savior, Jesus Christ. Yet the Bible promises that one of these virtues stands out above the others—and without it the others are empty. That virtue is *love.*

Love is the greatest virtue of all. As a Christian, you must cling to it and constantly convey it to people around you. Why? Because as the first part of 1 Corinthians 13 explains, love is what gives your words weight, your life significance, and your motives meaning. Anything said or accomplished without love is absolutely worthless.

Jesus said, "Your love for one another will prove to the world that you are my disciples" (John 13:35 NLT). Cultivating and sharing *faith* and *hope* certainly are important. But *love* is the greatest and most essential virtue for pointing others to Jesus Christ as Savior and encouraging them to surrender their lives and follow Him. Christians must cultivate and share it above all. There is no greater goal than to win others over to Jesus with your love.

Jesus, sometimes I get so focused on serving others or sharing the Gospel that I forget to just love people—right where they are. Help me to do that. Amen.

REAL LOVE

Beloved, let us love one another, for love is from God; and everyone who loves is born of God and knows God. The one who does not love does not know God, for God is love.

1 John 4:7–8 NASB

The world pretends to know what real love is. Secular culture has all kinds of ideas—some harmless, some not far off the mark, and some that are deceiving and dangerous. The basic reason humans are even looking for love is because God Himself is love and He instituted it among them when He created them in His image.

Authentic love is simply impossible to know without first knowing who God is and how He demonstrates His love to you. It's described so well in this passage: "God showed how much he loved us by sending his one and only Son into the world so that we might have eternal life through him. This is real love—not that we loved God, but that he loved us and sent his Son as a sacrifice to take away our sins. Dear friends, since God loved us that much, we surely ought to love each other. No one has ever seen God. But if we love each other, God lives in us, and his love is brought to full expression in us" (1 John 4:9–12 NLT).

Jesus, people show love in so many ways. Sometimes the way they use that word doesn't make sense to me. But I know real love only comes from You. Amen.

ACTIVE LOVE

We know what real love is because Jesus gave up his life for us. So we also ought to give up our lives for our brothers and sisters. If someone has enough money to live well and sees a brother or sister in need but shows no compassion— how can God's love be in that person?

1 John 3:16–17 NLT

Telling children they're loved but never playing with them or providing for them proves those loving words empty and gives them a false idea of love. The same kind of thing goes for relationships with spouses, extended family, and friends. Loving words in relationships are nice, of course, but they're hollow if not accompanied by action. Real love is active. Real love is sacrificial.

Christians who tell the world that they love others without actively helping brothers and sisters around them who are in need give a false idea of the love of the Savior. Jesus gave up His very life, and He calls His people to sacrifice in order to lovingly meet others' needs as well. First John 3 continues by saying, "Dear children, let's not merely say that we love each other; let us show the truth by our actions" (v. 18 NLT).

Father God, I don't want my words to be empty. Help me to show others love in real, meaningful ways. Amen.

Day 5

CONFIDENT LOVE

Our actions will show that we belong to the truth, so we will be confident when we stand before God. Even if we feel guilty, God is greater than our feelings, and he knows everything. Dear friends, if we don't feel guilty, we can come to God with bold confidence. And we will receive from him whatever we ask because we obey him and do the things that please him. And this is his commandment: We must believe in the name of his Son, Jesus Christ, and love one another, just as he commanded us.

1 John 3:19–23 NLT

It can be intimidating, even terrifying, to think of standing before Almighty God, the Creator of all the universe. Yet scripture promises that because of Jesus, Christians are made right with God (Romans 3), so you have no need to fear.

Believers will surely bow the knee (Philippians 2:10) in humility, respect, and awe before the King of all kings, but those who love God and obey His commands have no need to cower in fear. The passage above explains that believing Jesus and offering love to one another are what give Christians not just a little bit of assurance but *bold* confidence before their holy heavenly Father.

So, trusting in your Savior, go and boldly share His love, knowing that one day soon you can confidently stand before the one true God!

God, I'm awestruck that You allow me to stand before You, to tell about You, and to lead others to You. Help me to never take those duties lightly. Amen.

HELP FOR LOVING OTHERS

But concerning brotherly love you have no need that I should write to you, for you yourselves are taught by God to love one another.
1 Thessalonians 4:9 NKJV

Christians don't need instructions from other people on how to love, when God Himself is the very best teacher of love. He *is* love itself, after all!

Simply ask God for His help to love others. Do you have people in your life who are difficult to deal with, yet you know God is calling you to show them kindness and compassion? You don't have to take the time to read a pile of books on how to treat others well; simply ask God Himself day by day—sometimes moment by moment—to show you how to act and what to do for others, to give you the opportunities and the right words to say to share His love and point others to Him. Philippians 2:13 (NLT) promises that "God is working in you, giving you the desire and the power to do what pleases him."

Of Corrie ten Boom's many famous words, one quote stands out at this point. She prayed, "Dear Jesus. . .how foolish of me to have called for human help when You are here." A hearty "Amen!" to that.

Lord, I'm still trying to figure out how to love everyone like You do. It's not easy! Help me to keep trying. Amen.

Day 7

LOVE ABOVE YOURSELF

Be devoted to one another in love.
Honor one another above yourselves.
ROMANS 12:10 NIV

Secular culture has taken self-help to a cringe-worthy level for Christians. Of course, it makes worldly sense that a person must be healthy, happy, and well himself *first* for him to be able to help anyone else. Yet what does the Bible say about worldly wisdom? Read 1 Corinthians 3:18–19. Not to mention, how is the propensity for self-first kind of thinking consistent with the scriptures that say Christians should rejoice in suffering and trials? (See Romans 5, James 1, 1 Peter 4, 2 Timothy 3, and 2 Corinthians 4.)

Many times, the Bible talks about laying your life and selfish desires down and lifting others up. Take Philippians 2:3–4 (NIV) for example: "Do nothing out of selfish ambition or vain conceit. Rather, in humility value others above yourselves, not looking to your own interests but each of you to the interests of the others."

Loving others means sacrificing your own desires in order to help meet their needs (despite whatever trials and suffering you might be enduring yourself), just like Christ sacrificed to meet the world's greatest need—and thus saved humankind from sin. Thankfully God doesn't expect this kind of sacrificial love from your own ability. He urges His people to depend on Him for endless power and strength.

Lord, I am working on thinking of others more. I ask You to keep me so busy serving others, Lord, that I don't have time to dwell on myself. Amen.

GOD CARES FOR YOU

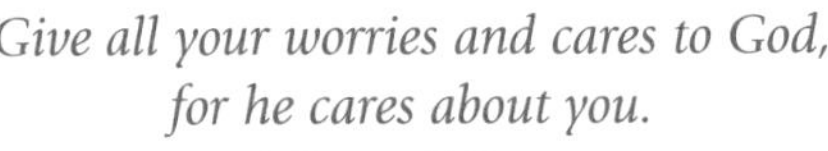

Give all your worries and cares to God,
for he cares about you.
1 Peter 5:7 NLT

You may feel like a hopeless mess, with a discouraged spirit, staggering through life burdened with countless cares and problems, isolated from friends and loved ones. You may seriously wonder if God even remembers you or cares about you. If so, where is He when you need Him most?

But be assured that God hasn't forgotten you—and He *does* care. His eyes are continuously upon your plight, and He hears all your groanings. He understands your frustration when your anguished prayers seem to be going unanswered, but He is working to *answer* your prayers, even if—from your perspective—He seems to be moving glacially slow.

Don't try to carry all your problems and concerns by yourself. Certainly, do your best to deal with situations you face, but you must also realize that one of the best things you can do is cry out to Him for *His* help in dealing with problems. Having done all that you can, give them into God's powerful hands and trust Him to work things out.

When you do that, He will send peace into your heart and comfort you, assuring you that everything will work out. . .even when the situation seems hopeless.

God, my list of cares is long! I know You can take them all.
I just need to let go of my worries and trust You more. Amen.

Day 2

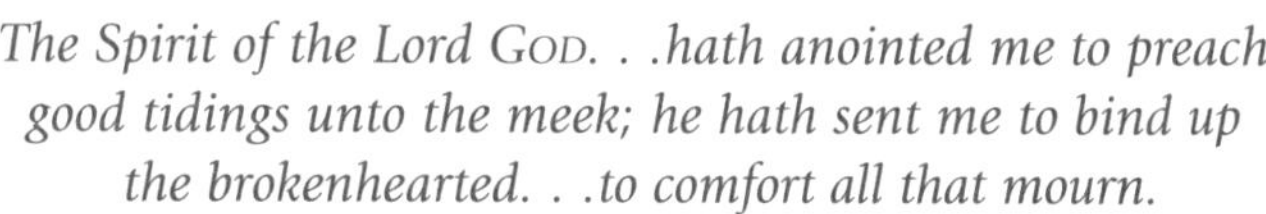

THE COMFORTING SAVIOR

The Spirit of the Lord God. . .hath anointed me to preach good tidings unto the meek; he hath sent me to bind up the brokenhearted. . .to comfort all that mourn.

Isaiah 61:1–2 KJV

In Luke 4:17–21 Jesus declared that this Old Testament passage was written specifically for Him and fulfilled by Him. It therefore describes what Jesus is like, giving you a look into His heart and the overwhelming love He had—and has—for people around Him.

Isaiah's prophecy went on to say that the Messiah would "provide for those who grieve in Zion—to bestow on them a crown of beauty instead of ashes, the oil of joy instead of mourning, and a garment of praise instead of a spirit of despair" (Isaiah 61:3 NIV). The people were despairing, figuratively smearing their faces with ashes in their deep mourning, but Jesus came along, anointed their heads with the oil of joy, and dispelled despair.

God's Holy Spirit anointed Jesus "to comfort all that mourn," so you should picture Him as gentle, caring, and continuously seeking to cheer people up. If you can understand and believe this one facet of Jesus' heart, you will have grasped His most basic thought toward you. No wonder He was constantly talking about His disciples experiencing joy!

Lord, it gives me so much peace to know that You will comfort me when I am sad and tired and when my heart is heavy. I count on that comfort! Amen.

Day 3

PROTECTED AND COMFORTED

Even when I walk through the darkest valley,
I will not be afraid, for you are close beside me.
Your rod and your staff protect and comfort me.
PSALM 23:4 NLT

David declared that the Lord's staff protected and comforted him, even when making his way through the darkest valleys. A shepherd used his staff as a deadly weapon against fierce animals, and knowing that their guardian was always looking out for them was a source of great comfort to the flock.

Jesus is the Good Shepherd, and He has promised to always be close to you, never to abandon you. But perhaps you worry that although He's been with you *this* far, He will eventually grow tired of you and bail out—most likely during your time of greatest need. But elsewhere He promised, "Surely I am with you always, to the very end of the age" (Matthew 28:20 NIV). He's with you *always*. He will never desert you.

You will be required to cross many dark valleys during your sojourn on this earth. May you find deep comfort in the fact that the Son of God will be with you every step of the way. And when you cross the final "valley of the shadow of death" (v. 4 KJV), He will usher you into the loving presence of His Father forever.

My Shepherd, I trust Your strength. I use Your wisdom
to guide my steps. Help me to face the dark paths
in my future. Give me courage. Amen.

Day 4

GOD WILL CONSOLE YOU

When anxiety was great within me,
your consolation brought me joy.
PSALM 94:19 NIV

Have you ever felt great anxiety? It can be a terrifying experience. When you're facing unrelenting stress or are under serious spiritual attack, anxiety can seem like a great wave rising, powerful enough to rip your boat completely from its moorings. In that moment, you feel as if it's all over. Fear and despair are flooding your mind and about to drive you over the edge, and you don't think you have the strength to resist.

An unknown psalmist was suffering terrible anxiety and cried out in anguish, "Who will rise up for me against the wicked?" He then flung himself upon God, declaring, "Unless the LORD had given me help, I would soon have dwelt in the silence of death" (v. 17). He knew that God was His *only* hope and was desperate for His help.

You too can cling to God when waves of anxiety strike with punishing force. God is your Rock. He will not be moved, and if you trust Him, you won't be moved either. He will come to your defense. He will protect you and comfort you, and in the place where you suffered great anxiety, He will surprise you with peace and joy.

Lord, when my heart starts thumping and my palms start sweating, remind me of what is real. Speak truth to my mind and quiet the voices of anxiety. Amen.

GOD COMFORTS THE MOURNING

"God blesses those who mourn, for they will be comforted."
MATTHEW 5:4 NLT

You typically think of a mourner as someone grieving the death of a loved one, and that's a large part of the picture. But people mourn many things—the death of a dream, the end of a relationship, financial loss, wasted years, or failing health. When you're mourning, there seems to be no reason to have hope, no reason to be happy.

You trudge through life empty, drained of goals and purpose. You're in survival mode, droning along on autopilot. But time after time, God reaches out to tenderly comfort you, to breathe hope into you again. He pierces the clouds of despair and a single, faint shard of light illuminates your darkness. At first, you're often almost too despondent to be cheered by it. But slowly the clouds part, the light returns, gathering in brightness and strength, and finally hope rises and you can see your way again.

It will be like that at the end of this weary, trouble-filled life. The glorious light of heaven will surround you and sweep you up into its embrace in a fantastic rush of beauty and love, dispelling all your sorrows and heartaches. And your heavenly Father will draw you close, wipe away your tears, and comfort you.

Lord Jesus, grief is such a long, lonely journey. It's hard to reach out for help sometimes. Remind me that I am never alone. Amen.

Day 6

THE TRUEST COMFORTER

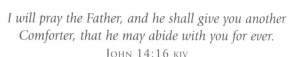

I will pray the Father, and he shall give you another Comforter, that he may abide with you for ever.
JOHN 14:16 KJV

After Job suffered great calamities, his three closest friends came "to mourn with him and to comfort him" (Job 2:11 KJV). Unfortunately, they soon forgot their initial mission and began calling his every motive into question and condemning him—so much so that Job lamented, "Miserable comforters are ye all" (Job 16:2 KJV).

There's *another* Comforter, however, who never condemns you or tears you down, but always seeks to take your side to comfort and restore you. He may frankly point out areas you need to change in, and urge you to turn to God, but He loves you deeply and always seeks your good. And He constantly assures you that you are God's beloved, saved child (Romans 8:15–16). This wonderful Comforter is, of course, the Holy Spirit.

The Greek word *parakletos* translated "Comforter" in this verse means "One called alongside." It's someone who pleads another's cause, or who helps them by comforting or defending them. The Holy Spirit feels deeply for you. He "prays for [you] with groanings that cannot be expressed in words" (Romans 8:26 NLT). You can be assured that this Comforter is *truly* on your side.

God, sometimes people say stupid things when they are trying to help. Help me to forgive them and see how they are trying to love me. Amen.

THE GOD OF ALL COMFORT

Blessed be. . .the Father of mercies and God of all comfort, who comforts us in all our tribulation, that we may be able to comfort those who are in any trouble, with the comfort with which we ourselves are comforted by God.

2 CORINTHIANS 1:3–4 NKJV

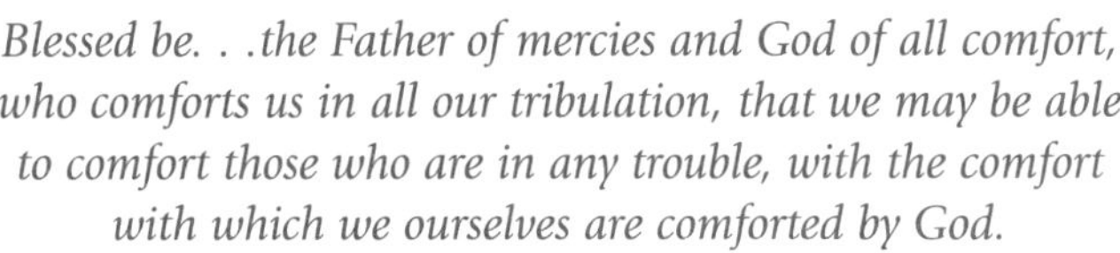

This scripture is a beautiful promise to cling to in time of need. God is truly the "God of all comfort" who "comforts us in *all* our tribulation." Whatever you're going through, your heavenly Father personally feels your pain and empathizes with you. When describing the afflictions of His people, scripture assures you, "In all their suffering he also suffered" (Isaiah 63:9 NLT).

And there is a second part to this promise. In the same epistle, Paul wrote, "God, who comforts the downcast, comforted us by the coming of Titus" (2 Corinthians 7:6 NKJV). First of all, Paul states the profound promise that "God. . . comforts the downcast," whoever they are and whatever they're going through.

But God has more than just your benefit in mind. After you've been touched and strengthened, He wants you to be moved by the same compassion that moves Him, to reach out to others and console them. You are to encourage others with the comfort with which you yourself are comforted by God.

Lord, I love the way You comfort me. Help me to comfort others with that same kind of quiet, persistent, peaceful care. Amen.

ASK, SEEK, KNOCK

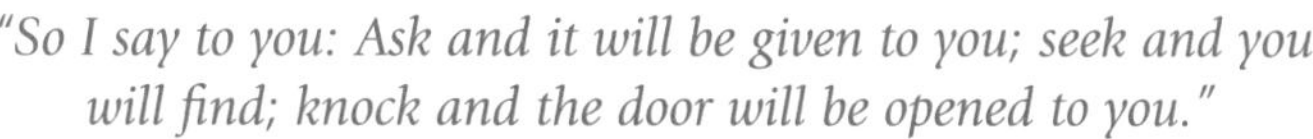

"So I say to you: Ask and it will be given to you; seek and you will find; knock and the door will be opened to you."

LUKE 11:9 NIV

When it comes to the promises of God, there are three key ways to watch them spring to action: Ask. Seek. Knock. It's impossible to see miracles come to pass in your life if you don't ask for them, so start by asking. Sure, God can read your mind. But speaking your request aloud bolsters your faith and reminds you that He is able. So, raise your voice. Speak it aloud. Watch your faith increase.

Next, seek God's will. Just because you ask for something doesn't mean it's God's best for you. When you seek Him with your whole heart, when His desire becomes more important than your desire, you'll be on the right path. He will reveal His good and perfect will to you, and it will be just what you need at this point in your life.

Finally, knock. Don't give up, even if the door doesn't open right away. Be like that persistent widow in Jesus' parable (Luke 18:1–8). Become a nuisance if you have to, but don't stop. Keep on knocking. Keep on seeking. Keep on asking. The Lord loves your persistence.

Thank You, Lord, for listening to my requests—
even the ones that come day after day. Help me
to know the plans You have for me. Amen.

Day 2

FIRST THINGS FIRST

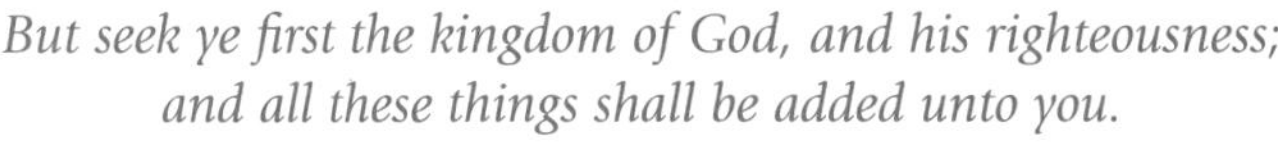

But seek ye first the kingdom of God, and his righteousness; and all these things shall be added unto you.

MATTHEW 6:33 KJV

Life is filled with exciting things, all vying for your attention. From the minute you wake up in the morning, distractions abound. Emails. Social media. Text messages. Phone calls. Bills. Spouse. Kids. Job. Car issues. Mortgage payments. On and on the list goes.

In the midst of the chaos it's easy to forget that you should be seeking God first. Before your feet hit the ground, begin to thank Him for the new day ahead of you. While you're brushing your teeth, praise Him for the opportunities He's about to give. While you're driving the kids to school, and as they head off to class, pray for God's best. Or as you drive to work, begin to speak His promises over your life.

In other words, give the choicest part of your day—the untainted first few minutes and hours—to the One who knows and loves you best. He's got your interests at heart. If you seek Him first, all of those other things on your to-do list will fall into perfect alignment.

God, my mind wanders and I get distracted so easily by things that just don't matter. Help me to find You in all this worldly mess! Amen.

Day 3

THE KINGDOM OF GOD

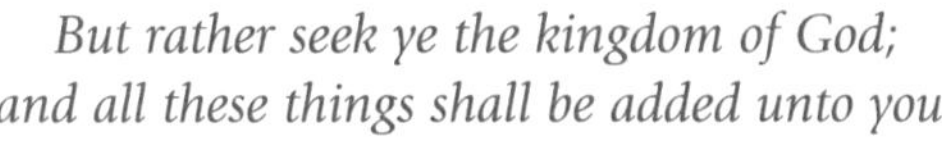

But rather seek ye the kingdom of God;
and all these things shall be added unto you.
LUKE 12:31 KJV

What comes to mind when you hear the words "kingdom of God"? Many people think of heaven, a place of eternal bliss. They think of white, fluffy clouds and pearly gates. Others think of a fairy-tale kingdom, with castles and knights, kings and queens. Some people believe it's a literal place; others argue that it's symbolic.

If you really want to know where the kingdom of God exists, take a look inside yourself. Jesus said that the kingdom of God is within you (Luke 17:21). When you "seek first the kingdom" (Matthew 6:33 NKJV) what you're really saying is, "God, I want Your will, Your kingdom, to take first place in my life, my family, my career, my friendships."

You're also saying, "I trust that all things (all of Your promises) will be added unto me when I seek Your kingdom first."

Why would your heavenly Father remind you that putting His kingdom first is key? Because His plans are far superior to your own. He's got amazing things in store for you. Those promises will come to pass in ways you never even imagined. So, hold on for the ride! "All these things" are about to be *added* unto you!

God, I want to be a good citizen in Your kingdom. I know Your ways are better than mine. Help me to seek those first. Amen.

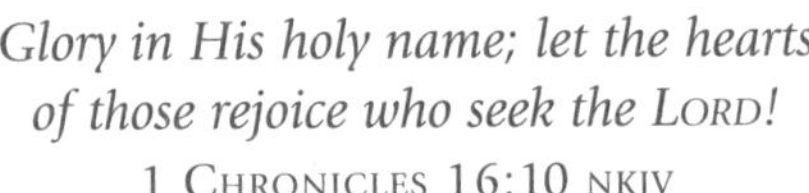

A HAPPY HEART

Glory in His holy name; let the hearts of those rejoice who seek the LORD!
1 CHRONICLES 16:10 NKJV

In this crazy, mixed-up world today, folks are looking to many different things to bring joy. Everywhere you look, promises abound! Television commercials. Magazine ads. Billboards. They all guarantee happiness and fulfillment.

However, you've learned the secret, one that doesn't require a slogan or advertisement: *nothing* can make you as happy as the kind of eternal joy that radiates from a heart fully linked with the Lord.

No matter how many cars you own, no matter how many vacations you go on, no matter how expensive the home you live in, you'll never truly be happy until you've accepted Jesus Christ as your Lord and Savior. Once you've crossed that threshold, a whole new world awaits.

When you put Him in His proper place—on the throne of your heart—you'll experience life-altering joy and enjoy peace as never before. His promises become real. Tangible. His Word springs to life. You begin to seek His perfect will for every area of your life because you know you'll find contentment and peace. And where peace reigns, joy abounds.

So, go on! Glory in His Name. Let your heart rejoice as you continue to seek His good and perfect will.

Lord, when I'm focused on worshipping You, I feel the most beautiful joy. Help me not to wait for that to happen. Help me to rejoice in You today! Amen.

Day 5

WITH ALL DILIGENCE

At night my soul longs for You, indeed, my spirit within me seeks You diligently; for when the earth experiences Your judgments the inhabitants of the world learn righteousness.

ISAIAH 26:9 NASB

Think back to your school days. Were you a diligent student, or one who procrastinated? If you gave yourself over to your studies, if you pursued every task with diligence, then the payoff came with better grades. (How fun to show *that* report card to your parents!) But if you waited until the last minute to do your homework or to study for a test, you paid the price with lower grades. (Hiding that report card never worked, did it? Mom always found out.)

That's how it is with the things of God too. When you become lackadaisical, when you forget to study His Word and pray, your faith begins to shrink. But when you seek Him with all due diligence, you grow stronger day by day.

Diligence is a critical part of your faith-walk. It bolsters your confidence so that you can stand in faith, believing God in good times *and* bad. Sure, there will be days when you don't feel like sticking close to God. Yes, there will be times that you grow weary. But diligence always has a pay-off.

Sovereign God, help me to work harder at knowing You than I work at knowing anything else. Help me to devote time every day to reading Your Word. Amen.

FINDERS KEEPERS

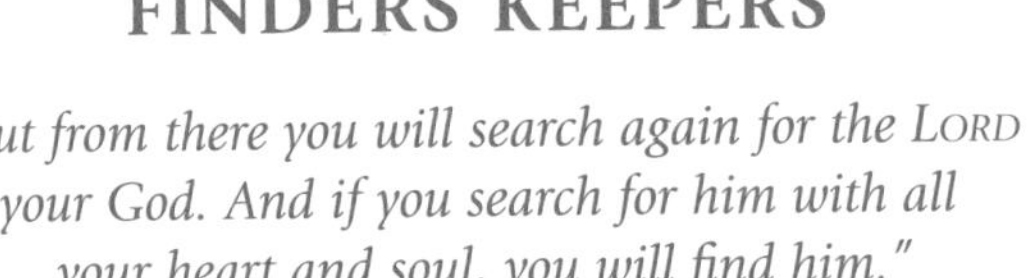

"But from there you will search again for the Lord your God. And if you search for him with all your heart and soul, you will find him."
Deuteronomy 4:29 NLT

Perhaps you grew up hearing the phrase, "Finders, keepers! Losers, weepers!" It's a familiar expression, albeit painful to the loser.

There's one area of your life where this phrase makes perfect sense: in your spiritual walk. When you seek God, when you spend time asking Him for His thoughts, His plans, His desires over your situation, you'll be a winner in the end. His faithfulness will astound you. The answered promises will invigorate you.

But when you rush ahead of God, convinced you have a better way, you'll end up on the losing end every time. In other words, you'll be disappointed and will wonder why He didn't come through for you. . .never realizing you didn't give Him a chance to do so.

Here's the key: don't be in a hurry. It's more important to be in sync with your heavenly Father than to strike out on your own and end up crashing and burning. Pace yourself. Then brace yourself for a great outcome. You'll be a finder who gets to keep the prize.

Lord, let me not worry about lists or schedules or worries. Let me put behind me anything that is keeping me from knowing You more. Amen.

THEN WILL I HEAR

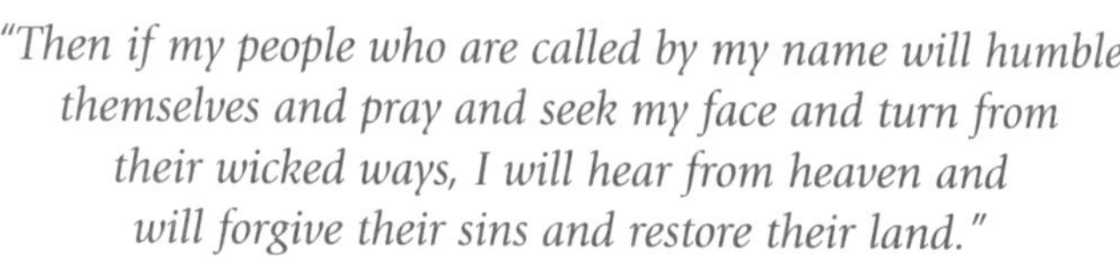

"Then if my people who are called by my name will humble themselves and pray and seek my face and turn from their wicked ways, I will hear from heaven and will forgive their sins and restore their land."
2 Chronicles 7:14 NLT

Have you ever been around a person who needed a hearing aid but refused to wear one? Chances are, you spent a lot of time with your voice raised. You probably ended up repeating phrases a lot too.

Aren't you glad that God doesn't need a hearing aid? Yet there are occasions when He seems to hear your requests louder and clearer than usual. There are times when the Lord calls you to seasons of specialized prayer for your family, your community, and your nation. He asks you to humble yourself and pray. When you're obedient—when you do what He asks—it's as if the volume on His "heavenly hearing aid" is turned way up! God is tuned in to your requests, He hears them with such clarity that He's compelled to move on your behalf by restoring and healing your land.

So, what are you waiting for? Today the Lord is calling you to bow down, to turn from anything holding you back, and to seek His face.

God, I don't want to disobey you. I do things without thinking. Humble me. Strip my heart of its pride. Forgive me. Amen.

BUILDING ON THE ROCK

"Therefore whoever hears these sayings of Mine, and does them,
I will liken him to a wise man who built his house on the rock:
and the rain descended, the floods came, and the winds blew and
beat on that house; and it did not fall, for it was founded on the rock."
MATTHEW 7:24–25 NKJV

When Jesus spoke the words in today's verses, He had just finished teaching about not judging others, the importance of diligent prayer, the Golden Rule, the narrow gate that leads to life, a tree being known by its fruit, and the separation that occurs between Christ and people who practice lawlessness.

Whoever hears these sayings of Jesus and *does* them will be considered wise by Jesus Himself. As such, that person will be able to withstand the disasters of life because they built upon a solid rock—that is, on Jesus Himself. Some of what He said are hard sayings, and all of them involve forsaking the flesh. But wisdom knows that this difficult battle won't last forever.

How are you doing when it comes to these sayings by Jesus? Are you resisting the flesh in favor of the narrow gate? What practical steps can you take today that will help you walk in wisdom going forward?

Lord, I need solid ground to stand on. Help me to plant
my faith firmly in Your Word and Your truth.
Let my actions be based on that. Amen.

....

....

....

....

....

....

....

....

Day 2

WISDOM FROM ON HIGH

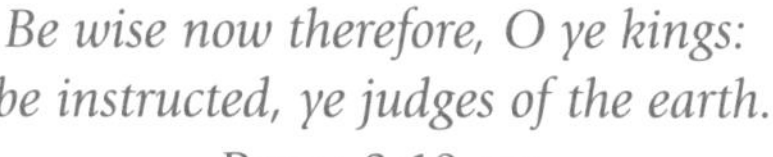

Be wise now therefore, O ye kings:
be instructed, ye judges of the earth.
Psalm 2:10 KJV

Scandals are nothing new. They've occurred in every generation and at every level of society. But the twenty-four-hour news cycle probably makes everybody more aware of them now as they occur, than they were of past indiscretions. At the heart of many scandals is the person's belief that they're above the law.

That's what was going on in Psalm 2:2–3 (KJV). It says, "The kings of the earth set themselves, and the rulers take counsel together, against the Lord, and against his anointed, saying, Let us break their bands asunder, and cast away their cords from us."

The psalmist says that even kings and judges of the earth are to receive instruction and therefore to become wise. The next verse (Psalm 2:11) explains where such instruction and wisdom should come from, saying leaders are to serve the Lord with fear, and to rejoice with trembling.

How are you doing in the leadership position(s) you find yourself in at work or school, in the community, at church, or in your home? Do you rule with an iron fist or with an open palm? Are you in it for your glory and for your gain, or for God's?

Lord, I want my life to be above reproach, so I can earn the respect and trust of those I serve. Help me not to hurt my witness through bad leadership. Amen.

SPEAKING WORDS OF LIFE

My son, pay attention to what I say; turn your ear to my words. Do not let them out of your sight, keep them within your heart; for they are life to those who find them and health to one's whole body.

PROVERBS 4:20–22 NIV

For better or worse, children remember what they are taught by their parents—both by word and by deed. If somebody were to ask you your philosophy about child rearing, showing emotion, or your work ethic, you might start with these words: "Well, I was raised to believe. . ."

But the philosophies you picked up during your childhood run even deeper than that. If you were raised in a family in which there was constant unrest in the home due to addiction, infidelity, abuse, or anger, then you may have either adopted those problems or you tend to keep people at arm's length trying to avoid such troubles.

Whatever the case, you have a chance to speak life into the next generation. Root yourself deeply in God's Word so you can pass that wisdom on to your children and grandchildren. In so doing, you'll be practicing Proverbs 22:6 (NIV): "Start children off on the way they should go, and even when they are old they will not turn from it."

Lord, I have not always had the best examples to follow. But I know I can always follow You. Help me to show others how to live through Your Word. Amen.

Day 4

THE WISE WILL SHINE

And they that be wise shall shine as the brightness of the firmament; and they that turn many to righteousness as the stars for ever and ever.
DANIEL 12:3 KJV

All of heaven takes note when God's people are under persecution. Daniel 12:1 speaks about such a time when Michael the Archangel will "stand up" (perhaps literally, but certainly symbolically) for the children of God to work for their deliverance. During that time, Daniel says some shall awake to everlasting life, while others to shame and everlasting contempt (v. 2).

Those who are abiding in Christ by feasting on His Word, staying in communion with Him, submitting to the Holy Spirit, fellowshipping with the saints, and living wisely during such difficult times will shine as the brightness of the firmament, turning many to everlasting life. That means it's possible, even under the hottest persecution, to shine for Christ. As you do so, people will notice—much like you can't help but notice the stars right now, even if you're not into astronomy. Their beauty causes you to look.

Do your neighbors currently see your light? How about your friends, coworkers, and family? Your job isn't to convince them to come to the light. It's to shine so they're attracted to the light.

God, I want to shine for You! Let my life be a light to others. Let my joy in You bubble up and be evident to all. Amen.

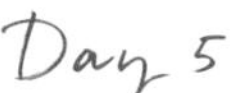

HEAVENLY CONVERSATIONS

However, we speak wisdom among those who are mature, yet not the wisdom of this age, nor of the rulers of this age, who are coming to nothing. But we speak the wisdom of God in a mystery, the hidden wisdom which God ordained before the ages for our glory, which none of the rulers of this age knew; for had they known, they would not have crucified the Lord of glory.

1 Corinthians 2:6–8 NKJV

Earlier in this epistle, Paul said the message of the cross is foolishness to those who are perishing, but to those who are being saved it is the power of God (1 Corinthians 1:18). Later, in 2 Corinthians 4:3, Paul alluded to the fact that the Gospel is veiled to those who are perishing. Even the rulers of this age can't understand it apart from the Holy Spirit.

"It is not the wisdom of politicians, nor philosophers, nor rabbis (see 1 Corinthians 2:6), nor such as they teach nor such as they relish; but the wisdom of God in a mystery, the hidden wisdom of God," writes Matthew Henry in his commentary.

Colossians 1:26 says this mystery has been revealed to the saints. Therefore, the conversations among God's people are to be on a higher plane. What a privilege to speak wisdom to one another!

Lord, I certainly don't understand everything in Your Word. But I know You will bless me if I keep trying. Help me to be filled with Your wisdom. Amen.

Day 6

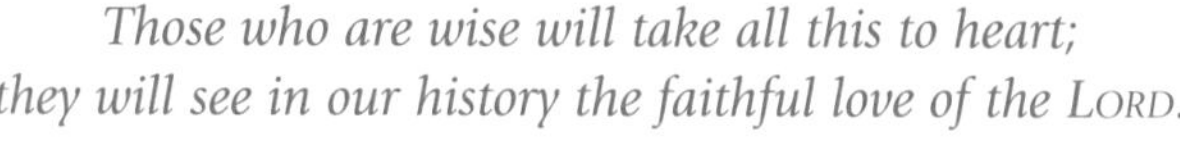

GOD'S FAITHFULNESS

Those who are wise will take all this to heart;
they will see in our history the faithful love of the Lord.
Psalm 107:43 NLT

The writer of this psalm takes inventory of the Lord's faithfulness for the purposes of giving people even more reason to praise Him.

Some were homeless, and others were hungry and thirsty. They cried out, and God rescued them (vv. 4–6). Some were depressed and their misery led them to rebel against God. When God weighed them down with hard labor, they cried out, and He saved them (vv. 10–13). Some were fools on the verge of death. They cried out for deliverance, and God healed them (vv. 17–20). Some traveled abroad to earn a living but encountered stormy seas. They cried out in their distress, and God saved them (vv. 23–29).

The Lord not only rescues and delivers His people in the short-term as they cry out to Him, but He also brings them to settle in cities (v. 36), blesses them with large families and heads of livestock (v. 38), and pours contempt on princes who oppress them (vv. 39–40). How can God's people do anything other than praise Him?

How has God been faithful to you and your family when you've cried out to Him? Praise Him for it!

God, Your Word shows me over and over again how faithful You were to Your people, even when they disobeyed. I know I can count on You! Amen.

Day 7

CULTIVATING WISDOM

For wisdom is protection just as money is protection,
but the advantage of knowledge is that wisdom
preserves the lives of its possessors.
ECCLESIASTES 7:12 NASB

You lock your doors before you go to sleep every night. You lock your car door, even when you're driving. You're careful about where you walk and the time of day you do it. And, whenever possible, you try to build up cash reserves as a hedge of protection for unexpected expenses.

As important as these measures are, Solomon advises that you also invest in wisdom because it too is a form of protection. You know this to be true. You teach your children not to play in the street, to avoid hot ovens, and to wear a helmet when they climb on their bicycles. They don't fully understand why, but you teach them as they grow and mature. Eventually, they realize the wisdom of such things.

Elsewhere, Solomon says wisdom is a tree of life to those who take hold of her (Proverbs 3:18). In John 6:63 (NASB), Jesus says: "It is the Spirit who gives life; the flesh profits nothing; the words that I have spoken to you are spirit and are life."

How are you currently cultivating wisdom? Are you paying as much attention to it as to building your nest egg?

Lord, when I am filled up with Your understanding,
I feel able to face any problem. Help me to find
new ways to learn more about You. Amen.

....

....

....

....

....

....

....

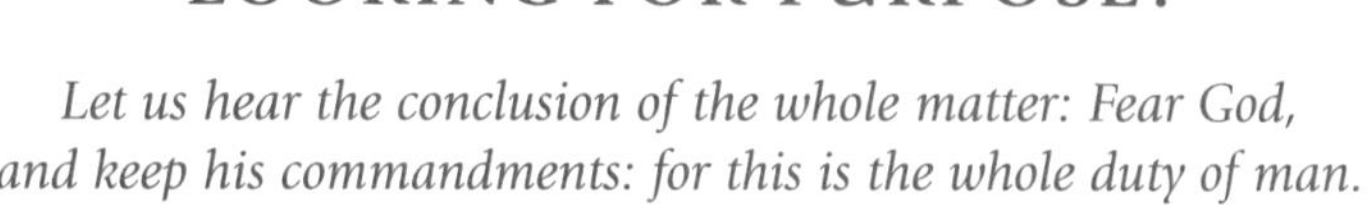

LOOKING FOR PURPOSE?

Let us hear the conclusion of the whole matter: Fear God, and keep his commandments: for this is the whole duty of man.
ECCLESIASTES 12:13 KJV

Isn't everyone looking for purpose in life? And the Bible has the simple yet profound, perfect answer—the *only* answer that they will genuinely find fulfilling, if only they will believe it and test it! Yet so many people try anything *but* the Bible for answers; they keep striving and toiling. . .and coming up empty.

Humanity's purpose in life is to fear (or respect) God and obey His commandments. This is the "whole duty" of man, says Solomon. The only authentic fulfillment people can ever find is to do what their Creator intended specifically for them, to obey Him in the things He designed and prepared. Ephesians 2:10 (NIV) says, "For we are God's handiwork, created in Christ Jesus to do good works, which God prepared in advance for us to do."

The greatest commandments are to love God with all your heart, soul, mind, and strength, and to love your neighbor as yourself (Matthew 22:35–40). Such obedience will cause everything else to fall in place, not always for an easy life but for a *good* life filled with purpose and satisfaction and sweet relationship with the Creator.

God, following commands seems so simple, yet it's so hard to do every day. But I trust that obedience to You is the best way. Amen.

Day 2

AUTHENTIC OBEDIENCE

"Not everyone who calls out to me, 'Lord! Lord!' will enter the Kingdom of Heaven. Only those who actually do the will of my Father in heaven will enter."

MATTHEW 7:21 NLT

The tongue can easily boast about obedience to God. There are all kinds of people today and throughout history pretending to obey the Bible and lauding themselves as true followers of Christ. But in the end, actions speak louder than words.

The Bible warns, "Watch out for false prophets. They come to you in sheep's clothing, but inwardly they are ferocious wolves. By their fruit you will recognize them. Do people pick grapes from thornbushes, or figs from thistles? Likewise, every good tree bears good fruit, but a bad tree bears bad fruit. A good tree cannot bear bad fruit, and a bad tree cannot bear good fruit. Every tree that does not bear good fruit is cut down and thrown into the fire. Thus, by their fruit you will recognize them" (Matthew 7:15–20 NIV).

Good fruit will result from obedience to God's commandments. The true Christian life is not made up of empty words that are easy to say, but rather, it is made up of challenging and rewarding obedience to God's good way in His Word—the best way to live.

God, I don't want to be confused by false messages about spiritual truths. Help me to think clearly about these things. Amen.

OBEDIENCE EQUALS PROSPERITY

"If you are willing and obedient,
you will eat the good things of the land."
Isaiah 1:19 niv

The Bible promises that obedience equals prosperity. Consider the verse above and also these: "Blessed are those who fear the Lord, who find great delight in his commands. Their children will be mighty in the land; the generation of the upright will be blessed. Wealth and riches are in their houses, and their righteousness endures forever" (Psalm 112:1–3 niv). "When the Lord takes pleasure in anyone's way, he causes their enemies to make peace with them" (Proverbs 16:7 niv).

The caveat is, sometimes the world's idea of prosperity confuses believers. Obedience to God does not necessarily mean riches and fun and constant good health and perpetually happy/peaceful relationships here on earth. It certainly can mean those things for this temporary life, but ultimately it means all these things and more in your *eternal* paradise home that God is creating.

It also means God's guidance and peace for any hard thing here in this sinful world as you obey His commands, no matter what the circumstances or how you're tempted to ignore them. Obedience to God means His constant, loving presence in your life because "the one who keeps His commandments abides in Him, and He in him" (1 John 3:24 nasb). There is no better prosperity than that!

My King and my Lord, so many people are confused about
what living a Christian life really means. Help me to
get my own mind straight on this! Amen.

DON'T DREAD DISCIPLINE

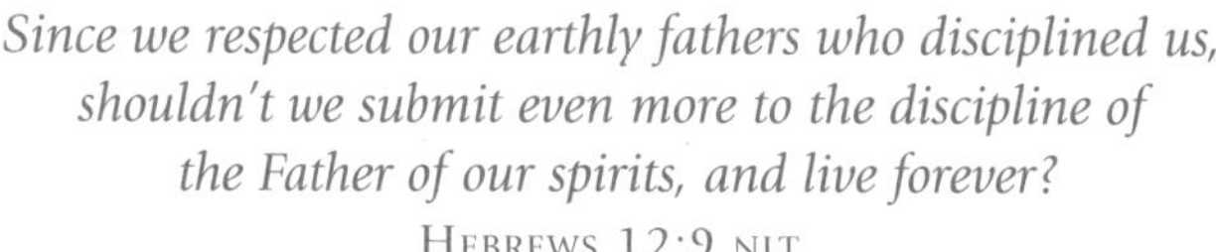

Since we respected our earthly fathers who disciplined us, shouldn't we submit even more to the discipline of the Father of our spirits, and live forever?
HEBREWS 12:9 NLT

If you were blessed with a loving father to obey, you realized he was worthy of respect. In fact, you probably realized as you became an adult that the purpose of his discipline was to protect you, train you, and mature you. If imperfect human fathers are capable of that, how much more so is the perfect heavenly Father?

And just like a good earthly dad disciplines his children, the heavenly Abba disciplines those He loves. Proverbs 3:11–12 (NLT) says, "My child, don't reject the LORD's discipline, and don't be upset when he corrects you. For the LORD corrects those he loves, just as a father corrects a child in whom he delights."

A vital aspect of being obedient to God and His commands is being subject to His discipline when you need it. God uses your mistakes and His correction to train and mature you. It produces the fruit in your life that advances His kingdom and brings Him glory. Remember, "No discipline is enjoyable while it is happening—it's painful! But afterward there will be a peaceful harvest of right living for those who are trained in this way" (Hebrews 12:11 NLT).

Lord, I don't think anyone likes being corrected. It's embarrassing and humbling. But I thank You for loving me enough to not let me keep making the same mistakes! Amen.

Day 5

A REAL SERVANT OF CHRIST

So then, my beloved, just as you have always obeyed,
not as in my presence only, but now much more in my absence,
work out your salvation with fear and trembling.
PHILIPPIANS 2:12 NASB

Did you ever have a classmate in school who acted perfectly obedient and sweet in front of the teacher, but whenever the teacher turned away or recess time rolled around, this classmate broke every rule but still cunningly managed to keep out of trouble?

God doesn't want the kind of obedience that is just for show or for selfish gain. He wants obedience that comes from a willing heart—a heart that loves Him and His Word and wants to produce the good fruit He has planned for those who follow Him. He wants obedience that seeks to please Him alone, no matter what people around you think or say. A question to ask yourself regularly in your walk with Jesus is the one Paul asks in Galatians: "Am I now trying to win the approval of human beings, or of God? Or am I trying to please people? If I were still trying to please people, I would not be a servant of Christ" (Galatians 1:10 NIV).

Be a genuine servant of Christ first and foremost, and then let Him help you to serve others as He directs.

Lord, I want to please You all the time, not just when I know
others are watching me. Help me to live right,
even in the secrets of my heart. Amen.

Day 6

DO THE WORD

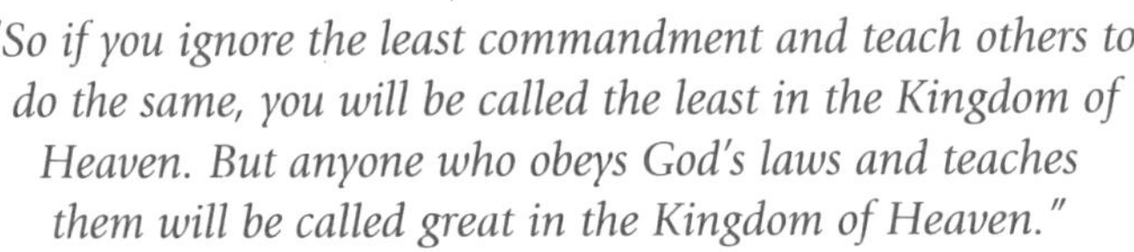

"So if you ignore the least commandment and teach others to do the same, you will be called the least in the Kingdom of Heaven. But anyone who obeys God's laws and teaches them will be called great in the Kingdom of Heaven."

Matthew 5:19 NLT

Believers will be held accountable for their response to God's commandments. It's easy to hear them and pay lip service to them. It's easy to attend church once in a while or even weekly and nod in agreement and sing praise and shake the pastor's hand at the end. It's easy to say that God is real and Jesus died on the cross. It's easy to make an appearance of being a Christian and leave it at that, never truly obeying God and serving Him wholeheartedly. Matthew 5:19 has a strong warning for this, especially for those believers who, by their example, teach others to disobey God.

James 1:22 (NLT) says, "But don't just listen to God's word. You must do what it says. Otherwise, you are only fooling yourselves." And Romans 2:13 (NLT) says, "For merely listening to the law doesn't make us right with God. It is obeying the law that makes us right in his sight."

God's Word is living and active (Hebrews 4:12), never just something to hear, but rather something to *do*.

I don't want to just go through the motions, Lord—acting like a believer but not really living for You. Help me to be a genuine Christian! Amen.

OBEY AND ABIDE

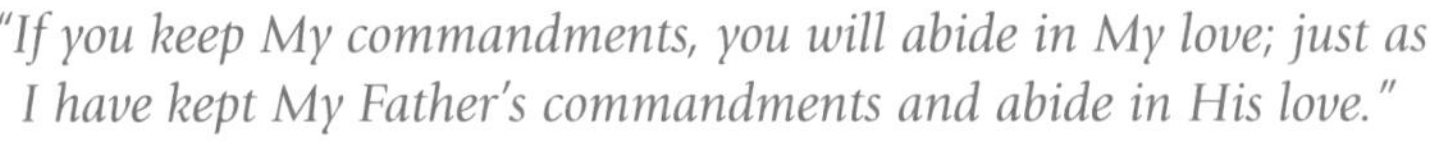

"If you keep My commandments, you will abide in My love; just as I have kept My Father's commandments and abide in His love."

JOHN 15:10 NASB

When people choose to live outside of God's commands, they then often complain that God would never want a relationship with the likes of them, or they complain about once-upon-a-time feeling close to Him but how they now feel far away. When someone feels distant from God or grumbles that a relationship is impossible, it's never because God has changed or become unreachable. In Malachi 3:6 (NASB), God promises, "For I, the LORD, do not change." And James 1:17 (NLT) says, "He never changes or casts a shifting shadow."

It's difficult to remain close to God in a fallen world. It takes determination and persistence to maintain close communion with your heavenly Father when the world constantly distracts you and Satan seeks to devour you (1 Peter 5:8). The solution is simple to explain—just keep God's commandments—yet difficult at times. It takes day-to-day diligence. However, you're never without God's help in doing so. Pray constantly, holding fast to His Word, asking for help to obey, and you'll surely abide in His everlasting love.

I want my life to be so entwined in Your Spirit, Lord, that I never stop feeling Your love and faithfulness. Help me to hold tight to You! Amen.

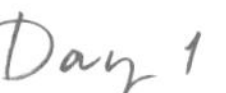

A GIFT GOD WANTS

Let us draw near with a sincere heart in full assurance of faith,
having our hearts sprinkled clean from an evil conscience
and our bodies washed with pure water.
HEBREWS 10:22 NASB

You have the ability to give God something that He's always wanted—your trust. He saves and wants you to trust that He saves completely. He gives and wants you to trust He'll give perfectly. He restores and wants you to trust that you're being made into a new creation.

Sin minimizes your ability to trust because sin always gives first place to what *you* want. Grace enhances your ability to trust because God's gifts are focused on your well-being while your focus shifts to God and away from self (because God is taking care of you). Faith is the key that unlocks grace, brings you into relationship with Him, and allows Him to begin restoring what sin has broken.

Faith is an offering of trust to God. It's a choice to believe the difficult. It's a decision to embrace the glorious impossible. It's easy to overlook, seems like a peculiar gift, and defies logic. Yet if you're ever to be made whole it's trust (faith) that gives permission to the Restorer.

Trust, together with obedience, make the perfect gift for the God who's given you everything else.

God, wash my heart clean.
Let me start new each day in You! Amen.

A MIRACLE'S WITNESS

*I have been crucified with Christ; and it is no longer I who live,
but Christ lives in me; and the life which I now live in
the flesh I live by faith in the Son of God,
who loved me and gave Himself up for me.*
GALATIANS 2:20 NASB

The Bible provides amazing benefits. You can read about the life of Christ, have a front-row seat to lessons Jesus taught, and witness the emotion of the final moments of His human existence. You can understand the sacrifice and how that gift offers forgiveness and eternal life.

It was in a reflective moment that the apostle Paul declared himself a follower of Christ. The apostle decided that he wouldn't live his life for himself, but he would put self aside in order to totally identify with the Author of Life.

When you do this, you recognize Jesus as the Son of God and realize that His sacrifice was accepted by God as payment for sin. You then live a life subject to God's plan and willingly submitted to His authority. Faith is the starting point of transformation, the declaration that you're a servant of God and a work under divine construction.

Without this transforming faith you can never truly accept the daily miracles God performs on your behalf.

When I think about what You gave up for me, I am rendered speechless. I can't believe You did that for me. You are amazing. I love You, Jesus! Amen.

Day 3

THE SIZE OF YOUR FAITH

Jesus overheard them and said to Jairus,
"Don't be afraid. Just have faith."
MARK 5:36 NLT

Was it a parlor trick, a cruel joke, or the mutterings of a madman? Jesus was asked to make a trip to heal the daughter of Jairus. Before He arrived, the young girl died. However, in the midst of those who'd gathered to grieve, Jesus told the parents, "Don't be afraid. Just have faith."

Had they ever witnessed someone raised from the dead? Death was something from which no one returned. Any hope they once held was dashed to the wastelands of internal grief and the external tears of mourning.

Yet faith suggested assurance and hope. How could this family possess what was gone? Faith spoke of impossibilities becoming living realities. They had heard the *Jesus stories*, trusted the truth of those stories, and they invited Him, the Story Creator, into their home. In the most unlikely of circumstances a young girl was brought back to life because the Son of God served the God of the impossible and performed a miracle.

Do you have a dream for your life and then conclude, "That could never happen"? If God's will and your plans connect then you can expect the miraculous.

Don't let limited faith hinder God's next great gift.

Lord, when I read about Your miraculous healings,
I'm always struck by Your powerful, but calm,
authority. You can truly do anything! Amen.

Day 4

BOLD AND BOLDER

He said to the woman, Thy faith hath saved thee; go in peace.
LUKE 7:50 KJV

Jesus arrived at the home of a religious leader. Simon made sure all preparations had been made. Or had he? Food? Check. Drinks? Check. Common hospitality? Ah, the missing piece.

She hadn't forgotten, and her hospitality was lavish. After a day of walking, Jesus' feet were tired and dirty. She arrived at the meal uninvited, but Jesus welcomed her. She wept and washed His feet with her tears. She kissed His feet and anointed them with expensive perfume. She was a sinner who understood that she needed rescue.

Simon was upset with the intrusion, but received a lesson in the value of forgiveness. Jesus contrasted Simon's hospitality with the gift of the sinner. Even though Simon was a religious leader he was also a sinner, and the anointing Jesus received was something Simon needed to witness. The faith of this one sinner has given hope to countless others from the first tear, drop of perfume, and radical act of worship.

An act of trust, acceptance, and conviction brought this woman to the feet of forgiveness and rescue. She wasn't afraid of what others would think; she was bold in her commitment, and she's remembered for her faith. What will *you* be remembered for?

Lord, I see how vulnerable this woman was with You, and how You lifted her up. I want to be like that. I want to risk everything for You. Amen.

FAITH AND GLORY

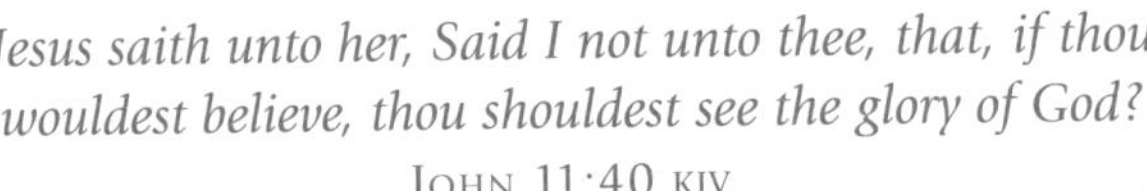

Jesus saith unto her, Said I not unto thee, that, if thou wouldest believe, thou shouldest see the glory of God?

John 11:40 KJV

Jesus received the first-century equivalent of a telegram. A friend was sick. Could He come? Would He heal? The request was simple and Jesus was willing, but He wasn't ready to visit. He had *God appointments* elsewhere, and His visit would be delayed. While Jesus was elsewhere, however, His friend Lazarus died.

When Jesus arrived, His friend had been in the tomb for four days. Jesus was greeted with a statement from his sister that ultimately led Jesus to weep. Martha said, "If You had been here, my brother would not have died" (John 11:21 NKJV).

A crowd gathered. Many had witnessed the miracles Jesus had performed. Most had heard His teaching. Some were convinced Jesus could have healed Lazarus, but hadn't He arrived too late? The crowd waited to discover the answer.

Martha continued, "Even now I know that whatever You ask of God, God will give You" (v. 22). This was a faith response inviting profound trust to meet God's provision.

Jesus prayed to His Father for help. *He helped.* Jesus called his friend to come out of the grave. *He did.* Jesus pinpointed the need for faith. *They believed. . .*and saw God's glorious miracle.

Jesus, I see You make despair disappear and replace it with pure joy. Please do that in my life. I know You can! Amen.

A TIME TO FOLLOW

By faith Abraham obeyed when he was called to go out to the place which he would receive as an inheritance. And he went out, not knowing where he was going.

HEBREWS 11:8 NKJV

He'd lived many years in the same place, Haran. It was familiar. It was home. Abraham had no children, but he had a promise. When God told this man it was time to move he must have felt a little apprehensive. Leave all that was familiar? Leave his family and relatives? Start over again at his age? So many questions.

But Abraham obeyed. He followed God to a new land. He had a determined faith that if God led then He would provide everything he and his wife needed. *God did.* In this new country Abraham and Sarah welcomed a son, built a life together, and witnessed the miracles of their Maker.

The Bible is filled with stories of people who expressed a total faith in God's plan for their lives. They had faith in a promise. They believed that what God said was what He would do. God called those who had such faith *righteous*.

Trust God. He never calls in sick, He works the night shift, and His love is beyond comprehension. If He says to follow, trust His leadership.

I am listening for Your call, Lord. Where will You send me today? Who do You want me to see? What do You want me to say? Speak, Lord. Amen.

Day 7

THE FAITH OF AN ANALYST

Jesus said to him, "Thomas, because you have seen Me, you have believed. Blessed are those who have not seen and yet have believed."
JOHN 20:29 NKJV

Thomas was an analyst. He paid attention to facts. He was the resident skeptic among Jesus' disciples. He spoke his mind. He wanted proof. Thomas was a lot like you.

It's easy to trust what your eyes see, ears hear, and hands touch. This is observable, scientific, and logical. Jesus was quick to point out that the logical approach missed out on the wisdom of God. When Thomas insisted that seeing was believing, Jesus said people were more blessed when they believed first. Without faith (a complete trust in God) they would always consider the possibility that God wasn't trustworthy. If you require that God prove Himself in every circumstance, you make Him small.

When you question every decision God makes you may be unintentionally saying that He isn't all powerful, all wise, and all knowing.

When you *can't* trust others, you *can* have complete confidence in God. When people let you down, He can lift you up. When you can't see the future, you can believe in the One who created time. When you don't have answers, you can have faith in the One who calls Himself Truth.

Believe. . .and see.

My Lord and Savior, I'm afraid I am just like Thomas— wanting so much to believe and yet being pulled back by my doubts. Open my eyes, Lord. Amen.

GUIDING LIGHT

Your word is a lamp to my feet and a light to my path.

PSALM 119:105 NASB

Picture yourself on a dark and winding path. There are no visible markers, so you're unsure of each step. To make things more challenging, the pathway is rough, filled with potholes. You ease your way along, praying that you won't take a tumble or make a wrong turn.

Think of your journey with the Lord in a similar light. When you don't take the time to study the Word of God, you find yourself on unsure footing, and when you don't have the illumination of scripture to guide your way, you're sure to stumble. Every fall leads to another spiritual bump or bruise.

There are so many amazing promises in the Bible, and they're there for the taking. But you have to open God's Word, study it, and apply what you've read to your daily life. When you take the time to do that, the promises spring to life. The road is made clear. The potholes are easier to navigate. Best of all, your faith is bolstered. You have the tenacity to keep going, even when you don't feel like it.

So, what are you waiting for? Open that Bible and get ready for an adventure!

God, I want to be able to see where I'm going and know if I'm headed in the right direction. Help me to understand Your Word and Your will clearly. Amen.

THE TREASURE TROVE

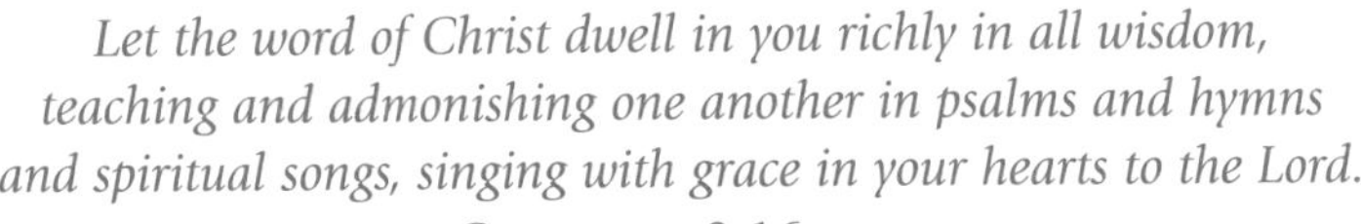

Let the word of Christ dwell in you richly in all wisdom, teaching and admonishing one another in psalms and hymns and spiritual songs, singing with grace in your hearts to the Lord.

COLOSSIANS 3:16 NKJV

Wouldn't it be wonderful to stumble across a treasure chest? Even before prying it open, your imagination would kick in. What will you find inside? Jewels? Gold coins? Family heirlooms? The possibilities are endless.

Now think about the Word of God. It's much like that treasure box, only it contains riches that can't be tallied in earthly dollars and cents. When you allow the words from the Bible to penetrate your heart, you find that they're like priceless jewels, worth more than diamonds and rubies.

The promises you find in the Word of God are treasures, and you can freely claim them. You can cash them in at any time. Best of all, the scriptures penetrate your heart and bring more changes than you'll ever understand. They "dwell in you richly."

You won't ever have to go looking for buried treasure. It's with you, wherever you go. And this is a gift you can share with everyone you come in contact with. Now that's a real gift!

Lord, Your Word is precious to me. Every time I look in it, I find something new and useful. Remind me to read it every day, Lord. Amen.

Day 3

AFFIXED AND ADHERED

Fix these words of mine in your hearts and minds; tie them as symbols on your hands and bind them on your foreheads. Teach them to your children, talking about them when you sit at home and when you walk along the road, when you lie down and when you get up.

DEUTERONOMY 11:18–19 NIV

If you've ever used superglue, you know how powerful it can be. Talk about a long-lasting adhesive! Perhaps you've inadvertently glued your fingers together, or maybe you pasted two items together accidentally. There's no turning back when you use superglue. Once those items are stuck, they're stuck!

That's how the promises in the Word of God are too. When you fix them to your heart and mind, they're permanent. They're superglued. Those promises become so much a part of you that you couldn't imagine living without them. Because of this, you naturally share them with everyone you come in contact with.

So, crack open your Bible today. Read it with new eyes—eyes wide open to the fact that the scriptures can and will have a lasting impact. God's promises will be stuck to you like glue.

God, help me to commit Your Word to memory, so I may always have Your wisdom ready at any moment. Amen.

Day 4

ALIVE AND POWERFUL

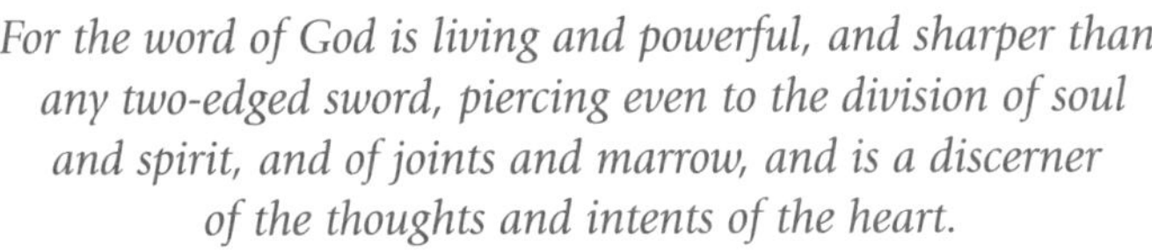

For the word of God is living and powerful, and sharper than any two-edged sword, piercing even to the division of soul and spirit, and of joints and marrow, and is a discerner of the thoughts and intents of the heart.

HEBREWS 4:12 NKJV

There's something incredibly moving about watching the human heartbeat on a hospital monitor. It confirms what you already know, that the person is alive and ticking. And the up and down motion of the graph brings hope.

Try to picture a similar monitor springing to life every time you open the Word of God. Maybe you're going through a rough time financially. You turn to a verse about the Lord's provision. The monitor kicks in. *Tick, tick, tick.* Perhaps you're walking through a deep valley, and you stumble across a scripture about hope. *Tick, tick, tick.* Maybe you've just lost a loved one and you read a verse that brings tremendous comfort. *Tick, tick, tick.*

The monitor sends a visible reminder that those words you've just read are more than words: they're life. Today, as you study the promises in the Word of God, remember this: they're alive and have the power to transform your life.

God, Your Word is living and breathing. And it gives life to me too. Help me to use it to examine my spirit. Help me to hear Your voice. Amen.

Day 5

A HOLY BOOMERANG

So shall my word be that goeth forth out of my mouth: it shall not return unto me void, but it shall accomplish that which I please, and it shall prosper in the thing whereto I sent it.

ISAIAH 55:11 KJV

It's great fun to play with a boomerang! You watch it whirl through the air, headed away from you, and then look on, mesmerized, as it turns back toward you. It's remarkable, if you think about it. That boomerang always wants to head back home again, to return to the one who sent it.

The same is true with the Word of God. When you study the scriptures and then speak them over your situation, you're sending them out to the great beyond. But they always come back home again, taking root in your heart.

So, speak the scriptures. Yes, speak them aloud. If you're going through a crisis, chose a verse that lifts your spirit. Speak the words over your situation and believe in your heart that they won't return void. Then watch as they rebound with life and energy, much like that boomerang, ready to do their work in your situation.

Remarkable! What great power is in the promises of God!

Speak, Lord. I am listening. Speak through the words on the page and through the words in my heart. Amen.

Day 6

HE'S STILL SPEAKING

God, after He spoke long ago to the fathers in the prophets in many portions and in many ways, in these last days has spoken to us in His Son, whom He appointed heir of all things, through whom also He made the world.
HEBREWS 1:1–2 NASB

How wonderful it must have been to sit at the feet of Jesus, gleaning from Him, witnessing miracles, seeing lives transformed. Can you imagine walking with Him, talking with Him, listening to Him pray for those in need? What a glorious experience to hear that voice, up close and personal. The disciples must have been in awe every step of the way.

We have the same opportunity. Did you know you too can hear His voice? When you open your Bible and read the scriptures, they come alive. The words jump off the page in much the same way that they radiated from the lips of your Savior two thousand years ago. They have just as much power, just as much energy.

It brings God pleasure to speak to His children. And what a creative God He is! First, He speaks through the prophets. Then, in person through His Son. Now, through the voice of His Spirit and through His Word. He's speaking, even now. Are you listening?

I'm so thankful, Lord, that You gave us Your Word to study and to get to know about You. With every story, I see a different aspect of Your majesty. Amen.

Day 7

DOERS OF THE WORD

"This Book of the Law shall not depart from your mouth, but you shall meditate in it day and night, that you may observe to do according to all that is written in it. For then you will make your way prosperous, and then you will have good success."

JOSHUA 1:8 NKJV

Remember that time you committed to lose weight? You had every intention of going to the gym several times a week to work out. Oh, you started off well, but after a while your *want-to* faded. It's one thing to say you're going to do something; it's another to actually follow through on it.

The same is true when it comes to reading the Word of God and standing on its promises. You can read all day long, but if you never apply what you've read, then you're a hearer only. The Lord longs for you to be a doer of the Word.

Sure, it takes work. Yes, you have to recommit daily. But oh, the joy of watching His promises fulfilled in your life! You'll bear witness to miracles when you commit to studying the Word.

So, grab your Bible. Meditate on what you're reading. Become like a sponge, happily soaking up the truth of what you're reading. Then, spring into action. Become a doer of the Word.

God, I don't want to speak empty promises. Help me to keep my word, like You keep Your promises to me. Amen.

Day 1

INFUSING OTHERS WITH COURAGE

Strengthen the weak hands, and make firm the feeble knees.
Say to those who are fearful-hearted, "Be strong,
do not fear! Behold, your God will come with
vengeance. . .He will come and save you."
ISAIAH 35:3–4 NKJV

To encourage someone means to infuse them with courage, and the above passage from Isaiah explains how to do this. When you see someone wearily stumbling under a heavy load of affliction, grief, or confusion, you are to come alongside them to strengthen their weary hands. You are to seek ways to make their failing knees firm so they don't collapse in the way.

One way you do this is by saying, "Be strong, do not fear!" Remind them that God will surely come and save them. If they lose hope that He's with them, it's all over. So give them renewed hope that He cares for them and will help them.

The patriarch Job had a lifelong habit of encouraging people. As one of his friends stated, "Your words have upheld him who was stumbling, and you have strengthened the feeble knees" (Job 4:4 NKJV). Again, note that he "made firm" their knees, a crucial point that was about to buckle under the strain.

If you "en-*courage*" someone, create courage in them, you're doing a very great thing.

Lord, I know so many people need a word of hope or cheer.
Help me to find these souls and give them peace and joy. Amen.

Day 2

CONFIRMING AND STRENGTHENING

Confirming the souls of the disciples, and exhorting them to continue in the faith, and that we must through much tribulation enter into the kingdom of God.

ACTS 14:22 KJV

It's a very beautiful and powerful thing to encourage others. After Paul and Barnabas had established new Christian communities in several Roman cities, they returned to those cities to strengthen the believers. They encouraged them so that they'd have the tenacity to stick to their professions of faith.

Barnabas' actual name was Joses, but the apostles named him "Barnabas" which means "Son of Encouragement" (Acts 4:36 NKJV). Barnabas was a positive and compassionate soul, always encouraging others. When the early church first heard about Gentiles becoming Christians, they sent out Barnabas to see what was happening. And he "encouraged them all that with purpose of heart they should continue with the Lord" (Acts 11:23 NKJV).

We need more Christians with a Barnabas anointing. To be this way, you need to first of all care deeply about others. Timothy was also like this. Paul said, "I have no one else like Timothy, who genuinely cares about your welfare." He said, "I hope to send Timothy to you soon for a visit. Then he can cheer me up by telling me how you are getting along" (Philippians 2:19–20 NLT).

God, help me to slow down so that I have time to really see people and ask how they are doing—and then wait for an answer. Amen.

Day 3

ENCOURAGE ONE ANOTHER

Therefore encourage one another and build each other up, just as in fact you are doing.
1 THESSALONIANS 5:11 NIV

What are some of the most important reasons that Christians are to meet together regularly, whether on Sunday or on other days of the week? You might think the main reasons are to hear biblical teaching and to sing worship songs—and no doubt these are important—but the Bible actually emphasizes another issue.

Paul wrote, "Let us not neglect our meeting together, as some people do, but encourage one another" (Hebrews 10:25 NLT). The main reason for meeting is to *encourage* each other. Paul wrote the Christians of Rome, "I long to see you so that. . .you and I may be mutually encouraged by each other's faith" (Romans 1:11–12 NIV).

In the first verse above, Paul urged the believers in Thessalonica to "encourage one another and build each other up." These two things are almost identical. To encourage someone is to buttress them so that they don't collapse. To build them up is to go beyond mere survival repairs.

Believers build up and strengthen others in the faith when they encourage those going through difficult times to keep their eyes on God. You often accomplish this by quoting them promises from God's Word.

Lord, when I meet with others to worship and learn about You, I have so much joy and peace. Thank You for making us into a family of believers. Amen.

Day 4

GOD STRENGTHENS YOU

He giveth power to the faint; and to them that have no might he increaseth strength.
Isaiah 40:29 KJV

God constantly whispers words of comfort with His Spirit. In Isaiah's day, He said, "This is the resting place, let the weary rest"; and, "This is the place of repose" (Isaiah 28:12 NIV). But God's people, then as today, often didn't listen. They continued on their weary way, trudging under the weight of heavy burdens.

Jesus still says, "Come to me, all you who are weary and burdened, and I will give you rest. Take my yoke upon you and learn from me. . .and you will find rest for your souls" (Matthew 11:28–29 NIV). Often, to build up your strength again, you simply need to rest. This is true with your physical body, and it's surely true of your spirit as well.

Find new strength today by resting close to God's heart. "He who dwells in the secret place of the Most High" (Psalm 91:1 NKJV) will not only find divine protection, but also renewed spiritual strength.

"Now may our Lord Jesus Christ himself and God our Father, who loved us and by his grace gave us eternal comfort and a wonderful hope, comfort you and strengthen you" (2 Thessalonians 2:16–17 NLT).

Lord Jesus, I am so tired. Please lift my burdens from my shoulders. Please help me to find rest in You. Amen.

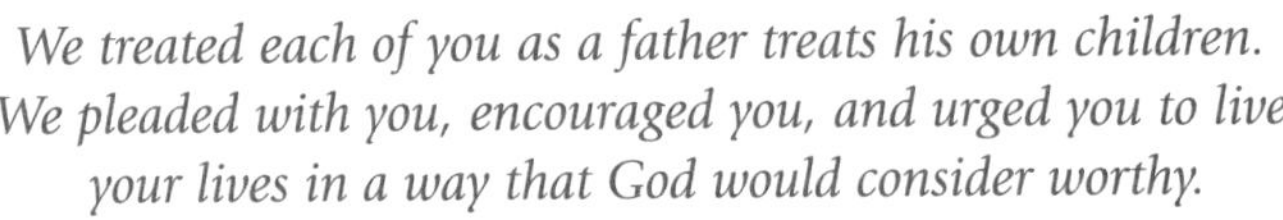

A FATHER'S ENCOURAGEMENT

We treated each of you as a father treats his own children. We pleaded with you, encouraged you, and urged you to live your lives in a way that God would consider worthy.
1 Thessalonians 2:11–12 NLT

Paul reminded the Christians of Thessalonica how he had conducted himself when he had been with them, treating each one of them as a father treated his own small children. Rather than scolding them, browbeating them, or shaming them into submission, Paul had focused on positive methods.

He had pleaded with them and urged them to live godly lives, and woven throughout all his entreaties were strong threads of compassion and encouragement. In so doing, Paul was reflecting the heart of the heavenly Father. "As a father has compassion on his children, so the Lord has compassion on those who fear him" (Psalm 103:13 NIV).

God is always merciful and encouraging, and wants you to relate to others the same way. Ask Him to transform you into His image. His goal is to help you to grow up into a mature woman of God, gentle, patient, and longsuffering.

Draw close to God and walk in the Spirit of Christ, and you'll become a positive, encouraging person, a joy to be around.

Father God, I want to see Your children as You see them. Please grow compassion within me, Lord. Amen.

THE GIFT OF ENCOURAGEMENT

"The Lord God has given Me the tongue of the learned,
that I should know how to speak a word
in season to him who is weary."
Isaiah 50:4 NKJV

You can claim this promise when you're aware that those around you are discouraged, but you don't know how to cheer them up. People you meet are often hurting, and you want to say the right thing at the right time, but may be at a loss for words.

At such times, you need God to inspire your words. Jesus promised that you could count on your heavenly Father to put His words in your mouth, so that "it will not be you speaking, but the Spirit of your Father speaking through you" (Matthew 10:20 NIV).

You may not have done an in-depth study of God's Word, but He's able to give you the tongue of the learned, so that you'll know what to say regardless. "The Holy Spirit. . .will teach you all things" (John 14:26 NKJV).

You can encourage others when they're anxious as well. "Worry weighs a person down; an encouraging word cheers a person up" (Proverbs 12:25 NLT). But as with any kind of encouragement, you need to speak it out loud for it to do any good. So don't be shy. Speak up.

Lord, I don't always know the right things to say when
I see someone who is feeling low. Help me to have
the courage to reach out anyway. Amen.

BRINGING OTHERS RELIEF

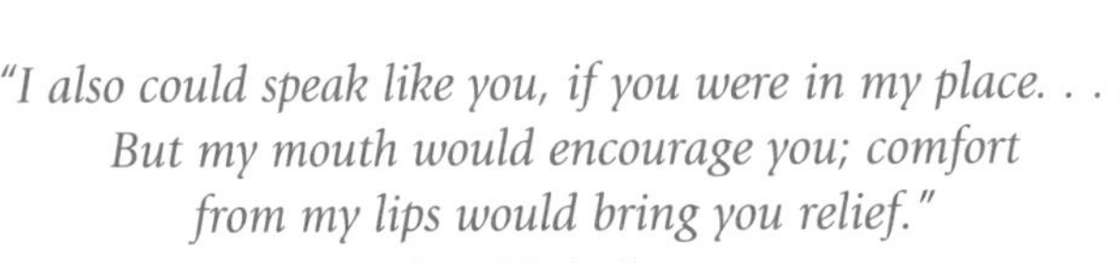

"I also could speak like you, if you were in my place. . . .
But my mouth would encourage you; comfort
from my lips would bring you relief."
Job 16:4–5 NIV

If you have a heart filled with compassion and love, they will naturally flow out of you to others. It's written of the patriarch Joseph, "And he comforted them, and spake kindly unto them" (Genesis 50:21 KJV). This was to his *brothers* who could hardly speak a civil word to him, who had betrayed him, and who sold him as a slave to the Midianites.

Often, the true test of your Christianity is seeing whether you will do good to those who have wronged you, and forgive them and love them. According to many people's way of thinking, after Job's fickle friends falsely accused him, he would've been perfectly within his rights to speak the same way back to them when they ran into trouble.

Many people relish getting in hurtful digs to their foes when they're down. But Job told his friends that this just wasn't his style. He assured them that if they were ever in pain, he would encourage them and bring them relief from their discouragement. He would seek to alleviate their grief. May you have the same attitude as he had.

God, erase bitterness and negativity within me.
When others insult me or snap at me, help me not
to snap back. Help me to show love instead. Amen.

MADE TO REJOICE

Rejoice in the Lord always; again I will say, rejoice!
PHILIPPIANS 4:4 NASB

There is something wonderful and mysterious about Christian joy. It's both emotion and deeply-rooted truth, both a command from God and a blessing to be received. To rejoice is to be happy because of who God is and what He has done, but it's different than the transient happiness that accompanies life's ups and downs. In fact, joy often results from tribulation, a by-product of the hope that God works out for you as you persevere through hardship (Romans 5:4).

Jesus covered joy's full scope in His teachings: "These things I have spoken to you, that My joy may remain in you, and that your joy may be full" (John 15:11 NKJV). He spoke words of instruction and caution, humbling words full of promise and hope—and His desire seems to be that, as you follow and obey Him, He rejoices in you, which is certainly cause for you to rejoice.

Rejoicing, then, is also both action and response. God rejoices when you abide in Him, bearing fruit by His power and grace (John 15:4), and you rejoice when you are of service to Him. To be joyful is to be actively obedient to God, even as you enjoy the peace and blessing of just belonging to Him.

When I am following You, totally focused on doing Your will,
Lord, that's when I feel my greatest moments
of joy. Help me to remember that. Amen.

Day 2

BY HOOK OR BY CROOK

Evil people are trapped by sin,
but the righteous escape, shouting for joy.
PROVERBS 29:6 NLT

When was the last time you rejoiced in your salvation? Some have more obvious reasons to give thanks and celebrate, simply because big sin makes for a big testimony. And while that is certainly something worth celebrating, remember that small sin still separates believers from their heavenly Father and still carries eternal consequences.

So, you have cause to rejoice, because you have all escaped sin's trap. If there weren't bright lights or angelic choruses accompanying the moment you received Christ, that doesn't make it any less a break from hell's clutches.

Take a moment to consider what Christ delivered you from. It might be a barnburner of a story, involving drugs, sex, and rock and roll, or it might be a quiet tale of a merciful release from pride, cynicism, and self-sufficiency. Now, consider (and pray for) those still caught in a web of their deception. Give thanks for your next breath, because it's the respiration of a freed child of God, given a gracious peace that the world can neither give nor remove (John 14:27).

No matter how you came to Christ, you came, and however you made it into His safe embrace, it's worth rejoicing!

God my Deliverer, thank You for rescuing me from my own darkness. Help me to keep walking in Your light. Amen.

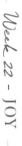

Day 3

DON'T HOLD BACK

Be glad in the LORD and rejoice, you righteous;
and shout for joy, all you upright in heart!
PSALM 32:11 NKJV

What makes you celebrate? Even if you're a typically under-control, what-would-they-say-at-the-club kind of individual, there's something in your heart of hearts that you know would get you fired up—that would elicit a tiny fist pump and an under-your-breath "Yes!" For others, celebration is a way of life; you've got a dance for filling up the gas tank for under thirty bucks and a ten-part handshake for two-for-one burger night.

Either way, how does your rejoicing translate when it's time to worship? You might attend the kind of church where outward expressions of joy are frowned on as drawing attention to oneself—and that's certainly something to be wary of, since God is the one who should be getting the attention.

Maybe you save it for when you get home, but here's the bigger question: why raise arms, clap, or shout for a touchdown or a guitar solo when you don't do it for God? Surely it's not because you think those things are more worthy of praise than He is. David is telling you to let loose, at least a little, when it comes to giving God His due and thanking Him for all He has done for you.

Lord, I want people to see peace and joy in the way
I live my life. I want them to see You! Amen.

JOY BOTH NEAR AND FAR

As sorrowful, yet alway rejoicing; as poor, yet making many rich; as having nothing, and yet possessing all things.
2 Corinthians 6:10 KJV

The scope of God's work in your life and in the world is overwhelming, something Paul captured in this list of paradoxes. By the world's standards, to be sorrowful and rejoice at the same time is contradictory, but under the banner of God's love and work in and through you, they represent the short and long view of life.

For instance, you can grieve the loss of a loved brother or sister in Christ wholeheartedly, weeping with those who weep, but even in that sad season, you can still have joy, knowing that you will see them again, happy and whole, in heaven.

Christian joy is a multifaceted gift. On one hand, it's supernatural, given by the Holy Spirit and founded on the grace that secured your salvation. At the same time, it's emotional, a heartfelt response to God and what He has done for you.

God enriches your spiritual poverty with His most lavish gift, the constant presence of His Spirit, and redeems the perishable possessions of this world with life eternal. His love for you never changes, and that's a good reason to rejoice.

Help me to find joy even in the hardest moments, Lord. Help me to feel Your peace even in the most stressful times. Amen.

Day 5

A NO-GOOD DAY CAN'T COMPETE WITH A REALLY GOOD GOD

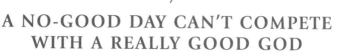

Frustration is better than laughter,
because a sad face is good for the heart.
ECCLESIASTES 7:3 NIV

Some days are not tailor-made for rejoicing. Some of the worst ones sneak up on you like the proverbial thief in the night. You couldn't possibly anticipate all the things that end up going badly, and you're left wondering what good could come from such a tornado of troubles. Your bones feel dried up, melted like wax, withered like grass, or any of those intense metaphors David came up with when he had a bad day.

Those days, you have to give it time. And then, when you can manage it, let God know what a crummy day you've had. He knows, but tell Him anyway. He can handle your frustration and hard questions; He's heard it all before. More often than not, once you've let it all out, you can look past it.

It becomes easier to remember how the Creator of the universe is your Dad, how He lets you vent because you need to, how your problems shrink in His hands. Somewhere in there, you make your way back to joy, not because your day wasn't so bad after all (it was a *terrible* day, wasn't it?), but because your God is so good.

God, I have good days and bad days. Help me to show kindness and patience no matter what kind of day I'm having. Amen.

SORROW'S SOLACE

A cheerful heart is good medicine,
but a crushed spirit dries up the bones.
Proverbs 17:22 niv

If someone were to come up to you on a rough day and offer a handy little slogan like, "A cheerful heart is good medicine," you might be tempted to offer a decidedly un-Christian response in a stream of typographical symbols. Later, though, after a nice long walk or hot bath, consider looking more closely at the word *cheerful*: in the original Hebrew, it means "joyful." And *joyful* is whole different matter.

Joy does come in happy times, but often, it comes disguised as sorrow. When you first read Paul's statement, "We also glory in tribulations" (Romans 5:3 nkjv), it seems like a really holy but wholly unrealistic response to hardship. But look at what's sandwiched around it: rejoicing in the "hope of the glory of God" (v. 2) and "knowing that tribulation produces perseverance; and perseverance, character; and character, hope" (vv. 3–4).

Astonishing, isn't it? You can have joy when life's going great because you have peace with God through Jesus, and you can have joy when life stinks because God uses trials to build Christlike character in you and pour out His love on you. Sometimes God's good medicine doesn't taste good, but it does the trick.

Lord, I do know what it's like to feel crushed. Help me to love people when they are at the lowest of lows. Let me show them that they are not alone. Amen.

Day 7

FULL ACCESS

"Until now you have not asked for anything in my name. Ask and you will receive, and your joy will be complete."
JOHN 16:24 NIV

As Jesus prepared His disciples for His departure, He encouraged them with a remarkable promise: they were now to ask God directly for whatever they needed, and when they asked in Jesus' name, they would receive it. And the reason they were to ask? So that they could be full of *joy*.

Joy is an essential part of the work God is doing in your life. Because it comes from Him, the world can't produce or replicate it. When you think of prayer as a way of making your joy complete, rejoicing becomes part of the proof that there is more of Jesus in you and less of you. That doesn't mean that you go around acting happy just to impress others with your spiritual depth; that move is straight out of the Pharisee playbook.

Rather, you seek God more and more, through prayer, by His Word, in fellowship, and by sharing your gifts in ministry and investing in others' best interests. As you fill yourself with more of the things that are dear to His heart, rivers of living water will flow from you (John 7:38) and you will rejoice in being a conduit of God's blessing.

Father God, help my heart's desires to become aligned with Yours. I want to be filled to the brim with the joy that comes from knowing You. Amen.

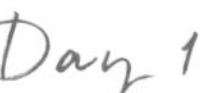

Day 1

WORLDLY PEACE VS. GOD'S PEACE

And the peace of God, which passeth all understanding, shall keep your hearts and minds through Christ Jesus.
PHILIPPIANS 4:7 KJV

What do you consider your most peaceful place? A serene beach with salty breezes and the soothing sounds of the ocean? A scenic mountainside with crisp air and near silence? Relaxing on a porch swing, or even just wrapped in a cozy blanket in your own living room? Whatever the places and circumstances that bring you a sense of peace, they don't compare to the peace of God that passes all understanding.

Worldly peace is temporary and conditional, based on circumstances and feelings. The peace of God is constant; it keeps (guards) your heart and mind, protecting them from the worries of the world.

The scripture prior to the one above says that prayer and thanksgiving are the way to get the peace of God. If you aren't feeling the constant, unexplainable peace that God offers, ask yourself: "How are my prayer life and my time in the Word?" You can't receive anything from Someone you're ignoring. Draw near to God this moment and during this week as you read about peace. Then stay in constant communication with your heavenly Father who loves you dearly and wants you to experience His wonderful peace!

Whenever my world is spinning with stress, Lord, whisper to me. Remind me to stop and spend time with You. You are my only source of peace. Amen.

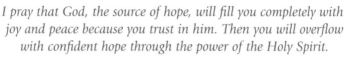

BECAUSE YOU TRUST IN HIM

I pray that God, the source of hope, will fill you completely with joy and peace because you trust in him. Then you will overflow with confident hope through the power of the Holy Spirit.
ROMANS 15:13 NLT

This verse says, "Because you trust in him. . ." But *do* you? It's a good question to ask yourself, especially if you're lacking peace or having doubts about your faith. Remind yourself why you trust the Lord. Think of all the reasons to believe that His Word is true, that the salvation He offers through the death and resurrection of Jesus is real, and that He constantly works in and through His people, drawing sinners to Him and building His eternal Kingdom. Meditate on the ways God has revealed Himself to you in the past, has provided for you, and has answered your prayers.

If you're still struggling, then simply go outside and look at His Creation, for "since the creation of the world God's invisible qualities—his eternal power and divine nature—have been clearly seen, being understood from what has been made" (Romans 1:20 NIV).

"Because you trust in him" you can be completely filled with joy and peace. The one true everlasting God of all peace is worthy of your total trust!

Lord, I admit that sometimes I struggle with feeling You near.
But if I keep praying and keep reading Your Word,
peace comes to my heart. Thank You. Amen.

Day 3

PEACE AMONG BELIEVERS

Behold, how good and how pleasant it is for brethren to dwell together in unity!
PSALM 133:1 KJV

It's incredible to think of the peace there will be in heaven—no more wars, terrorism, or violence of any kind. And do you ever think how incredible it will be to simply have peace and no more dissension among believers—to live in perfect, sinless relationship and fellowship with one another and our Creator? Amazing!

Psalm 133:1 says how good it is for believers to live together in unity. Sadly, in today's fallen world, disagreement and division even in the Church are common, often giving a poor testimony to unbelieving bystanders. God will ultimately judge everyone's hearts and motives, but each of us are to do our part to seek unity as brothers and sisters in Jesus Christ.

Until you reach your heavenly home, you must do as Paul urged: "Make every effort to keep the unity of the Spirit through the bond of peace. There is one body and one Spirit, just as you were called to one hope when you were called; one Lord, one faith, one baptism; one God and Father of all, who is over all and through all and in all" (Ephesians 4:3–6 NIV).

God, it's so terrible when Christians are fighting. I hate it. Help me to be an instrument of peace instead of a voice of division. Amen.

Day 4

PEACE TOWARD UNBELIEVERS

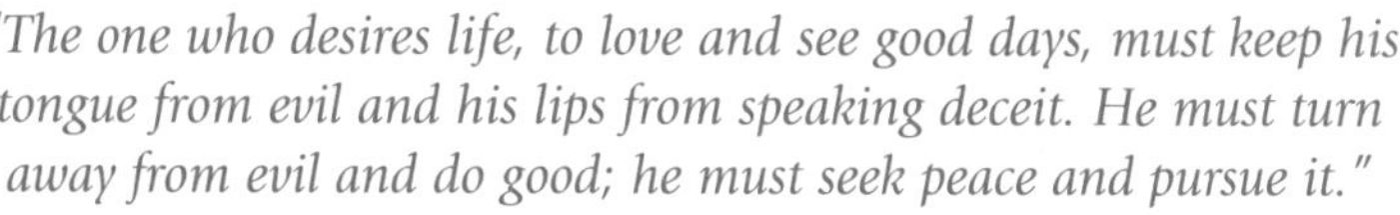

"The one who desires life, to love and see good days, must keep his tongue from evil and his lips from speaking deceit. He must turn away from evil and do good; he must seek peace and pursue it."
1 PETER 3:10–11 NASB

Unbelievers are watching how you act and react. As today's scripture indicates, hopefully they see you keeping your lips from lying. Hopefully they see you turning from evil and toward good, and seeking peace and pursuing it. You can't do any of these perfectly on your own, of course, but with your Savior's help you can show unbelievers what it means to depend on the God of grace. You can show them what it means to strive to live a life that's pleasing to Him—full of the peace that comes from Him and that extends to others around you.

First Peter 2:11–12 (NLT) advises believers to keep peace in the world and toward unbelievers in this way: "Dear friends, I warn you as 'temporary residents and foreigners' to keep away from worldly desires that wage war against your very souls. Be careful to live properly among your unbelieving neighbors. Then even if they accuse you of doing wrong, they will see your honorable behavior, and they will give honor to God when he judges the world."

Lord, I wrestle with holding my tongue every day.
The temptation is strong to say whatever is on my mind,
good or bad. Help me to have self-control, Lord. Amen.

Day 5

PEACE IN THE MIDST OF FEAR

For God has not given us a spirit of fear,
but of power and of love and of a sound mind.
2 Timothy 1:7 NKJV

If you let it, the world can seem scarier day after day. Alarming news is thrown at you from every angle and every media source—everything from natural disasters to terrorist attacks. Sin and evil are running rampant and, worse, are often widely celebrated.

From a natural perspective, it certainly seems that you have reason to fear. But despite all this, you can have tremendous hope! You have a God who is bigger and stronger than the worst kind of evil, and who shelters you under His wings (Psalm 91:4). This same God will one day eradicate all evil.

Until that day, He's called you to accomplish good things which He prepared for you to do despite everything that's happening around you. And He hasn't left you alone. He's given you His Holy Spirit, not a spirit of fear, but His own Spirit "of power and of love and of a sound mind."

You never have to fear *any* kind of evil. You can have abiding peace in the midst of a scary world, because "if God is for us, who can ever be against us?" (Romans 8:31 NLT).

Lord, I confess that sometimes I let the foolishness
and tragedy of this world sweep my peace away.
Help me to focus on You as I navigate chaos. Amen.

Day 6

FIGHT FOR PEACE

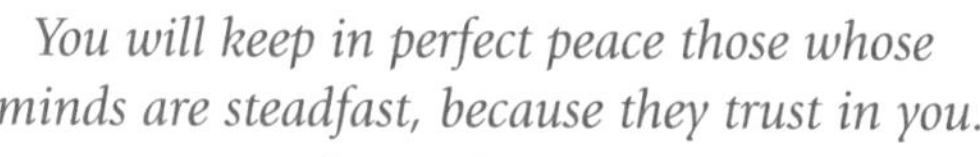

You will keep in perfect peace those whose minds are steadfast, because they trust in you.

ISAIAH 26:3 NIV

When your mind is full of worry and anxious thoughts, the very best thing you can do is to fill it with God's Word, which can powerfully fight the anxiety threatening to overcome you. God's Word is the "sword of the Spirit" (Ephesians 6:17 NIV) and is "sharper than any double-edged sword" (Hebrews 4:12 NIV). It's ready to do battle to win peace for you! When worry is attacking you, it's effective to repeatedly pray verses like Isaiah 26:3. Here are more scriptures to commit to memory and have at the ready:

"The Lord is near. Do not be anxious about anything, but in every situation, by prayer and petition, with thanksgiving, present your requests to God" (Philippians 4:5–6 NIV).

"Cast all your anxiety on him because he cares for you" (1 Peter 5:7 NIV).

"In peace I will lie down and sleep, for you alone, LORD, make me dwell in safety" (Psalm 4:8 NIV).

"So do not fear, for I am with you; do not be dismayed, for I am your God. I will strengthen you and help you; I will uphold you with my righteous right hand" (Isaiah 41:10 NIV).

Lord, when my anxiety is rising and negative thoughts threaten to overwhelm me, let Your Word rise up in my mind. Remind me that peace is found in You. Amen.

PEACE OF MIND AND HEART

"I am leaving you with a gift—peace of mind and heart. And the peace I give is a gift the world cannot give. So don't be troubled or afraid."
JOHN 14:27 NLT

In the time leading up to Jesus' crucifixion, His disciples were confused about how everything would play out, but He explained to them that He wouldn't be leaving them alone. He was sending the Counselor, the Holy Spirit, to guide them and be God's presence among them—not in quite the same way that Jesus had walked among people, but to indwell all believers and spread the Gospel far and wide. Jesus also promised a gift that the world couldn't give them, a gift of peace to their minds and hearts, a gift that would keep them from being troubled or afraid.

The Holy Spirit wasn't just for the believers of bygone days. No, He's *your* Counselor too, God's very presence working within you. The gift of peace of mind and heart is for you as well. Receive it. Know that the Holy Spirit is with you and that Jesus' peace is constantly available to you. Ask Him to fill you and strengthen you with it. He is very happy to oblige.

What a gift-giver You are, Lord! You gave us peace. Your peace. Not the world's weak version that cannot stand up to real troubles, but powerful peace in Your presence. Amen.

GENTLY HARSH?

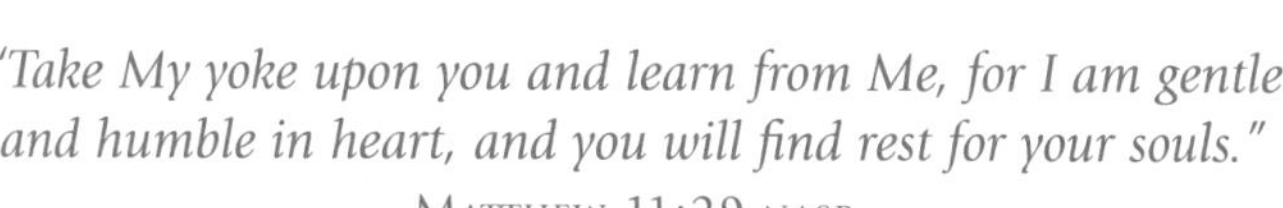

"Take My yoke upon you and learn from Me, for I am gentle and humble in heart, and you will find rest for your souls."
Matthew 11:29 NASB

Jesus promised to be your teacher—not drill instructor. Jesus promised you could learn from Him—not be belittled for what you don't know. Jesus promised a gentle approach—not harsh criticism.

Gentleness should be liberally applied to your relationships. Harshness invites the fighting stance of defensiveness. Any benefits harsh knowledge might offer are dismissed as rude and insensitive. There may be a time for strong words and confrontation, but even these difficult moments can be marked with a gentleness that provides evidence of compassion.

This biblical approach to relationships can be hard in a culture dominated by sarcasm, rude comments, and disrespect. You must remember you're called to respond differently than the culture around you. One of those differences is to be gentle when it would be much easier to interact in ways that burn bridges of friendship, boardwalks of opportunity, and platforms of love.

It's easy to apply crushing words to those who fail you. God's grace never does this. If the God you learn from is gentle, then your interactions should benefit from following His example.

Lord, soften my tongue. Lord, banish my bitterness. Lord, humble my hands. Lord, shape me into a person of gentleness and humility, that I may manifest Your grace. Amen.

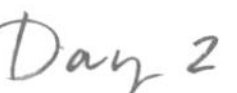

A STRONG GENTLENESS

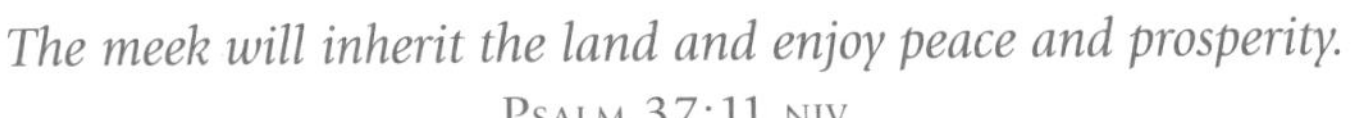

The meek will inherit the land and enjoy peace and prosperity.

PSALM 37:11 NIV

Meekness is described as strength balanced with gentleness. Meekness is the picture of a perfect leading man. He's strong, but gentle when he needs to be. He doesn't let emotions dictate his response. He overlooks offenses, but stands up when he needs to. He's not bent on proving himself, but on standing up for the defenseless.

Many great heroes and heroines could be described as meek. They stood up for justice, but sought peaceful solutions over aggression. They related to others in such a way that their example changed hostile hearts and minds. To be gentle is not to be weak—it is to be in control of a power that could destroy, choosing a path of restoration.

When Jesus is referred to as *meek and mild* it's not an insult. It doesn't mean He had no backbone. It doesn't mean He was weak.

Jesus fasted forty days in the desert, was betrayed by one of His disciples, and endured the verbal abuse of those who would crucify Him. In the end, He was meek enough to say in His final breaths, "Father, forgive them" (Luke 23:34 KJV).

You would find it hard to come to God if you felt intimidated. Perhaps that's why He chose gentleness.

Almighty Father, help me to stand up for others and stand firm in You. Help me not to seek glory for myself in doing so but always seek to honor You. Amen.

Day 3

A FRUIT STAND

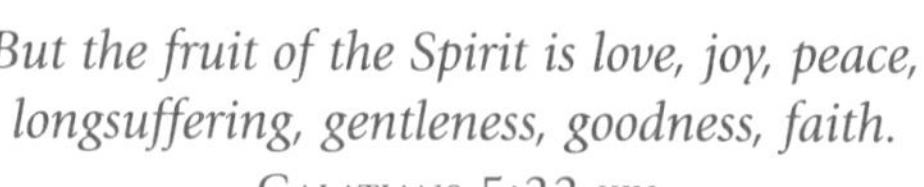

*But the fruit of the Spirit is love, joy, peace,
longsuffering, gentleness, goodness, faith.*
GALATIANS 5:22 KJV

Jesus is described as a vine and Christians are referred to as branches attached to the vine (see John 15:5). He states that Christians will be known by their fruitfulness (see Matthew 7:16). If you ever wonder what kind of fruit others should be able to identify in your life, the leading verse above names each fruit one by one.

The spiritual fruit you're to grow includes "love, joy, peace, long-suffering, gentleness, goodness, faith." You might sometimes act as if you get to pick and choose which fruit you allow to grow, but Galatians 5 is pretty clear that the fruit comes from God's Spirit, so they're *all* supposed to grow. You're to bear *each* fruit. It won't happen overnight. You need to grow. Make no mistake, God wants you to thrive and the fruit is the evidence of your growth.

You might agree that fruit like love, joy, peace, and faith are pretty important, but might be more reluctant to claim the fruit of longsuffering (patience), gentleness, and goodness. God never made such distinctions. He wants each fruit to be evident in your life. He wants others to recognize them. He wants you to accept the value of His fruit.

*Lord of all creation, sometimes it's hard for me to see
any good things growing in me. Help me to recognize
the fruit of the Spirit in my life. Amen.*

Day 4

STOP THE HYPOCRISY

The wisdom from above is first pure, then peaceable, gentle, reasonable, full of mercy and good fruits, unwavering, without hypocrisy.
JAMES 3:17 NASB

Gentleness is a by-product of wisdom. Wisdom also delivers the qualities of purity, peace, and a personality that's easy to get along with. Wisdom shows mercy and relies on a sure and steady moral compass. Wisdom is a good thing and a *God gift*.

It's possible to fake these qualities for a limited time. You might behave pretty godly in the right crowd for a while. The switch of peace, knob of mercy, and touchscreen of purity can read, "All systems go," but in your own strength and with enough time you'll fail to continue acting out these traits. God calls this *hypocrisy*.

You don't like to have others see you as a failure so you try to impress them, only to be caught in the state of being human. Far better to let God's Spirit develop these traits so you don't have to claim to be wise. You *will* be.

Gentleness shouldn't be a by-product of personal effort. Gentleness lives in peace, seeks out the reasonable, and chooses mercy. Gentleness shows that God's wisdom still finds a home in the heart of the faithful—and He's still working on you.

God, I'm glad You are unwavering. Me, though? I'm full of wavers! Take charge of my life, Lord. Help me to be a steady, faithful, godly witness for You. Amen.

Day 5

SUSTAINED IN HUMILITY

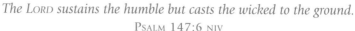

The Lord sustains the humble but casts the wicked to the ground.
Psalm 147:6 NIV

Someone is weak. They're injured. They won't get very far without help. So they rest their arm around another. They are helped to move from one location to the next.

"The Lord sustains the humble" is a promise that provides incredible benefits. Gentleness is a key element of humility. It offers an honest assessment of who you are. . .and who God is. Only those who recognize they need help will actually ask for it. They are the people God desires to help. Why? He doesn't ask you to come to Him in perfect condition. Because you sin, you can't expect perfection from your own efforts.

When you admit that you can't do it all, when you understand you need help, and when you ask God for assistance, you've discovered humility. In that moment, God takes the opportunity to help.

How can you learn to rely on God when you constantly do everything yourself? Trusting in your efforts, decisions, and strength doesn't provide any room for God to work on your behalf. When you believe you can do it all you don't allow God to do anything. Falling is always the result of refusing God's help.

Lord, I am aware of my weaknesses. Why then do I think I can handle things on my own? Help me to remember to call on You first, and always. Amen.

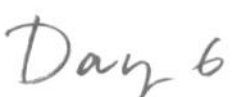

GENTLENESS: A NEW NORMAL

Remind the believers to submit to the government and its officers.
They should be obedient, always ready to do what is good.
They must not slander anyone and must avoid quarreling.
Instead, they should be gentle and show true humility to everyone.
Titus 3:1–2 NLT

Christ-followers should be shaped by something remarkably foreign to what is considered normal. While you can fight for your rights, it shouldn't be at the expense of relationship. Your words and actions should reflect biblical gentleness.

This may be in conflict with the way you're conditioned to think of your government. You may have firm opinions. You have a resolute grip on who you're for and what you're against. You believe debating with those who disagree with you is just the trait of good citizenship.

Today's verses instruct you to humbly submit to the government and those who lead. Arguing means you lose the ability to carry on a meaningful conversation. Defensiveness follows quarrels, sometimes putting distance in your relationships.

Gentleness doesn't remove conviction from your mind or diminish the power of your vote, but it does help you to remember that God's in control and His love for others is infinitely greater than your political analysis.

Prescription: Apply generous amounts of gentleness to what you say and do. This results in improved friendship.

God, I get it. I can't be obedient unless I submit my
will to Yours, which means submitting to other
authorities too. Let me follow Your lead. Amen.

AN INTENTIONALLY GENTLE RESPONSE

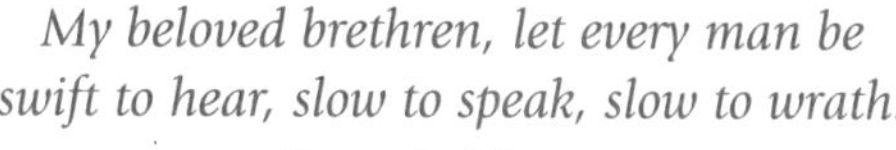

My beloved brethren, let every man be swift to hear, slow to speak, slow to wrath.

James 1:19 NKJV

God promised to deal gently with you through His love, mercy, and grace. He asks you to follow His lead by showing the same gentleness to others. Today's verse points directly to the reason it's so important.

If you don't aim for gentleness in your relationships, you may tend to respond with wrath. Coming from the desperately wicked heart of man (see Jeremiah 17:9), wrath leads to violations of God's laws. You can't demonstrate love in the midst of wrath. When your decisions are defined by rage there are additional actions that lead to a poor outcome. Bitterness, clamor, slander, and malice (see Ephesians 4:31–32) bubble to the surface and spill out on unsuspecting victims.

God was very clear: "The wrath of man does not produce the righteousness of God." Why? It keeps forgiveness at arm's length, refuses correction, and impairs godly wisdom.

You should listen more, speak thoughtfully, and never base your actions exclusively on emotions. Unlike wrath, gentleness leads with compassion, inspires with kindness, and befriends with mercy. Making gentleness an intentional response is a choice you never have to regret.

Lord of all, be Lord of my temper too. Harness my anger into righteous, good actions. Stop my hot words from setting fires. Rescue me from my rage, Lord. Amen.

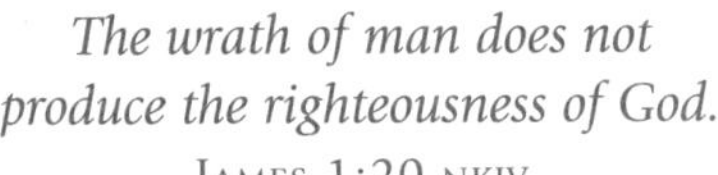

BE SLOW TO WRATH

The wrath of man does not
produce the righteousness of God.
James 1:20 NKJV

Anger is not, in itself, a negative thing. It's right and important to be angry at injustice and wickedness. But if you're too easily aroused to anger and if you don't control it, this tendency will wreak havoc in your life and relationships.

Long experience with a quick, hot temper may have convinced you that you simply can't control your angry outbursts, but James says, "Let every man be. . .slow to wrath." The ability to control your temper is not just something that a *few* people can master. It's something God expects of "*every* man." So you can control it.

Several other scriptures point out that one of the most important Christian virtues is self-control (Galatians 5:23; 2 Peter 1:6), which means the ability to choose what is right and to stick to it, even if strong emotions are surging inside. This, again, is something that God expects of every believer.

It might not come easily. It will probably take concerted and persistent effort, but keep at it, stay determined, and with God's help, you *can* control your temper. That's a promise.

Word of life, help me to listen before I speak, even in my head.
Help me to overlook petty offenses and save my
energy for fighting true evil. Amen.

Day 2

BETTER THAN THE MIGHTY

He who is slow to anger is better than the mighty,
and he who rules his spirit, than he who captures a city.
PROVERBS 16:32 NASB

Solomon made a profound observation: he pointed out that, as most people in his day were aware, certain outstanding warriors could do astonishing feats when waging warfare. Then he stated that if you refrained from being easily aroused to anger, you were doing even better than these super soldiers.

Likewise, a highly-disciplined siege army could—with carefully executed planning and great daring—conquer a heavily fortified city, but if you ruled over your own temper, you'd accomplished even more than them.

If you work out a plan and have the guts to stick to that plan, you can succeed. A plan can be as basic as knowing what kinds of things trigger you and thinking of methods ahead of time to defuse your anger in such situations instead of being simply swept along by strong emotions.

You may have an ongoing problem with your temper, and mastering it may be almost more than you can hope for now, but don't give up. Proverbs 20:18 (NKJV) states, "Plans are established by counsel; by wise counsel wage war." This works for besieging a city and for conquering your anger.

Lord, I want to be a warrior You can count on. Let me not be so interested in fiery anger as I am in fierce faith. Amen.

Day 3

TURNING AWAY WRATH

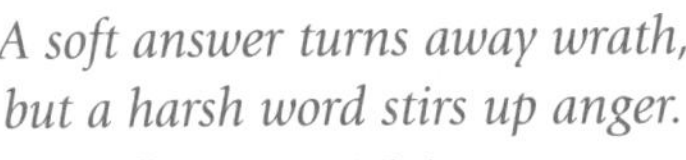

A soft answer turns away wrath,
but a harsh word stirs up anger.
PROVERBS 15:1 NKJV

At times, you may have to tell someone things they don't want to hear, and that may cause them to become upset. But if you use consideration and wisdom, you can defuse much of their anger.

If someone lashes out at you or verbally assaults you, the temptation will be strong to answer back in a belligerent tone of voice. Don't. You'll only stir up their anger. Respond in a calm, nonthreatening tone and choose your words carefully.

If you're insecure, you may insist that you're not going to put up with verbal abuse from anyone—and immediately give people both barrels in return. But the mature refuse to respond in anger. You let it pass. "Sensible people control their temper; they earn respect by overlooking wrongs" (Proverbs 19:11 NLT).

Have empathy. Think how you would feel if *you* were in their situation. "So in everything, do to others what you would have them do to you" (Matthew 7:12 NIV). You would prefer to be handled with love and respect, so treat others that way. If you put forth an effort to treat others gently, it can make a huge difference in them, and calm the whole situation.

Lord, if I truly have nothing nice to say, shut my mouth, please. But help me to find the nice things to say too! Amen.

Day 4

CONTROLLING YOUR TONGUE

Do everything without complaining and arguing.
PHILIPPIANS 2:14 NLT

It's easy to recognize a blatant verbal outburst as anger. But it's often harder to put a finger on subtly expressed anger, the kind that escapes your lips as sullen grumbling or a constantly contentious attitude. You may even *deny* that you have issues, though it's obvious to those around you that something has ticked you off or is eating away at you.

Paul said, "Do everything without complaining and arguing." You may find that much easier said than done. Bellyaching and snapping back at others may be such an ingrained habit that they seem like a part of your nature and personality.

You can't simply put a Band-Aid on a festering wound and try to keep your mouth shut. You have to deal with the underlying issues. That means admitting that you *are* angry, then facing the "root of bitterness" (Hebrews 12:15 KJV) that's the source of your anger. And then you must forgive and let go of the offense.

When you've done this, you'll finally get a handle on the slow-burning anger that's been expressing itself in complaining and arguing. And you can overcome it. God's Word commands, "Do *everything* without complaining and arguing," so He will give you the grace to do precisely that.

Lord, I confess that I struggle mightily with complaining.
I know it's useless—words without action. Help me to use
my time and my mouth in more productive ways. Amen.

Day 5

LET GOD GET MAD

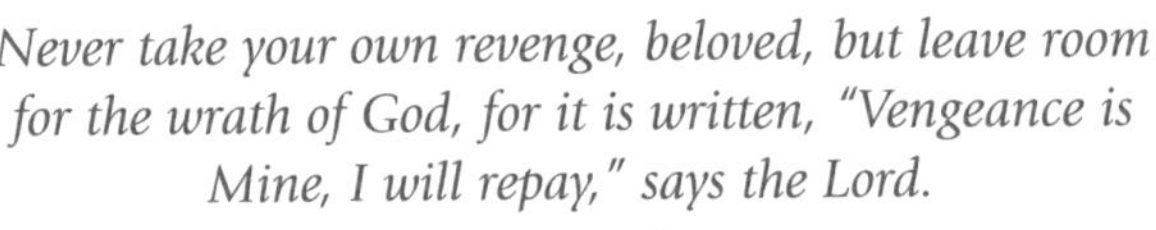

Never take your own revenge, beloved, but leave room for the wrath of God, for it is written, "Vengeance is Mine, I will repay," says the Lord.

ROMANS 12:19 NASB

The Bible says to never seek your own revenge, but to step back completely out of the picture and let God be the one to act on *His* anger. His anger is always perfectly fair and is motivated by deep love and justice. So don't try to take matters into your own hands. Let God be the one to repay the wrongs others do to you.

Leviticus 19:18 (NKJV) says, "You shall not take vengeance, nor bear any grudge. . .but you shall love your neighbor as yourself." People who bear grudges invariably plot revenge. A grudge is slow, simmering anger. It's anger on a back burner, stewing on a low flame, but it's anger just the same.

When you seek revenge, you're desiring to do violence to someone, except, instead of acting in the sudden heat of angry passion, you're acting in cold, calculating malice. The end result, however, is the same.

Instead of hating your enemies and plotting to harm them, you are to "love your enemies" (Matthew 5:44 KJV). Pray that God changes their hearts and has mercy on them.

Lord, any time I try to get revenge, I make a mess. But even when I harbor vengeful thoughts, my heart gets messy. Clean out these hateful feelings, Lord. Amen.

Day 6

HANDLING ANGER PROPERLY

"In your anger do not sin": Do not let the sun go down while you are still angry.
Ephesians 4:26 NIV

If you grew up in a home where you were exposed to constant angry outbursts, you might have difficulty believing that there's *ever* an acceptable time to express anger. Some Christians even doubt that believers should feel *sad*. But like happiness, anger and sorrow are valid emotions. "To every thing there is a season. . .A time to weep, and a time to laugh; a time to mourn" (Ecclesiastes 3:1, 4 KJV).

In certain circumstances, anger is an appropriate response. Paul knew that all believers would experience it at times; he just wanted to be sure that they handled it properly. So his first advice was, "In your anger do not sin." Don't get carried away with rage. Godly anger is a catalyst for change, but human temper tantrums don't accomplish God's purposes (James 1:20).

Paul's second piece of advice was: "Do not let the sun go down while you are still angry." Deal with the situation. Express your anger, work through the issues, and then let your anger go. Don't let it continue smoldering inside for months or years—even if all the issues aren't resolved immediately. God often takes time to work things out.

Lord, I am sorely tempted at times to mope and sulk and pout. Help me to deal with my irritation in a more healthy and godly way. Amen.

Day 7

ANGER AND HELLFIRE

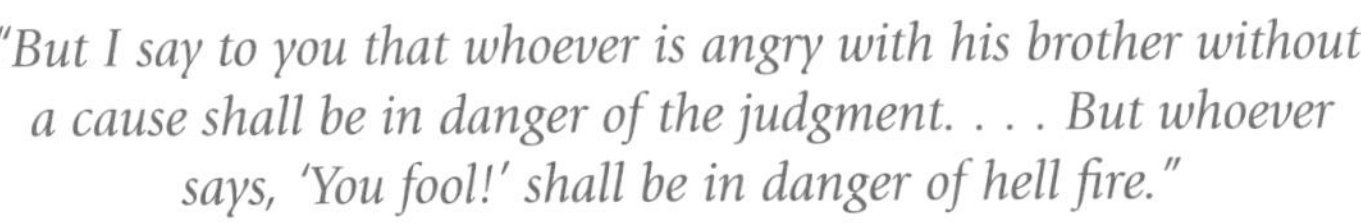

"But I say to you that whoever is angry with his brother without a cause shall be in danger of the judgment. . . . But whoever says, 'You fool!' shall be in danger of hell fire."

MATTHEW 5:22 NKJV

Like most people, you've heard your share of curses and name-calling. Some people, when upset, demand that God damn people to hell. They say it so often and so freely that it loses its ability to shock—but this is truly a terrible thing to utter. As a Christian, you might not say such things, but you may be guilty of related sins.

Jesus said that "anyone who is angry with his brother will be subject to judgment." He then said if you even call anyone "fool" you're in danger of hell. The danger of losing your temper is that you often utter ill-advised words, and Jesus warned, "The words you say will either acquit you or condemn you" (Matthew 12:37 NLT). James adds that "the tongue is a fire, a world of iniquity. The tongue. . .is set on fire by hell" (James 3:6 NKJV).

You can wound people deeply with words spoken in anger, and the best way to avoid doing this is not to give in to wrath in the first place. Guard your tongue. You'll be glad you did.

Lord, it's so hard to control my tongue. And it's much harder to control what words come to mind. Help me today. Fill my mind with Your Word. Amen.

Day 1

UNLOCKING HUMILITY

Humble yourselves in the presence
of the Lord, and He will exalt you.
JAMES 4:10 NASB

Humility is the gateway to God's grace. Pride, however, is the lock that keeps you from entering. Where God could rightfully demand total obedience from you as His creation, He instead gave you free will, so that you could choose to love Him. Faced with that choice, though, you may think, as Satan once did, that you know better than your Creator. But rather than leave you to your just deserts—sin's fatal wages—God stooped, reaching down to you and making a way back to Him.

You can do nothing to patch things up with Him—it's not in your nature—so He did everything. The one thing He requires, though, is enough humility to see that you are a sinner, that you have fallen and there is no way you can rise on your own merits. Small and great, poor and rich, everyone is on the same footing before God.

And while it would be enough to surrender your pride and trade your condemnation for His salvation, He offers you more. When you humble yourself, placing Him first and loving others more highly than yourself, He will lift you up. Let God cut the lock of pride off and open the floodgates of peace and blessing.

God, I know I am nothing without You.
Never let me forget that. Amen.

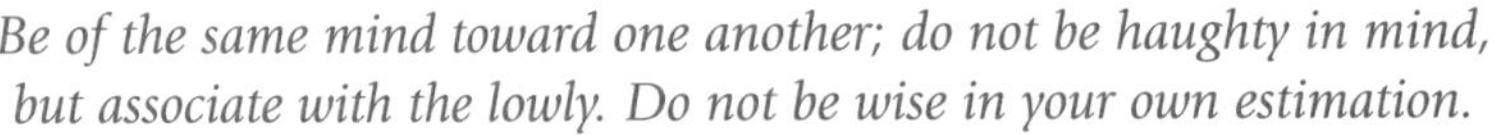

TRUE INFLUENCE

Be of the same mind toward one another; do not be haughty in mind, but associate with the lowly. Do not be wise in your own estimation.
ROMANS 12:16 NASB

Humility involves a great paradox: you gain influence through serving others. If you're like most people, you want your life to count, to make a difference and have an impact in some way. But whether you want do so globally or locally, true impact starts with influence, and true influence begins with love.

True love requires putting someone else's interests ahead of your own, ahead of your feelings for and about them. You have to listen and discern and be ready to wade through the muck and mire of difficult choices. You have to be ready to learn before you can teach. In short, love requires humility.

Nothing derails humility more than pride. If you're just for yourself, others will know. But when someone else discovers that you are for *them*, it makes all the difference. Empathy is a huge tool in building relationships, but even where you don't have shared experiences to draw on, you can share the comfort of knowing that most people just want their lives to carry meaning and purpose. Few things are more Jesus-like than getting down into the nitty-gritty of life with others.

God, it can be hard to commit to real involvement in someone's life. Remind me that the best things come when I let You lead me, even through difficult places. Amen.

SHIFT YOUR MIND-SET

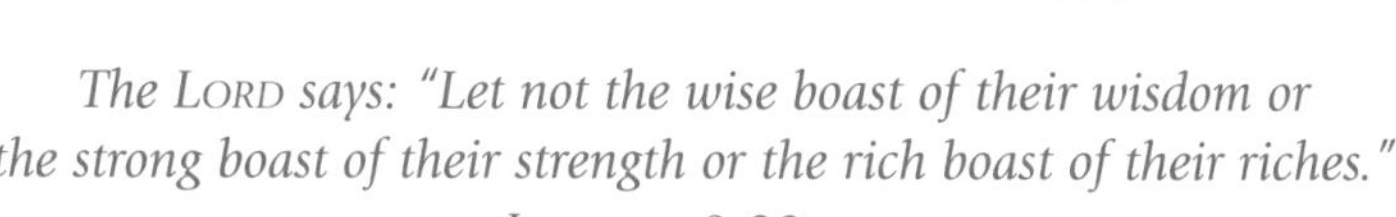

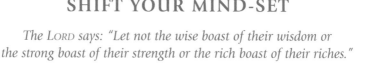

The Lord *says: "Let not the wise boast of their wisdom or the strong boast of their strength or the rich boast of their riches."*
Jeremiah 9:23 niv

Even under the grace of the cross, you still have to adjust your mind-set. The things that once served as markers of your strength and self-sufficiency—your accomplishments, education, wealth, or status—now serve as signposts along the wider path of destruction that you have abandoned to walk the narrow way of Christ.

Too often, even after they've been saved, people put their trust in money and possessions: the investment portfolio that secures their present or the retirement account that secures their future. But it doesn't take much to turn things upside down—the loss of a job, a market decline or crash, a lengthy illness—and there it all goes.

In contrast, what God has to offer never loses its value, never wavers with society's changing tides, because of the One who guarantees His promise: "Let the one who boasts boast about this: that they have the understanding to know me, that I am the Lord, who exercises kindness, justice and righteousness on earth, for in these I delight" (Jeremiah 9:24 niv). Humility means you shift your thinking from what you have done to what God has done.

Lord God, sometimes I get caught up in wanting what others have—an image of success. Help me to want to succeed in the pursuit of humility instead. Amen.

Day 4

PREPARATION AGAINST PRIDE

Clothe yourselves with humility toward one another, because, "God opposes the proud but shows favor to the humble." Humble yourselves, therefore, under God's mighty hand, that he may lift you up in due time.

1 Peter 5:5–6 NIV

There are many good reasons not to go out naked: culturally, you avoid embarrassment; practically, you avoid sunburn or frostbite; and spiritually, you avoid vulnerability. If you're not careful to arm yourself each day with prayer and the knowledge of God's Word, you're heading onto a battlefield in your skivvies. And of all the enemies that await you, your own pride may be the most dangerous.

Pride keeps you from putting others first, from serving wholeheartedly, from being willing to go unrecognized, and from seeing that you're not always right. To be clothed with humility is to be approachable, to listen well, and to curtail complaint.

Humility is deliberate preparation to put things in perspective: you are a saved sinner, going out into a world of lost souls, whom God wants to reach, possibly through you. Your agenda, whatever it may be, comes second. Be ready to do what you need to do today—at work, with the family, when juggling activities—but keep God's priorities first. Determine to be an instrument of God's grace, and you will find yourself a recipient too.

I don't ever want my pride to get in the way of loving others, Lord. Help me to get past silly grievances and pet peeves. Help me to love well. Amen.

THE BLESSING OF SPIRITUAL BANKRUPTCY

"Blessed are the poor in spirit,
for theirs is the kingdom of heaven."
MATTHEW 5:3 NASB

Bankruptcy is a scary word financially, but a huge blessing spiritually. When Jesus said "poor in spirit," He was referring to humility. Spiritually speaking, you have nothing to offer God; you are bankrupt before Him. There is nothing you can do to enrich Him or to pay the price for your sin.

Your spiritual debt actually dwarfs any physical debt you might have. No one can afford the arrogance of thinking prosperity or possessions will impress God or relieve them from the responsibility of using what He has given them—no matter how small or great—in the service of building His kingdom.

In fact, just as financial bankruptcy can be a tremendous relief from the pressures of trying to catch up and climb out of a debt-dug hole, acknowledging your spiritual insolvency before God is a healthy, pressure-relieving measure. Of course, just as you must avoid any of the irresponsibility that might have contributed to your monetary debt, you have to be careful to keep walking humbly before God. Comparatively, it's a small matter to turn all you are and have over to God, secure in the assurance of your salvation and the work to which He wants you to commit.

God, I come to You with empty hands and an open heart.
Take me and use me in Your kingdom today. Amen.

Day 6

POWER UNDER CONTROL

And being found in appearance as a man, He humbled Himself and became obedient to the point of death, even the death of the cross. Therefore God also has highly exalted Him and given Him the name which is above every name.

PHILIPPIANS 2:8–9 NKJV

There's a fine line between pride and humility. It centers on the idea of meekness, which is often misunderstood to mean being a doormat. In the ancient world, meekness was seen as a vice, not a virtue—associated with people deemed unfit for proper society.

God turned that notion on its head, making it one of those great paradoxes of faith: to be great in God's eyes, you have to humble yourself. If "humble yourself" sounds like a deliberate act, it is. *Meekness* captures the idea of a mustang broken to be bridled. The horse has lost none of its power or majesty; it could break out any time, but instead has submitted to the will of another.

There is no finer example of meekness than Jesus Christ. The One who could have forced every knee to bow (and one day will!) instead focused on the mission at hand, accomplishing the will of the Father at the cross. As His child, you have access to His power, both to submit to and do His will.

God, I don't know why You gave up so much. I am not worthy of Your sacrifice, and yet, You love me anyway. Help me to love like You. Amen.

THE COMFORT OF CONTRITION

This is what the high and exalted One says—he who lives forever, whose name is holy: "I live in a high and holy place, but also with the one who is contrite and lowly in spirit, to revive the spirit of the lowly and to revive the heart of the contrite."

Isaiah 57:15 NIV

Humility requires an act of submission—a desire to keep the focus on others rather than yourself. God's very interest in humankind is your example. That He who is perfect and complete all by Himself should show such deep interest in your well-being is humbling enough, but that He rewards you for following His lead is even better.

Because of God's generosity, when you humble yourself—prioritizing and contending for others' best interests—He promises to be with you. It's a good promise because it's not natural to be unselfish, and it can even put you in a vulnerable position with coworkers or family members who don't share your commitment to God.

Take comfort in knowing that your desire to be humble draws God's approval and His presence. That includes confessing the times when your pride gets in the way. He will lift your spirits and rejuvenate your heart, just because He loves that you're trying to be like Him.

When I stand on a high place, Lord, I see how small the world looks. You see my small world too, and You fill it with Your huge holiness. Thank You, Lord. Amen.

THE FINEST MOMENT

For to this you were called, because Christ also suffered for us,
leaving us an example, that you should follow His steps:
"Who committed no sin, nor was deceit found in His mouth";
who, when He was reviled, did not revile in return;
when He suffered, He did not threaten, but committed
Himself to Him who judges righteously.
1 Peter 2:21–23 NKJV

Jeff Bloemberg spent most of his hockey career during the 1980s in the minor leagues. He did finally get a shot with the New York Rangers, where he saw action in forty-three games over four seasons. But he's probably most remembered for something he didn't do.

The *New York Times* chronicled the events of a playoff game in 1990 in which an opposing player (referred to in the article as "a brawler on skates") went looking for a fight, and he found Bloemberg. Instead of fighting back, though, Bloemberg hunkered down and took a flurry of punches to his head and body.

The article quotes him as saying he was a born-again Christian and he wanted to let his light shine. The *Times* called it the "finest moment" of the opening round of the playoffs. As such, his self-control is a living example of 1 Peter 2:21–23. How would you react in such a situation?

Lord, when others accuse me or want to hurt me, help me to
answer with love. Help me to come to You for strength.
Help me to have self-control. Amen.

Day 2

AN IMPERISHABLE CROWN

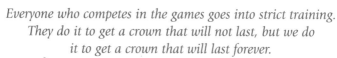

Everyone who competes in the games goes into strict training.
They do it to get a crown that will not last, but we do
it to get a crown that will last forever.
1 CORINTHIANS 9:25 NIV

After failing to qualify for the 2012 Summer Olympics in the *heptathlon* (a contest that includes seven different events), Heather Miller-Koch scaled back her schedule as a full-time nurse so she could train for the 2016 Summer Olympics in Rio. For the year leading up to the games, she trained full-time.

Her efforts paid off. She finished second at the Olympic trials, securing her spot on Team USA. She was set to compete in the Rio games and considered her many hours of training to be well worth it. And she should be proud of her accomplishment, even though she never went on to win a medal. Very few people are talented and disciplined enough to even qualify for the Olympics.

If she was willing to undergo such a strict training and nutrition regimen to compete for a perishable crown, how much more ought the Christian be willing to train for an imperishable crown? How about you? What are you willing to abstain from in order that the Gospel message might prevail in your life?

God, I spend all kinds of time working on things that will
not last. Help me to work harder at the things that
will build up Your eternal kingdom. Amen.

Day 3

DEVOTED TO GOD

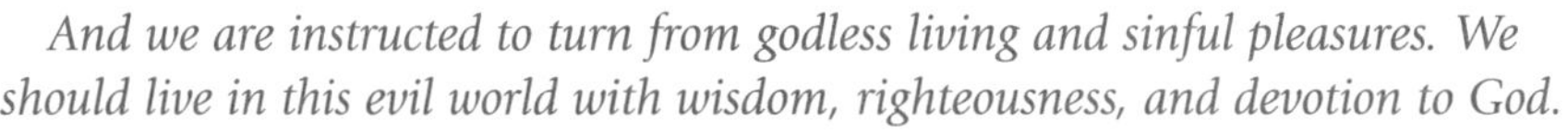

And we are instructed to turn from godless living and sinful pleasures. We should live in this evil world with wisdom, righteousness, and devotion to God.

TITUS 2:12 NLT

If you became a Christian later in life, then you can remember how it feels to live without any regard for God. Before Christ, you never gave your vices much thought. You simply engaged in them because they were pleasurable. After Christ, a battle ensued. You felt empowered to reject those activities and you desired to do so because you'd rather please God than yourself.

Sadly, though, you may have returned to your vices when the stresses of life came, and justified your actions, saying that you deserve some happiness. We've all been there. So, what's the antidote? Paul offers it in the second half of today's verse: to live with wisdom, righteousness, and devotion to God.

Wisdom comes from scripture, from the insights of pastors/teachers, and from fellow believers. Don't be shy about asking for help. Righteousness, in this context, refers to properly performing your duties as a Christian. When you live out your faith, you strengthen it. And devotion to God comes by surrendering your desires for self-pleasure in favor of pleasing God.

God, I don't want to return to living in darkness—outside of Your light, unaware of Your love. Help me not to let any temptation take me away from You. Amen.

Day 4

MODERATION IN EVERYTHING

Do you like honey? Don't eat too much, or it will make you sick!
PROVERBS 25:16 NLT

Judea was known for its abundance of honey. First Samuel 14:24–25 says Saul's men, who were pressed to exhaustion from a lack of food, even found honeycomb on the ground in the forest. And, of course, the Promised Land was often described in scripture as a land flowing with milk and honey.

Honey, which was in no short supply, was sweet and invigorating, and it provided a boost of energy. It was a good thing—a resource provided by God. But too much of it would make a person sick. This is a clear metaphor for the pleasures of this world. Many are accessible, fulfilling, and even allowable—in moderation—but excess is never a good idea. They will make your soul sick.

Which worldly pleasures have you yet to master? Food? Drink? Sport? Hobby? Television? Some other form of entertainment? Whatever it is, be willing to name it and then put boundaries on it which you will stick to in the future. Seek an accountability partner. Or be publicly accountable on social media. Exhibit self-control and your soul will benefit. The sheep who willingly follows God lacks for nothing (Psalm 23:1).

I'm sure You know my weaknesses, Lord. You know the indulgences I am most guilty of. Help me to create healthy boundaries that will keep me focused on You. Amen.

A TIME FOR SILENCE

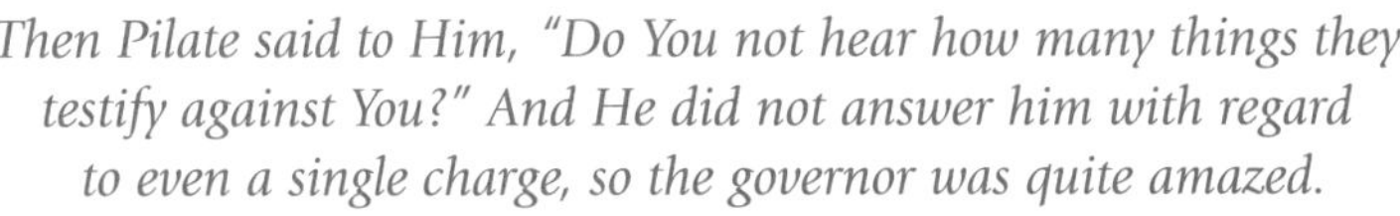

Then Pilate said to Him, "Do You not hear how many things they testify against You?" And He did not answer him with regard to even a single charge, so the governor was quite amazed.
MATTHEW 27:13–14 NASB

The person who lacks self-control is quick to defend himself. Jesus, on the other hand, was the model of self-control when He was arrested and faced accusations by the chief priests and the elders. They accused Him of stirring up people to revolt against civil authority, but He didn't respond to these false accusations. Pilate was incredulous. Why wouldn't Jesus defend Himself?

And does His action set a precedent for His followers? Is the Christian always to remain silent?

Let's answer the last question first. Paul didn't remain silent when charges were brought against him by the Jews (Acts 22). He respectfully laid out his case. Stephen spoke up at his own trial, also doing so in a respectful manner (Acts 7). So, there's a time to speak up and a time to be silent. But in all cases, it should be done respectfully and with a complete exhibition of self-control.

How do you typically respond when you're accused of something—either justly or unjustly? Do you need to improve in this area?

Lord, You used silence powerfully, and the world listened, and is listening still. Help me to know the power of silence. Help me to control my tongue. Amen.

CORAM DEO

Let your gentle spirit be known to all men. The Lord is near.
PHILIPPIANS 4:5 NASB

Gentleness is easier for some personality types than others. But that has no bearing on Paul's command to the Philippian church. He wanted them to let their gentle spirit be known to *all* men—and it probably didn't come naturally for some of them. But how's the world supposed to believe that the Gospel contains any power unless they see it in the church?

What might a "gentle spirit" look like in your life? How might you live that out in front of the world? Maybe it will include a tamer tongue, a less critical spirit, a more generous ear, an even temper, or a willingness to care less about who gets the credit and more about the final result. Whatever the case, how might committing your weakness to prayer change things in your office, your church, or your home?

Coram Deo means "in the presence of God." The Lord's return is near, as Paul points out in today's verse, and it should reorient the way you live today. Theologian R. C. Sproul words it this way in a blog post: "To live coram Deo is to live one's entire life in the presence of God, under the authority of God, to the glory of God."

Lord, You were gentle when You walked on the earth—and yet never weak. You had compassion. You cared for those without power. Show me how to be like You. Amen.

Day 7

BE ALERT

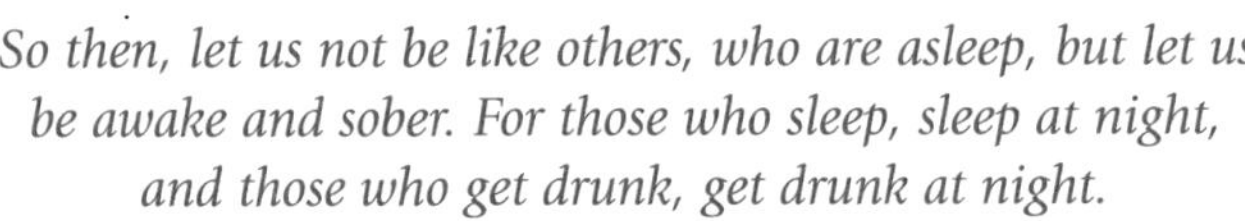

So then, let us not be like others, who are asleep, but let us be awake and sober. For those who sleep, sleep at night, and those who get drunk, get drunk at night.

1 THESSALONIANS 5:6–7 NIV

Jesus' disciples often struggled to understand basic spiritual concepts, such as living water, the bread of life, and being born again. They were constantly attempting to understand them through the physical, rather than the spiritual. But eventually, they caught on. The Peter of the Gospels sees the world much differently in the book of Acts and in his later epistles.

In today's verse, Paul spoke to the Thessalonian church about not sleeping like others do. Of course, he was asking them to be aware that Jesus was sitting on His throne and might return at any moment. Thus, living in any other way than being alert and self-controlled is a dangerous state—because you know better.

Some of your coworkers and neighbors are sleeping. They're living as if nothing is at stake, other than the next moment of fun. They're heading for a cliff and have no idea how close it is. You, on the other hand, are fully aware of its proximity. How can that not change the way you live today or prompt you to warn them?

Wake me up, Lord! Don't let me sleep on the job—
the job of bringing people to know You. Amen.

Day 1

CHOOSING COURAGE

So be strong and courageous, all you who put your hope in the LORD!
PSALM 31:24 NLT

When you're facing a threat, you may pray for God to give you courage, and He may supply it—but that's not always the way He works. He doesn't necessarily give you a download of bravery before you even face the enemy. Instead He commands *you*, "Be strong and courageous, all you who put your hope in the LORD!" Initially, the onus is on you to *choose* to trust the Lord and be courageous.

Focusing on trusting Him makes you aware of the Lord's great power and of the fact that He will defend you. As God told one king, "Do not be afraid nor dismayed because of this great multitude, for the battle is not yours, but God's" (2 Chronicles 20:15 NKJV). God *first* commanded His people to master their fear, and they were able to do so because they trusted in Him.

If God is on your side, you're well able to overcome your enemies. Ask yourself this: "If God is for us, who can be against us?" (Romans 8:31 NKJV). You can safely choose to be courageous, and then as you step out, God anoints you with extra courage and boldness. He will be with you and empower you.

Lord, when I am facing discouragement or fear, I know You are with me. Help me to feel bold and to stand tall, firmly grounded in You. Amen.

Day 2

REMEMBER GOD AND FIGHT

"Do not be afraid of them; remember the Lord who is great and awesome, and fight for your brothers, your sons, your daughters, your wives and your houses."
NEHEMIAH 4:14 NASB

It's a natural human tendency—when confronted by overwhelming force, or something startling or dangerous—to experience fear, to want to simply give up and hide in some hole. That's why, throughout the Bible, God constantly commanded people, "Fear not" (Luke 1:13, 30; 2:10; 5:10 KJV).

Frequently the enemy tries to get you to back down and run away with nothing more than threats and empty words. He often doesn't even need to attack you to cause you to experience anxiety. But God commands, "Do not be afraid because of the words that you have heard" (2 Kings 19:6 NASB).

You need to remember not only that God is great and has tremendous power, but you must remember your loved ones who are depending on you to protect them. Though it may be difficult, you must stand up and fight for their sakes. You won't have to do it alone. God has repeatedly promised to give you strength and to shield you from evil, so count on Him to be with you. If you will do this, God *will* be with you and help you to overcome.

Father God, I feel so afraid when someone I love is suffering. I wonder what will happen. I wonder if I'm helping. Remind me that worrying doesn't help anyone. Amen.

Day 3

WHEN YOU'RE AFRAID

Whenever I am afraid, I will trust in You.
PSALM 56:3 NKJV

King David didn't say, "I shall never fear," but confessed that he *did* fear at times, saying, "Whenever I am afraid. . ." He was an outstanding warrior, mighty in battle, and very courageous, but even he frequently got in over his head. When circumstances looked bleak and death seemed imminent, David too knew fear.

But he also knew what to *do* in such times. He focused on God and determined to trust in Him. He did this each time that fears threatened to overwhelm him. That's how he found peace. "Thou wilt keep him in perfect peace, whose mind is stayed on thee: because he trusteth in thee" (Isaiah 26:3 KJV).

Whenever you fear, make it a habit to turn to God—and *keep* your eyes fixed on Him. As you look steadfastly His way, you bathe your spirit in the light of His presence and partake of His strength. "They looked unto him, and were lightened" (Psalm 34:5 KJV).

But you must make a conscious effort to trust, even if your circumstances don't change for a while and your emotions are still being blasted by the storm. Fears can be very powerful and often are only calmed after a sustained determination to trust God.

My stomach shudders. My fingers pick. My neck tightens.
Sometimes my body knows I'm anxious before I do, Lord.
When I start feeling this way, I'll turn to you. Amen.

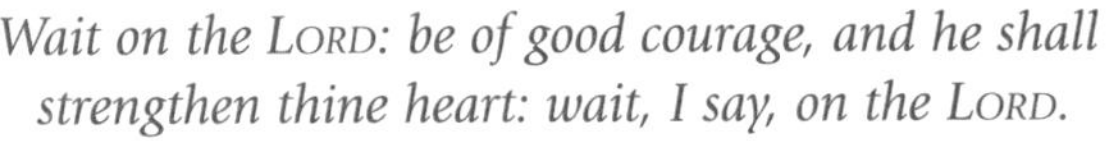

STRENGTHENED BY COURAGE

Wait on the LORD: be of good courage, and he shall strengthen thine heart: wait, I say, on the LORD.
PSALM 27:14 KJV

Sometimes when you desperately need God's help, it doesn't seem like He's coming through for you. You appear to be out in the open, unprotected, facing adversity or enemies by yourself. You wonder where God is. After all, didn't He promise to be there for you? The Bible has one clear piece of advice for you during such times—*wait on the Lord*. God says it twice in this one verse.

If you make the effort to "be of good courage," God will come alongside you, well up within you, and strengthen your heart. It's a promise. Give Him time, and He will strengthen you. A beautiful companion promise, found in the New Testament, says: "The Lord is faithful, and he will strengthen you and protect you from the evil one" (2 Thessalonians 3:3 NIV).

There may be special times of testing, often in lonely, discouraged hours when you feel beaten down and people have abandoned you, when you will be attacked by the forces of evil. At such times, you have to resolve to stand firm. God will then show up, make His presence known, work within you, and strengthen you.

Some things take time. I know this, Lord. But I forget.
Help me to be patient and wait for what
You have to give me. Amen.

Day 5

NOT FEARING MAN

*We say with confidence, "The Lord is my helper;
I will not be afraid. What can mere mortals do to me?"*
HEBREWS 13:6 NIV

When you ask yourself, "What can man do to me?" you might think, "Lots. People can do plenty to bring grief and fear and pain into my life." That's often enough true. The Bible even says, "Many are the afflictions of the righteous" (Psalm 34:19 KJV). But it goes *on* to promise, "but the LORD delivereth him out of them *all*" (emphasis added).

The point is: the Lord Almighty is your helper. He's on your side. He may permit enemies to attack you—why, you can't understand—but He will always get the upper hand in the end and bring you through to victory, one way or another.

Jesus said, "My friends, do not be afraid of those who kill the body, and after that have no more that they can do" (Luke 12:4 NKJV). Jesus taught a Gospel where the meek, the weak, the poor, and the downtrodden are truly blessed, despite the fact that they're beaten down, because in the end they will be truly victorious.

You may not always be victorious in this world, but your true home and treasure aren't in this life, but in the coming Kingdom of God.

*Lord, I know You won't always save me from the
consequences of sinful acts in this world. I understand
that. But I'm glad You won't ever leave me. Amen.*

Day 6

HOW TO CAST OUT FEAR

There is no fear in love; but perfect love casts out fear,
because fear involves punishment, and the one
who fears is not perfected in love.
1 JOHN 4:18 NASB

This is a powerful promise: "perfect love casts out fear." Two verses previously, the Bible declared, "God is love" (v. 16). This means is that if you live in God and He lives in you, you're filled with love and "perfected in love." The result is that you'll have "confidence in the day of judgment" (v. 17).

When you're filled with God's love, you no longer fear being rejected by Him. You can be confident that He's on your side; you no longer need fear that you'll be punished for your sins. This confidence then fills you with the courage and positive attitude you need to face life's many problems.

In the beginning, the apostle Peter was very conscious of his sins. After Jesus did a great miracle in his presence, Peter cried out, "Depart from me; for I am a sinful man, O Lord" (Luke 5:8 KJV). But instead of rejecting and punishing Peter, Jesus put His Spirit on Him and made him one of His closest followers.

Be filled with God's perfect love today, and it will cast all fear from your heart!

God, I know You love me perfectly. And that means no
matter what happens You'll keep loving me, caring for me,
and wanting what's best for me. I love that! Amen.

Day 7

COURAGE AND FEAR

The wicked man flees though no one pursues,
but the righteous are as bold as a lion.
PROVERBS 28:1 NIV

After God did miracles to bring the Israelites into Canaan, Rahab told the two spies, "When we heard of it, our hearts melted in fear and everyone's courage failed because of you" (Joshua 2:11 NIV). God had removed their spiritual defenses, and "their protection [had] departed from them" (Numbers 14:9 NKJV).

The wicked also fear because they have a troubled conscience; "the sound of a shaken leaf shall cause them to flee; they shall flee as though fleeing from a sword, and they shall fall when no one pursues" (Leviticus 26:36 NKJV). "There were they in great fear, where no fear was" (Psalm 53:5 KJV). Today it's called paranoia.

The situation is just the opposite for the righteous. God strengthens their spiritual defenses and they're as bold as a lion. The Lord can anoint you with supernatural confidence and courage. After the early Christians were filled with the Holy Spirit, they preached the Gospel with great boldness (Acts 4:31).

If you lack courage and confidence, ask God to give you the confidence to step out. And *keep* praying! It may not happen right away, but don't give up. Even though it takes a while, God is able to transform you.

Lord, let me live an honest life—I don't want to hide things from anyone. I want to be able to step out as an ambassador for You. Amen.

....

....

....

....

....

....

....

Day 1

IN EVERY SEASON

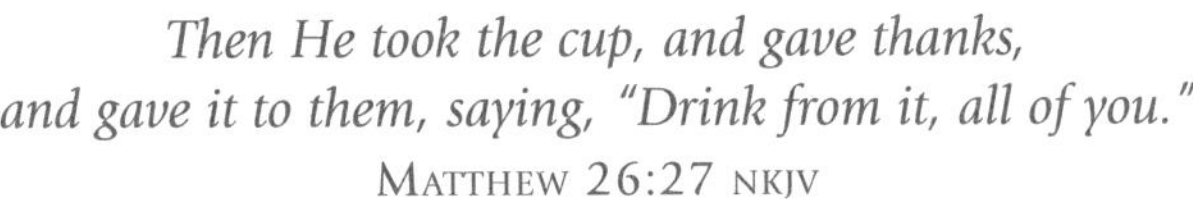

Then He took the cup, and gave thanks,
and gave it to them, saying, "Drink from it, all of you."
MATTHEW 26:27 NKJV

During the Last Supper, Jesus followed the standard protocol for blessings—one over the bread and another over the wine. But this time, when He gave thanks, it wasn't a typical premeal gesture of gratitude for the food. It was loaded with significance, as Jesus knew that He was headed to the cross—the painful, bloody fulfillment of His mission on earth.

And yet He gave thanks.

It's easy to be grateful when things are going well, when you're gainfully employed, well-fed, and healthy. But to thank God when the horizon is dark with peril, when the future is unclear, is to show a heart committed to trusting God.

It's good to thank God for all the ways He provides on a daily basis, especially over a meal as you prepare to enjoy both the food and the fellowship that comes with it. It's crucial, though, to do so when things aren't going well—in the midst of illness, loss, or doubt. The promise of Jesus' cup is that God can use all your suffering to good ends, to help you grow, to demonstrate His grace to others, or to check your priorities. God is good in every season.

Lord, when I participate in communion, I remember what You sacrificed. Thank You for suffering for me. I could keep thanking You forever and it wouldn't be enough. Amen.

....

....

....

....

....

....

....

....

HEARTSONGS

Singing a song of thanksgiving and telling of all your wonders.
PSALM 26:7 NLT

When was the last time you got a good song stuck in your head? There's something comforting about a familiar melody humming on your lips as you go about your day, like a tether anchoring you to good memories or a pleasant moment.

When David wrote a psalm, the words and harmonies tied him to his relationship with God, often giving him a lens through which to view God's faithfulness throughout his life. In both the good and bad times, David turned his heart toward God, commemorating His love, vowing his trust, confessing his sins, and declaring his commitment to follow. It was such a habit to put God first, to involve Him in every part of his life, that David couldn't help but put it in song.

What would it mean to worship God like that—not to compartmentalize His songs into the musical portion of a church service or a radio playing in the background, but to let the music of His work resonate every day, in every moment? It might be a familiar tune that's striking a chord at a particular moment, or it might be a new song, something coming from your heart alone, thoughts and words of gratitude and praise for your good God.

Father, when I sing in worship I feel close to You—
even though I don't sound very angelic! Hear my
voice as a sign of my love for You. Amen.

TRUSTWORTHY

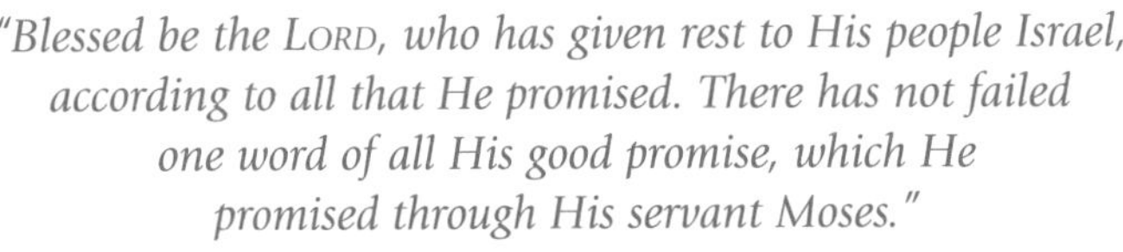

"Blessed be the Lord, who has given rest to His people Israel, according to all that He promised. There has not failed one word of all His good promise, which He promised through His servant Moses."
1 Kings 8:56 NKJV

People let you down. They may not want to or mean to. . .*or* they may not care about how you're affected at all. But as God is pushed further out of society, a promise means less and less. What used to be a typical expectation is more and more a shot in the dark. You want to trust others but it feels risky, especially once you've been burned.

What that also means is that someone who *keeps* a promise has impact. Being trustworthy used to be pretty standard, but these days it's a distinct characteristic. Everyone has been let down by a broken word, so much so that the assumption is that people *should* probably be honest but they probably *won't* be.

God, however, keeps His promises, and He expects you to, as well. A promise kept is a reflection of the Great Promise Keeper Himself. It breaks through cynicism, creating unexpected bonds based purely on trust. It enables you to reach people you've never met in ways you'd never anticipate, which is at the heart of the Gospel itself.

Lord, I want to keep my promises. Sometimes circumstances get in the way, but that's no excuse. Help me to be more devoted to keeping my word. Amen.

ALWAYS MEANS "ALWAYS"

Giving thanks always for all things to God the Father in the name of our Lord Jesus Christ.

EPHESIANS 5:20 NKJV

To give thanks all the time in every situation is something that most Christians agree with more in principle than in practice. It's easy to see why—when you've suffered a shock or a sudden loss, it's hard to say, "Thanks for the cancer, God," or "I'm so grateful to get fired."

Those words Paul used for "always" and "all things" actually mean "always" and "all things"! But that's impossible, right? Yes. . .unless you have faith. Unless you truly believe that God is in control, that nothing happens to you except what He allows, and that He loves you and wants what is best for you. Otherwise, you can't be thankful for adversity.

Remember, often all you can see is the problem in front of you—the tragedy or pain or hardship. But God has the broadest, most comprehensive perspective imaginable, and that's where you put your trust. When you thank Him in the midst of suffering, it's not the illness or joblessness or uncertainty you're thankful for. It's the belief that God is bigger than any of it, and that, no matter what, He can work things out.

When things are hard, help me to find reasons to be thankful, Lord. Remind me to point those out to others, so they can see Your love shining through the rain. Amen.

Day 5

AN ATTITUDE OF GRATITUDE

"I thank and praise you, God of my ancestors, for you have given me wisdom and strength. You have told me what we asked of you and revealed to us what the king demanded."
DANIEL 2:23 NLT

Prayer so often begins with gratitude, and gratitude often begins with awareness. How many things will God do for you today? Some of them are lasting and ongoing, like salvation and sanctification.

Others are more in the moment, like that "daily bread" that helped you pay a bill or meet a need, or those small but crucial encounters that God has in store for you on any given day—a chance meeting at the grocery store or in the hallway at work where God wants you to be available to listen, to speak an inspired word, to share a laugh, or to commiserate a loss. Just to be a part of what God is doing beyond your life, using you to help or touch others' hearts, is humbling and fulfilling.

Set your day on a path of gratitude. Paul wrote, "Devote yourselves to prayer, keeping alert in it with an attitude of thanksgiving" (Colossians 4:2 NASB). Take a moment to appreciate God's provision in your life, and then ask Him to prepare you for a day of divine appointments.

God, when I look at my family's history, I see many times You came through for us and rescued us from trouble. I thank You for those times today. Amen.

Day 6

PULL OVER AND PRAY

It is good to praise the Lord and make music to your name,
O Most High, proclaiming your love in the morning
and your faithfulness at night.
Psalm 92:1–2 NIV

When was the last time you stopped and counted your blessings? Daily life is a lot like Germany's autobahn—eighty miles an hour, all the time, a constant race of pass or be passed, full of noise and pollution and emergency phone calls. If you manage to squeeze in a prayer on your way to whatever's next, it feels like a small miracle.

At that pace, your time with God gets left at the roadside, lost in all the busyness of everyday life. You lose more than devotional time, though; you lose perspective. God's faithfulness, His daily mercies, go whizzing by, till it's easy to take them for granted. Then, when you're running on fumes, you wonder where God is.

Make a habit of gassing up spiritually before you go out each day. Carve out a few minutes in the morning to thank your heavenly Father for the blessings He daily provides, for His presence in the work you have ahead of you, for the unknown opportunities to be about His business—that amazing work of being His ambassador to the world, that unique privilege you have as His child.

God, help me to start my morning right—by starting
it with You. I can begin by saying thanks for
letting me have another day! Amen.

Day 7

A THANKFUL HEART TRUMPS A NERVOUS MOMENT

Be anxious for nothing, but in everything by prayer and supplication, with thanksgiving, let your requests be made known to God.

PHILIPPIANS 4:6 NKJV

Telling someone not to be anxious about a nerve-racking situation is similar to telling someone not to look down from a high place. It's almost impossible to avoid, especially when you're aware of the situation—a presentation or a deadline, or a conversation that might potentially become a confrontation.

And what if God doesn't work things out the way you thought He might, or the way you want Him to? That feeling in your stomach can become a hand over your eyes, blocking your view of God. Two little words, smack dab in the middle of this familiar verse, can break anxiety's grip and point you to God's peace: *"With thanksgiving."*

When you're stressed out, it's hard to think of being thankful—but it's essential. No matter what you're facing, God will still be God, sovereign and unchanging—and that means you will still be His beloved child, still the subject of thousands of good thoughts, still the precious heart He gave His Son to win back. So, when you face anxiety, thank God for who He is in the midst of it, and who you are to Him.

God, I don't want to be anxious for nothing, I want to be peaceful for a purpose! Help me to rely on You fully in every situation. Amen.

Day 1

GENEROSITY—MORE OR LESS

[Those who fear the Lord] share freely and give generously to those in need. Their good deeds will be remembered forever. They will have influence and honor.
Psalm 112:9 NLT

It's easy to succumb to selfishness. As a child you refused to share your treasures, and if you don't change, that attitude can follow you to the grave. You have and want more. You may borrow to get and then spend most of your life working to untangle your future from past debt.

While wrapped up in such an attitude of selfishness you might come face-to-face with someone in need and find yourself crippled by a resistance to share your *more* with those who have *less*. You might even be reluctant to give to God and come up with plenty of excuses why you shouldn't.

Generosity is less about your ability and more about bringing godly character to life using the resources and talents God has given you. The issue is never about the money. It's always about the way you respond to God's commands to live generously.

God's promises to supply *all* your needs are lavish and generous (Philippians 4:19). By understanding His love and care for others as well, you can begin to practice generosity with the awe and willingness to share that God always intended.

Lord, let me hold the things of this world loosely, so that I may always be ready to give them away to a person in need. Amen.

THE GIVING MOTIVE

"When you give to someone in need, don't do as the hypocrites do—blowing trumpets in the synagogues and streets to call attention to their acts of charity! I tell you the truth, they have received all the reward they will ever get. But when you give to someone in need, don't let your left hand know what your right hand is doing. Give your gifts in private, and your Father, who sees everything, will reward you."

MATTHEW 6:2–4 NLT

When God is generous, you know it. A gift comes from an unanticipated source. An unexpected check arrives in the mail. Relief is perfectly timed. Your conclusion? Your help came from the generous hand of God. James 1:17 (NKJV) says, "Every good gift and every perfect gift is from above, and comes down from the Father."

Did someone have to announce the news? Did God use social media to let others know He was generous? Were letters sent to family and friends announcing the blessing? No, He quietly provided for your need and invited you to get in touch.

God is generosity's best example. Give, expecting nothing in return, in order to help where help is most needed. Share, without drawing attention to the gift, because God is the only One who needs to know what was done, and He already does.

Lord, help me to give with no strings attached. Let me give out of a grateful heart, instead of having other motives. Amen.

A WIDOW'S FAITH

[Jesus] saw also a certain poor widow putting in two mites. So He said, "Truly I say to you that this poor widow has put in more than all; for all these out of their abundance have put in offerings for God, but she out of her poverty put in all the livelihood that she had."

LUKE 21:2–4 NKJV

God wants you to be generous, but He also wants you to pay attention to your motives for giving. Today's verses demonstrate how Jesus reacted to one incredible act of faith and generosity.

Imagine this widow coming to the temple. She doesn't own much. She can't earn much. Her current bank account? Two small coins. She isn't drawing attention to herself, but Jesus notices. He describes her gift as "more than all." Why?

There were people at the temple who gave *much* larger gifts, but she gave in great faith. All the money the widow had was two small copper coins—and she gave them *both*. Her future then rested in the hands of God. If He didn't provide, the widow wouldn't eat.

One small monetary gift was singled out for the message it sent about faith, and Christians today still pay attention. It's good to give from a generous heart; it's even better when that heart is overflowing with faith.

Lord, help me to get my priorities straight. I don't want to be thinking about who sees me giving or how my gift compares to another's. Help me to give with joy! Amen.

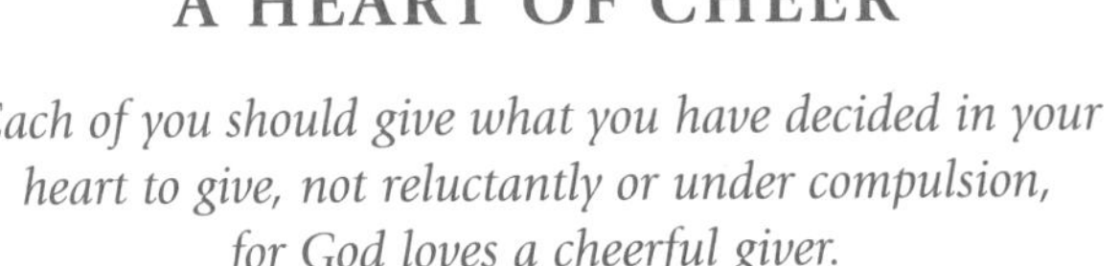

A HEART OF CHEER

Each of you should give what you have decided in your heart to give, not reluctantly or under compulsion, for God loves a cheerful giver.
2 Corinthians 9:7 NIV

God promised to meet the needs of His people, but He's asked His people to be generous. In scripture we're told that giving to the needs of the church is a priority with God, but He's looking for cheerful givers, not duty-bound supporters.

True, churches can use the money whatever people's motives for giving, but the difference is in the heart of the giver. One who is reluctant or gives under compulsion may view the *joy of giving* as a mistitled obligation.

When you're generous because you view sharing as an act of worship to God there is a spiritual bonus. Giving will actually bring joy instead of a dread that looks at what could have been purchased if the gift hadn't been given.

God doesn't want you to experience regret when you give. Perhaps that's why He wants you to focus on giving in order to see His ability to provide. Giving brings you in line with God's will, exposes you to His work, and brings you to the observation deck of His heart. When you connect with this journey you come face-to-face with your own *cheerful* heart.

God, I can feel my reluctance about giving. I can feel how I'm not trusting You fully. How I'm holding on to what I have. Help me to let go! Amen.

Day 5

DON'T MISS THE POINT

"Give, and it will be given to you: good measure, pressed down, shaken together, and running over will be put into your bosom. For with the same measure that you use, it will be measured back to you."

LUKE 6:38 NKJV

God has never been the originator of the *get-rich-quick* scheme. However, it could be inferred that this verse is suggesting that when you give $100 to God then He is going to give you at least $100 in return, but read carefully. There's more to it.

Whenever God provides a gift it's always the gift you really need. When you give as an act of worship to God He could return a gift of a blessing, like encouragement from a friend, the help of a neighbor, or the restoration of a relationship. These items are only a few examples of the gifts God might give to those with a generous spirit.

The *measure* you use might very well be the *cheerful* nature of your giving or the sense of *obligation* felt when you offer a gift. Money could be the least valuable gift God could offer back to you when He offers a gift of "good measure, pressed down, shaken together, and running over."

When you *give to get* you miss the point of generosity.

God, I can honestly say that every single time I've given myself, or my money, or my time, or my talents to You, You have given me even more. I can't out-give You! Amen.

Day 6

LENDING TO JESUS

If you help the poor, you are lending to the Lord—and he will repay you!
Proverbs 19:17 NLT

Jesus said that one day when His disciples saw Him enthroned in heaven, He'd tell them, "I was hungry and you gave Me food; I was thirsty and you gave Me drink; I was a stranger and you took Me in; I was naked and you clothed Me; I was sick and you visited Me; I was in prison and you came to Me" (Matthew 25:35–36 NKJV).

This statement would confuse many disciples in that day because they wouldn't be able to recall Jesus having need for clothing or health care. They certainly hadn't heard that He had served time in prison. They may have known Him to have been thirsty or hungry, but that was about it.

Then Jesus said that He'd explain that anytime they'd been generous to those in need it was as if they were generous to Him personally. His disciples would have recalled a similar thought from the writings of Solomon: "If you help the poor, you are lending to the Lord—and he will repay you!" (Proverbs 19:17 NLT).

Jesus wanted His disciples to be identified by their generosity, love, and compassion. So He made it clear that He Himself is always the object of your generosity.

Jesus, You gave so much to everyone around You. You shared Your wisdom and Your power, without hesitation. I want to be generous with everyone, just like You! Amen.

TRUE LIFE GENEROSITY

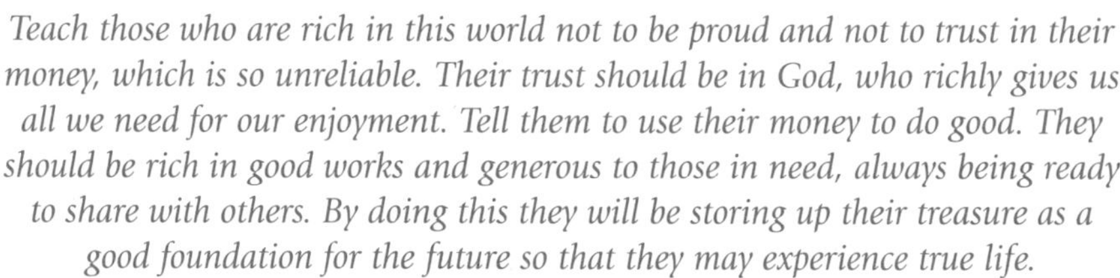

Teach those who are rich in this world not to be proud and not to trust in their money, which is so unreliable. Their trust should be in God, who richly gives us all we need for our enjoyment. Tell them to use their money to do good. They should be rich in good works and generous to those in need, always being ready to share with others. By doing this they will be storing up their treasure as a good foundation for the future so that they may experience true life.

1 Timothy 6:17–19 NLT

Economies collapse, markets crash, and currencies tumble. Yet people keep reaching for enough money to help navigate troubled times. Yes, saving is biblical. Managing money is too. You're asked to be wise, but money is not God, and God is not defined by money.

Your faith isn't to be anchored to cash reserves, but in the God who owns everything.

No amount of money can buy a sunset, the miracle of life, or the love of a spouse. God's best gifts are extremely lavish and can't be bought. The demonstration of your gratitude is linked to a generous heart. You're hospitable because generosity is relational. You're kind because generosity isn't defined by anything but love. You give because generosity is part of living "true life."

Lord, sometimes I get concerned about not having enough. But You've never let me down. Help me to give beyond what I think I can, trusting You to bless my efforts. Amen.

WILLING OR WHINING?

Be still in the presence of the Lord, and wait patiently for him to act. Don't worry about evil people who prosper or fret about their wicked schemes. Stop being angry! Turn from your rage! Do not lose your temper—it only leads to harm. For the wicked will be destroyed, but those who trust in the Lord will possess the land.

Psalm 37:7–9 NLT

A hungry child has to practice patience if Mom says he can't have a snack right before supper. Whether he likes the rule or not, he can choose to wait for food quietly and peacefully until mealtime (plus maybe earn a treat for good behavior), or he can choose to mope around the kitchen whining, "I'm *soooo* hungry." If you've been around young children much, you know they often choose the latter response.

God doesn't want childish bad attitudes while you wait. That's not true patience. The above passage says to "*be still* in the presence of the Lord, and wait patiently for him." And another well-known scripture says, "Be still, and know that I am God" (Psalm 46:10 NLT).

Being still in times of waiting means you have a chance to listen to what God wants to teach you during the downtime. So don't whine; rather, be pleasantly willing to wait.

Sometimes I fill up my waiting times with worrying and fretting. That's no good, Lord! I know it! Help me instead to be still and sure of You. Amen.

Day 2

WE ALL WAIT

For whatever things were written before were written for our learning, that we through the patience and comfort of the Scriptures might have hope. Now may the God of patience and comfort grant you to be like-minded toward one another, according to Christ Jesus.

Romans 15:4–5 NKJV

Hardship and waiting—no one escapes these, no matter what walk of life you come from. Are you waiting for a hardship to end or be resolved? Or waiting and working toward a new goal? Or waiting on God to answer a prayer? As a believer, you're always waiting and watching for a world dominated by sin and death to end with Jesus' return and the establishment of God's eternal and perfect kingdom.

Through any type of pain and need of endurance, God gives hope through His Word and through His presence. He is the God of patience and comfort, and He offers them in all your circumstances. He calls you to wait patiently on Him while at the same time caring patiently for others. This week, may you be encouraged as you learn about God's promises regarding the patience He desires from you and gives you. May your prayer be, "I wait for the Lord, my soul waits, and in His word I do hope. My soul *waits* for the Lord" (Psalm 130:5–6 NKJV).

Father God, help me to remind my brothers and sisters in Christ that even when we have to wait a long time, You are with us—teaching us and loving us. Amen.

Day 3

PATIENT FRUIT

"But the ones that fell on the good ground are those who, having heard the word with a noble and good heart, keep it and bear fruit with patience."
LUKE 8:15 NKJV

Have you encountered people who proclaim to know Jesus and are gung ho about their faith. . .for a little while? Then when they don't feel blessed enough with prosperity or resolution to their problems, they turn away from following Christ? The parable of the sower talks about all the different kinds of folks who hear the Word of God. The ones who succeed are those who hear the Word with good hearts, keep it, and bear fruit *with patience.*

Jesus truly is a quick fix for the problem of sin—because the moment anyone genuinely repents, He wipes out their sins, changing them from scarlet to white. He is able to do this because He triumphed over sin and death on the cross. However, a relationship with Jesus is not always a quick fix for all the consequences of sin. Sincere relationships with Jesus take patience, not demanding instant results and immediate miraculous interventions.

God certainly can do all things, and He promises to work all things for good for those who love Him (Romans 8:28), but He will work according to His own perfect timing. True believers must patiently trust His direction and schedule.

Jesus, I know that nothing really worthwhile happens overnight. Certainly that's true about my life in You. Each day, bit by bit, I'm learning how to love You more. Amen.

Day 4

PATIENT SUFFERING

Of course, you get no credit for being patient if you are beaten for doing wrong. But if you suffer for doing good and endure it patiently, God is pleased with you.

1 Peter 2:20 NLT

This scripture doesn't mince words. If a person does the crime, he pays the time, and there's no honor in patiently enduring it. But patiently suffering through punishment or a trial that was in no way warranted shows God you know the real meaning of patience, and He's pleased.

The Christian life offers no guarantee that you won't suffer in this life. Quite the contrary. You will suffer, and the Bible says to rejoice in your sufferings because God builds your character through them (Romans 5).

But the Bible does guarantee God's constant presence with you, no matter what trial you're facing or pain you're feeling. Isaiah 43:2–3 (NIV) says, "When you pass through the waters, I will be with you. . . . When you walk through the fire, you will not be burned; the flames will not set you ablaze. For I am the Lord your God, the Holy One of Israel, your Savior." (Notice that these verses say *when*, not *if*.)

Whatever your lot, wait patiently on God to deliver you from it, because He absolutely will, if not in this world then in His perfect kingdom to come.

Suffering is hard, Lord. Sometimes I feel so broken and weary. It helps me to know that You suffered too—You know what it's like. Stay with me, Lord! Amen.

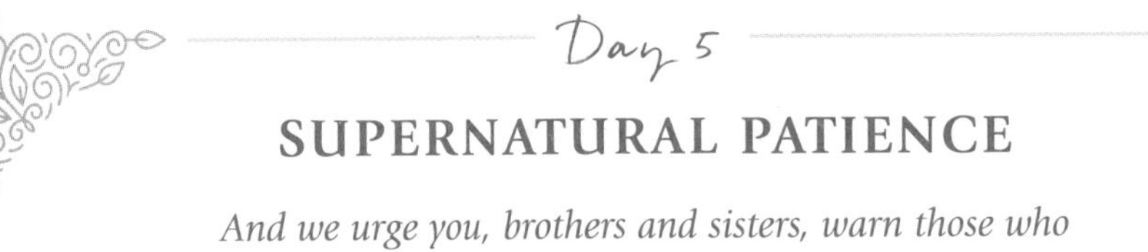

Day 5

SUPERNATURAL PATIENCE

And we urge you, brothers and sisters, warn those who are idle and disruptive, encourage the disheartened, help the weak, be patient with everyone.
1 THESSALONIANS 5:14 NIV

Be patient with *everyone*? Seriously? You might be thinking, "God, You know my coworkers, right? Or what about my neighbor and his ever-barking dogs?" But yes, God wants your patience with *everyone*. Ephesians 4:2 (NIV) says, "Be completely humble and gentle; be patient, bearing with one another in love." It sounds so utterly impossible to be patient with all the different types of people in the world. And it really is impossible for you alone. But as God's Word promises, all things are possible with Him (Matthew 19:26).

Second Thessalonians 3:5 (NLT) says, "May the Lord lead your hearts into a full understanding and expression of the love of God and the patient endurance that comes from Christ." Make sure you catch that it "comes from *Christ*." You can't have patient endurance without His help. God doesn't expect it from you in your own sinful human nature. Consistent patience with others is a supernatural phenomenon, truly a miracle from God in your life.

Depend on Him for patience with people He has placed around you, sharing His love with them and offering compassion and a listening ear, and encouragement when needed. Then just watch and see how God works!

Lord, when I think about how You love me, with all my faults, then I have a harder time being irritated with others. Your patience and kindness inspire me. Amen.

Day 6

WAIT ON GOD'S JUSTICE

Better is the end of a thing than the beginning thereof: and the patient in spirit is better than the proud in spirit. Be not hasty in thy spirit to be angry: for anger resteth in the bosom of fools.

ECCLESIASTES 7:8–9 KJV

Are you naturally hot-tempered or more easygoing? Whatever the case, this world is full of anger-inducing topics and experiences. Even if you're the most laid-back person on the planet, there's bound to be something that eventually pushes all your buttons. This scripture in Ecclesiastes reminds you not to be quick to anger, as do many other scriptures. (Check out Proverbs 14:29; 15:18; 16:32; 29:11; James 1:19–20; to name a few.)

For the minor offenses and the major ones, it's God's job to bring them all to justice, not yours. Romans 12:17, 19 (NIV) says, "Do not repay anyone evil for evil. . . . Do not take revenge, my dear friends, but leave room for God's wrath, for it is written: 'It is mine to avenge; I will repay,' says the Lord."

Remember every day that "a person's wisdom yields patience; it is to one's glory to overlook an offense" (Proverbs 19:11 NIV). Don't let anger overtake you; rather let God's supernatural patience overwhelm you in the times you're upset.

God, when I've lashed out in anger, I've felt like a fool later. I hate that feeling. Remind me of that when the anger starts bubbling up inside me! Amen.

Day 7

PERSPECTIVE ON PATIENCE

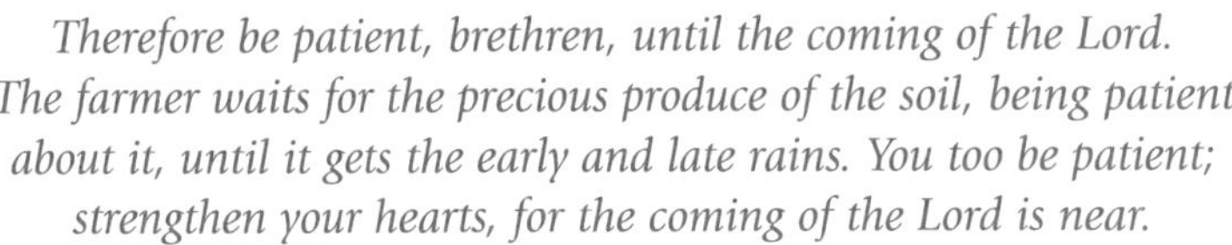

Therefore be patient, brethren, until the coming of the Lord. The farmer waits for the precious produce of the soil, being patient about it, until it gets the early and late rains. You too be patient; strengthen your hearts, for the coming of the Lord is near.

James 5:7–8 nasb

Jesus *is* coming, fellow believer! You must keep faith in that, even when the world gets you so discouraged and you wonder, "How long, Lord?"

It's essential to remember that God's timing and His perspective are so much bigger than yours. There's much more to His plans and purposes than you will ever be able to know on this side of heaven (Isaiah 55:8–9; 1 Corinthians 13:12–13).

Take some time to read all of 2 Peter 3 and especially note verses 8–9 (niv): "But do not forget this one thing, dear friends: With the Lord a day is like a thousand years, and a thousand years are like a day. The Lord is not slow in keeping his promise, as some understand slowness. Instead he is patient with you, not wanting anyone to perish, but everyone to come to repentance."

It's hard to wait on Him. (No kidding!) But He is good. He is patient with you. He wants *everyone* to come to repentance. And He goes with you on every step of your journey through life.

Lord, I want time to hurry up. I want You to come and make everything right. But I can't see things the way You do. Help me to be patient. Amen.

Day 1

IF YOU HAVE FAITH

*"You can pray for anything,
and if you have faith, you will receive it."*
MATTHEW 21:22 NLT

When you pray, do your words rise from a foundation of firm faith? Do you *know* that God will hear and answer? Or do you just *hope* He'll answer?

The scriptures are overflowing with heavenly promises—promises that God hears, that He answers, that He provides, that He cares. As your petitions align with your Father's perfect will, you will begin to experience a faith that blooms in heavenly harmony with your trust in His promises. Meditate on these scriptures, and let their truths refresh your spirit:

God hears: "We are confident that he hears us whenever you ask for anything that pleases him" (1 John 5:14 NLT).

God answers: "Ask and it will be given to you; seek and you will find; knock and the door will be opened to you" (Matthew 7:7 NIV).

God provides: "This same God who takes care of me will supply all your needs from his glorious riches" (Philippians 4:19 NLT).

God cares: "Cast all your anxiety on him because he cares for you" (1 Peter 5:7 NIV).

Believe without doubting that you will receive good things from your heavenly Father. You won't be disappointed. He never fails to keep a promise!

Gracious God, I know in my head that You are ready to supply me with anything I need. Help me to know it in my heart too. Amen.

Day 2

SECURITY IN TIMES OF TROUBLE

"He shall call upon Me, and I will answer him; I will be with him in trouble; I will deliver him and honor him."
PSALM 91:15 NKJV

When you're struggling with a troublesome issue, what kind of feelings do you encounter? It's likely you experience sadness, depression, doubt, anger, loneliness, fear, or anxiety (to name a few), and whether it's just one or a combination of many, you know how difficult it is to overcome those negative feelings.

It may seem near-impossible to crawl out of the dark hole you've dug yourself into—until you see the light and you remember God's promise to you and *all* believers: "Have I not commanded you? Be strong and courageous. Do not be afraid; do not be discouraged, for the LORD your God will be with you wherever you go" (Joshua 1:9 NIV).

Cry out to your heavenly Father, the One who listens, the One who hears your every prayer, the One who is always there. He will replace your anxious feelings with peace, hope, joy, and the calm assurance that everything is going to be just fine. It really will be okay, because God works *all things* together *for good* (Romans 8:28).

Praise Him today for His unending love and care, for the peaceful assurance He gives His children.

Lord, there are days when I feel like I'm drowning.
The ocean of trouble surrounds me and I can't breathe.
Rescue me from my own darkness, Lord. Amen.

Day 3

REFOCUS!

Be anxious for nothing, but in everything by prayer and supplication with thanksgiving let your requests be made known to God. And the peace of God, which surpasses all comprehension, will guard your hearts and your minds in Christ Jesus.

PHILIPPIANS 4:6–7 NASB

Worry distracts you from God. And when you're distracted from your relationship with Him, it's easy to forget that He alone is in control of everything. Then your mind becomes bogged down with anxious thoughts. You mistakenly begin to believe you must be in control, which only creates additional anxiety—and more insecurity—in your life.

When you become distracted in your faith, it's time to refocus. Whether you're facing a crushing disappointment, a scary diagnosis, or fear of the future, spend time in prayer and reflection. Your quiet conversation with God will redirect your thoughts and your feelings to Him—in whom there is complete security and trust. The result? Your heart and your mind will do an about-face.

As His peace becomes your peace, you'll want to shout from the rooftops that you've experienced the unexplainable goodness and grace of God. You will become a light to others, who will want to experience a worry-free life in Christ as well. "Let your light shine before others, that they may. . .glorify your Father in heaven" (Matthew 5:16 NIV).

Lord, I don't know why, but I keep forgetting how much it helps just to talk things out with You. Thank You for being a faithful listener. Amen.

....

....

....

....

....

....

....

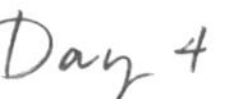

WHEN YOU CAN'T FIND THE WORDS

In the same way the Spirit also helps our weakness; for we do not know how to pray as we should, but the Spirit Himself intercedes for us with groanings too deep for words.
ROMANS 8:26 NASB

Have you ever felt a need to pray. . .a profound longing deep within your soul, yet you couldn't find the words to talk to God? Maybe you have struggled with praying for a friend who has received a daunting health diagnosis.

Or maybe you have personally experienced a difficult life circumstance—financial turmoil, divorce, death of a loved one, job loss—and for some reason, every time you fall to your knees, you feel nothing but utter weakness. You feel incapable of producing any kind of meaningful communication between your heart and your heavenly Father.

When you feel weak, rest in the holy promise of Romans 8:26, knowing that when you don't have the words, you have a heavenly intercessor, the Holy Spirit. And the Spirit knows your heart. As God's Word says: "When my spirit grows faint within me, it is you who watch over my way" (Psalm 142:3 NIV). The Spirit will bring you and God closer together, even in your weakness. When you can't find the words, the Spirit Himself will intercede on your behalf—every single time!

Thank You, Lord, for sending Your Spirit, who comforts me and teaches me how to comfort as well. Amen.

Day 5

CONFIDENT PRAYER

And this is the confidence that we have in him, that, if we ask any thing according to his will, he heareth us: And if we know that he hear us, whatsoever we ask, we know that we have the petitions that we desired of him.

1 John 5:14–15 KJV

If you're ever thirsting for assurance—to know with 100 percent confidence—that God is attentive to you, His child, repeat aloud this promise from 1 John 5. Let the words sink deep into your soul. Then quiet your heart and send this prayer heavenward:

Father God, do You hear me when I pray? Not just hear, *but* listen *to every word? Sometimes I experience uncertainty, wondering if You will answer my prayers. Help me to know, God, that I can pray confidently. Because I am Yours, Father, You will never fail to hear, to listen, to answer, to care. . .to love. I pray for Your will to be done in my life, today and always. In Jesus' name I pray. Amen.*

God desires for your heart to be overflowing with faith, for His Word says, "Without faith it is impossible to please God, because anyone who comes to him must believe that he exists and that he rewards those who earnestly seek him" (Hebrews 11:6 NIV). Believe, and pray confidently today!

God, when I doubt that You hear me, it's because I can't believe that You'd pay any attention to me at all. But You do. And that's amazing! Amen.

RESULTS

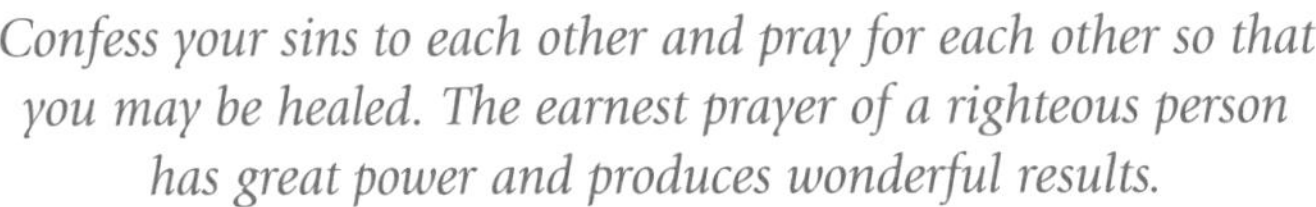

Confess your sins to each other and pray for each other so that you may be healed. The earnest prayer of a righteous person has great power and produces wonderful results.

James 5:16 NLT

As a Christ-follower, you know prayer is important. It's a necessary line of communication between your heart and God's that helps you maintain a growing, thriving relationship with the heavenly Creator. However, it's easy to fall into a routine where you breeze through your prayers. . .never fully thinking about the impact of your words or the powerful potential packed in just one single prayer.

So much good can be accomplished through prayer. The Bible says that the prayers of the righteous produce results—in fact, James 5 calls them "*wonderful* results." Those positive outcomes include:

- a right standing with God (1 John 1:9)
- wisdom (James 1:5)
- a changed life (James 4:2)
- peace beyond all understanding (Philippians 4:6–7)
- increased faith (Matthew 21:21–22)
- less stress (Psalm 55:22)
- forgiveness (James 5:15)
- healing (James 5:16)

If there is power in one single prayer, imagine how much power there is when *many* prayers are being sent heavenward on your or another's behalf! Today share your heart. Be open with your brothers and sisters in Christ. Wonderful results are sure to follow!

God, it's hard to work up the courage to confess my weaknesses to someone—even to You! Help me to find accountability partners I can trust. Amen.

HE IS NEAR

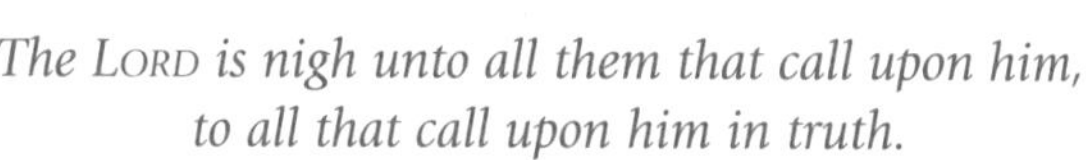

The Lord is nigh unto all them that call upon him, to all that call upon him in truth.
Psalm 145:18 KJV

Some days God seems so very far away, doesn't He?

When life isn't quite going as planned. . .

When you've reached the end of your rope. . .

When you're convinced that things are never going to get any better. . .

When you're completely exhausted from trying to control, well, *everything*. . .

It sometimes feels as though God has made Himself scarce, and you're on your own—drowning as wave after wave of despair comes crashing down upon you and you're left gasping for air.

In trying times, it's tempting to just give up hope. But in life's difficult moments it's more important than ever to keep praying. Keep reaching above the waves for the hand of your heavenly Father, the only One who is able to rescue you. "Be strong and of a good courage. . .for the Lord thy God is with thee whithersoever thou goest" (Joshua 1:9 KJV). "Fear thou not; for I am with thee. . . I will uphold thee with the right hand of my righteousness" (Isaiah 41:10 KJV).

Call out to God. And like David, in Psalm 145, feel His nearness. He is never more than a prayer away.

Creator God, sometimes I feel so small and You seem big and far away. Help me to get past these feelings and keep talking to You, no matter what. Amen.

PROOF THAT GOD LOVES YOU

"I correct and discipline everyone I love.
So be diligent and turn from your indifference."
REVELATION 3:19 NLT

You probably wish that God hadn't *made* a promise like this. He assures you, "I correct and discipline everyone I love." You may think this sounds more like a threat than a promise. But it *is* a promise.

If you're like most believers, you long to experience God's love, but your default assumption is that if God feels tender compassion for you, He will manifest it by blessing you with health, abundant financial provision, and joy-filled personal relationships. So when you suffer sickness, lack, and trying times instead, you doubt that God loves you. You think He must hate you and be angrily judging you for your sins.

But know this: God's discipline in your life is *proof* that He loves you. It's simply a wise, loving Father correcting your errant behavior, pointing out your need to return to Him, and keeping you on a short leash. He cares enough about you to discipline you and bring you closer to Him. It's where you're truly blessed.

This promise might not bring you much comfort at first glance, but when you truly grasp what it's saying, it has the power to give you great strength and reassurance during troubled times.

God, does anyone really like discipline? But I know I need it.
Every day! Guide me, Lord, now and always. Even when
I grumble. Especially then! Amen.

Day 2

PAINFUL BEATITUDES

"Blessed is the one whom God corrects; so do not despise the discipline of the Almighty. For he wounds, but he also binds up; he injures, but his hands also heal."
Job 5:17–18 NIV

On a flower-festooned hillside in Galilee, Jesus preached difficult teachings such as, "Blessed are those who mourn, for they shall be comforted" (Matthew 5:4 NKJV). Two thousand years earlier, in the neighboring land of Uz, one of Job's counselors stated a similar beatitude: "Blessed is the one whom God corrects" (Job 5:17 NIV).

Blessed to mourn? Blessed to be poor? Blessed to be persecuted? Blessed to be corrected by God—often with pain and grief? It surely doesn't *seem* like this is how a loving God would deal with His children, does it? Nevertheless, it's how you frequently experience His presence in your life.

You must be able to see beyond the discomfort and gaze into the Father's heart of love that moves Him to take such corrective measures. Yes, He wounds you—and wounds usually involve pain—but He's often operating to remove the darts and thorns of the enemy. Yes, He temporarily injures, but His motive in doing so is so that His tender hands can bring healing to festering wounds.

Have faith. Don't despise the difficult process God puts you through.

Healer and Lord, I know very well that mending wounds can be a painful process. Don't give up on me. Help me to become stronger through Your kind correction. Amen.

Day 3

THE PROCESS OF PRUNING

"My Father is the gardener. He cuts off every branch in me that bears no fruit, while every branch that does bear fruit he prunes so that it will be even more fruitful."
JOHN 15:1–2 NIV

In the parable of the vine, Jesus described the process of pruning. Pruning is quite a bit more involved than simply lopping off an entire branch. Pruning involves selectively cutting useless, dead wood, leaving the productive, fruitful parts of the branch. If a branch could feel pain, it would experience a great deal of it when pruned.

Unlike a branch, you *do* feel pain, anguish, and grief as God cuts dead wood from your life. He demands you surrender sinful habits and unproductive activities and pastimes to Him. You're often passionate about them, and they consume much of your time and energy, but bear no fruit for eternity. So God determines to snip them off—while you often fight to spare them from His shears.

God accomplishes most of His pruning in your life by discipline and scourging. He frustrates your wayward plans and brings your errant dreams to nothing. He often forcibly removes things from your tightly-clutching fingers. You wonder why God isn't giving you the desires of *your* heart? He has a higher good in mind.

Master, pruning is never a comfortable experience. But I'm certain I need it. And I definitely want to grow. Help me to grow in my faith. Amen.

Day 4

A FATHER'S DISCIPLINE

Know then in your heart that as a man disciplines his son,
so the Lord your God disciplines you.
Deuteronomy 8:5 NIV

Sometimes when you're undergoing God's discipline, you mistakenly think that He's angry with you, judging you, and about to thrust you out of His Kingdom. How quickly you forget that you're a born-again child of God whom He has promised to never abandon or cast out (John 6:37; Hebrews 13:5).

The heat of God's rebukes can be intense. "When with rebukes You correct man for iniquity, You make his beauty melt away like a moth" (Psalm 39:11 NKJV). But He's rebuking you *because* you're His child. It doesn't mean that He's done with you. It's proof that He's dedicated to you and loves you—in fact, that He *delights* in you. "For whom the Lord loves He corrects, just as a father the son in whom he delights" (Proverbs 3:12 NKJV).

You may know this fact, but easily forget it. That's why the Bible tells you to know it *in your heart.*

It pays to meditate on the depth of love that God has for even His wayward children. Remember the prodigal son, and how the father longed for him and welcomed him back. He had never ceased to be a son of the father.

Lord, this is no surprise, but sometimes I rebel against
Your discipline. I don't want to suffer. I don't want to go
through hardship. Please help me to see the benefits. Amen.

Day 5

BLESSED BY HARD DISCIPLINE

Blessed is the man whom You chasten, O Lord, and whom You teach out of Your law; that You may grant him relief from the days of adversity.
Psalm 94:12–13 nasb

God often sends you "days of adversity" which last for *months*. Why does He allow unpleasant circumstances to come into your life and go on and on? Because that's often what it takes to teach you deep lessons. When you've learned what He wants to teach you, He turns off the heat and grants you relief.

"We give great honor to those who endure under suffering. For instance, you know about Job, a man of great endurance. You can see how the Lord was kind to him at the end, for the Lord is full of tenderness and mercy" (James 5:11 nlt). God allowed Job to experience intense suffering, but afterward gave him relief and turned his situation around.

The Lord teaches you from His Word during chastening, reminding you of passages that relate to what you're going through. These are the lessons you desperately need to grasp, and you're blessed if God puts you through this difficult school. You probably don't *feel* blessed when you're in the middle of being chastised, but that's the end result, just the same.

God, I want to be the kind of person who faces adversity with peace and patience. But I'm not there yet. Help me to learn from You. Amen.

NECESSARY DISCIPLINE

No discipline is enjoyable while it is happening—it's painful! But afterward there will be a peaceful harvest of right living for those who are trained in this way.

HEBREWS 12:11 NLT

There's a beautiful worship song, popular some years ago, called "Refiner's Fire," which states the audience's desire to be made holy, purified, and drawn near to God. It's not sung too much these days, not because it went out of style, but because when it dawned on people that they were praying for God to put them through the *fire*, they hesitated to sing it.

If you ask God to purify and chastise you, He will do exactly that. It will make you a better person, but the process can be quite painful. It's worth it though. You might not care to repeat the experience, but if you're honest, you're thankful for when you went through such things. You learned lessons you wouldn't have learned otherwise.

This verse talks about "those who are trained in this way." The Bible even says of Jesus, "Though he were a Son, yet learned he obedience by the things which he suffered" (Hebrews 5:8 KJV). If Jesus Himself learned deep lessons of obedience through suffering, you should expect God to work the same way in your life.

Lord, I'm almost afraid to ask for this, but I do want You to purify my heart. I want so much for my desires to match up with Yours. Help me, Lord. Amen.

Day 7

SEVERE CHASTENING

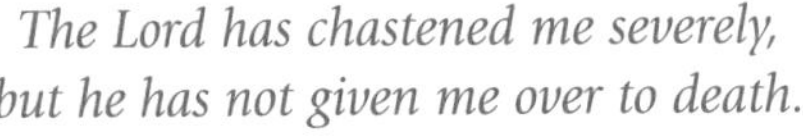

The Lord has chastened me severely,
but he has not given me over to death.
PSALM 118:18 NIV

This is a promise you may have occasion to quote at some point in your life. You almost hope not, but there are times when God leads you through deep, dark valleys and you feel like you're almost dying. At times like these, cast yourself upon the mercy of God. When David realized that he had seriously sinned, he prayed, "O LORD, do not rebuke me in Your anger, nor chasten me in Your hot displeasure" (Psalm 6:1 NKJV).

Sometimes you too will need to be chastised, and it won't be something you can avoid. God knows when discipline is necessary, but He does it in mercy and with great restraint. . .even though you're "sick almost unto death" (Philippians 2:27 NKJV). God told His people, "I will correct you in justice, and will not let you go altogether unpunished" (Jeremiah 30:11 NKJV).

God doesn't want to take you home before your time, but wants you to live a full life. Learn your lesson quickly so that He can bring the chastening to an end. Ask God to search your heart, convict you of sin, and lead you to repentance.

Even the deepest, darkest experiences have bright sides.

Lord, search the deep, secret places of my heart. Look into
my innermost thoughts. Reveal to me any sinful patterns
that I need to get rid of. Heal me. Amen.

Day 1

UNDERSTANDING THE LORD'S WILL

Therefore do not be foolish, but understand what the Lord's will is.
Ephesians 5:17 NIV

In a report about television and health, California State University cites these statistics: "According to the A.C. Nielsen Co., the average American watches more than 4 hours of TV each day (or 28 hours/week, or 2 months of nonstop TV-watching per year). In a 65-year life, that person will have spent 9 years glued to the tube."

Meanwhile, *Christianity Today* cited a study by the Evangelical Alliance recently that said: "The average length of time [evangelicals] spent studying the Bible was between 10 and 20 minutes per session, and over half (57 per cent) said they spent time reflecting on what preachers or speakers have said."

Don't draw the wrong conclusions here, though. TV isn't necessarily foolish. It can be educational and even spiritually edifying, depending on the program. But much of what is available probably *does* indeed fall into the foolish category, doesn't it? And watching television is often a passive activity.

Understanding the Lord and His will, on the other hand, only happens when you're actively seeking Him, much like knowing your spouse only occurs when you spend time in conversation together. What are you doing today to go deeper with God to understand His will?

God, I am nowhere close to being able to understand everything You've said in Your Word. Help me to make time to study Your Word intently. Amen.

Day 2

GLORY IN UNDERSTANDING

But let him that glorieth glory in this, that he understandeth and knoweth me, that I am the LORD which exercise loving-kindness, judgment, and righteousness, in the earth: for in these things I delight, saith the LORD.

JEREMIAH 9:24 KJV

For too long, God's people boasted (gloried) in their wisdom, their might, or their riches (v. 23)—all of which are indicators that they had more faith in their own abilities than they did in Him. In today's verse, the Lord says that if people "boast"—that is, publicly and firmly claim ability in some area—they should do so in their right understanding of Him and the way He exercises lovingkindness, judgment, and righteousness on earth.

"To glory in a thing is to depend on it as the means or cause of procuring happiness," wrote Adam Clare in his commentary. "But there can be no happiness but in being experimentally acquainted with that God who exercises loving-kindness, judgment, and righteousness in the earth."

To be able to "boast" that you truly know God, you will first have to go through the fires of testing, walk through dark valleys of "the shadow of death," and battle through raging floodwaters that seek to drown you. You will then walk closely in God's presence. That is something truly worth boasting about.

Father, I wish I could boast that I know You. But I feel like I'm just beginning to have a glimpse of who You are. What will You show me today? Amen.

Day 3

HIDING FROM JUDGMENT

A prudent man foreseeth the evil, and hideth himself: but the simple pass on, and are punished.

Proverbs 22:3 KJV

A careful believer can see sin on his horizon and he changes course, even going so far as to hide for a season, when necessary. It is far better to flee and hide than to face judgment for engaging in the evil or sin.

You'll find many evidences of this in scripture, from Noah, to Joseph, to Abraham and Lot, to God telling His people to flee Babylon because He was about to send a destroying wind (Jeremiah 51:1–6), to the church in Corinth whose members were engaged in sexual immorality (1 Corinthians 6:18).

In so doing, none of these people necessarily experienced physical protection, although there certainly was an element of protection on them as they fled. Instead, they were saving themselves from the judgment that was due to those who continue in sin. Only the wise take such action.

What are you doing to hide yourself from judgment while still engaging the culture around you? Knowing when to do what can be difficult to discern. If you need help, seek out a mature Christian to aid you in working through your circumstances. And take what that friend says to heart.

Lord, sometimes I fear that I am not nearly wary enough of the sources of evil thoughts and motivations. Help me to be able to both recognize evil and avoid it. Amen.

Day 4

BECOMING PRUDENT

The simple believe anything,
but the prudent give thought to their steps.
PROVERBS 14:15 NIV

When people refer to someone today as a "simple man," they mean someone who has simple tastes and a clear focus in his life. He doesn't need riches or fame. He only needs dreams, love, and a strong work ethic. That's *not* what the writer of today's verse meant.

The Hebrew word for "simple" means this: silly, seducible, foolish. On the periphery, a simple man in this context is one who believes in wild conspiracy theories because they appeal to his fears or worldview. But anyone can fall for a falsehood if he isn't prudent. Being prudent includes having good judgment. Having good judgment includes a willingness to investigate, question, and search out the truth.

As it relates to matters of faith, a prudent man listens to others intently, but then sets out to examine the scriptures for himself. He asks himself whether this doctrine is consistent with the totality of scripture, whether it is shallow or strange, whether it appeals to the spirit or the flesh, and whether it glorifies man or God.

How are you doing in this area? How are you showing prudence toward the doctrines you believe? Can you defend your beliefs from scripture? If so, you're on the right track.

Lord God, the last thing I want to be is a fool. Let me not believe everything I hear but instead have careful thought and a discerning heart. Amen.

STRENGTHEN THY BRETHREN

I will instruct thee and teach thee in the way which thou shalt go: I will guide thee with mine eye.

PSALM 32:8 KJV

When sinners becomes penitent, the next step is often for them to teach other sinners to walk in the way of the Lord. Psalm 32 describes this very scenario for David. His bones grew old (v. 3) because of his unconfessed sin. God's hand was heavy on him (v. 4). But when he acknowledged his sin, he found forgiveness (v. 5) and God became his hiding place (v. 7).

But David didn't stop there. In verse 8, he promised to teach others in the way they should go, much like he promised to do in Psalm 51:13 after repenting of sin. Solomon did the same thing, referring to himself as a preacher in Ecclesiastes 1:1. Jesus instructed Peter likewise, saying: "And when thou art converted, strengthen thy brethren" (Luke 22:32 KJV).

Who has been your teacher in your faith walk? If you haven't found one, seek someone out. Who have you mentored in the faith? In both cases, the relationship doesn't have to be a formal one. The key is to either receive or convey godly wisdom that is rooted in a repentant heart.

Lord and Teacher, if there's anything good that can come of my past mistakes, please let it come through me. Help me to lead others to You. Amen.

Day 6

STAYING WISE

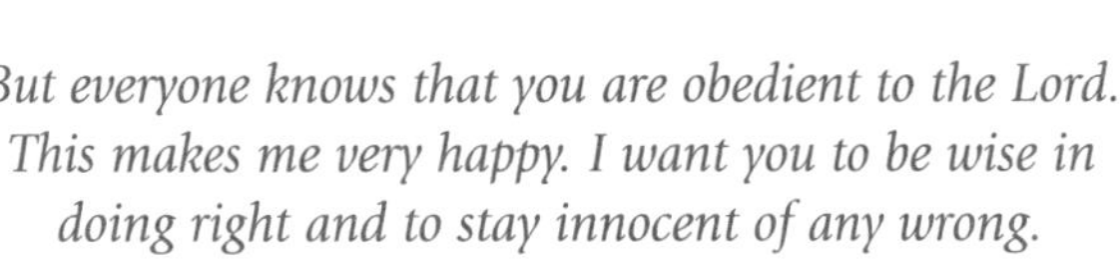

But everyone knows that you are obedient to the Lord. This makes me very happy. I want you to be wise in doing right and to stay innocent of any wrong.
ROMANS 16:19 NLT

In this day and age, individual churches are sometimes known for pastors who have fallen or for ugly splits rather than for their obedience to the Lord—especially in the opinion of a watching world. The same could be said even among the brethren. How many churches can you name in your local area that have a reputation in which "everyone" knows about their obedience to the Lord?

And yet, the church in Rome had this reputation. As important as this was, Paul didn't want them to rest on their reputation. He wanted them watch out for people who caused divisions—especially those who taught doctrine that was contrary to what they had originally been taught (vv. 17–18). They needed to stay wise in doing right, and one of the ways they were to do so was to stay true to orthodox teaching.

Can this be said about your faith tradition or the church where you're a member? Are you, as a member of that church, submitting yourself to quality teaching and then passing it along to others?

To be known as helpers, as leaders, as truth-tellers.
That's what I want for the body of believers, Lord.
And that's what I want for me. Amen.

Day 7

THE FOUNTAIN OF LIFE

The law of the wise is a fountain of life, to turn one away from the snares of death. Good understanding gains favor, but the way of the unfaithful is hard.
PROVERBS 13:14–15 NKJV

The law of the wise (biblical truth) is a fountain of life, bringing renewal, much like water revives a dying plant. One Bible commentator, Dr. John Gill, says doctrinal truth is a means for quickening dead sinners and of refreshing the souls of weary saints.

You've experienced such refreshing in your own life—first at your conversion and multiple times afterward as the Word spoke to your soul. The wise person is never far from biblical truth. She drinks of it daily, speaks of it among friends, and meditates on it during good times and bad. When the storms come, these wise people are firmly rooted and unbending. Yes, the winds blow and often cause damage, but the wise spiritually prosper anyway. To travel any other path is far more difficult, especially if the believer has to journey alone.

Would the Christians in your life consider you wise based on what they see and hear from you? Do they hear you citing biblical promises during the storms of your life? Do they find comfort when you offer such promises during their storms?

Lord, I want biblical truth to come to my mind faster than any movie quote or the latest commercial jingle. Help me to study Your Word. Amen.

Day 1

THE LAW OF KIND WORDS

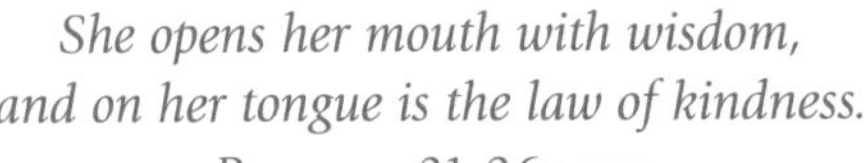

She opens her mouth with wisdom,
and on her tongue is the law of kindness.

PROVERBS 31:26 NKJV

One of the most prominent and important ways you show kindness is by your speech. Words carry power. They can harm or heal, help or hurt; indeed, "the tongue can bring death or life" (Proverbs 18:21 NLT). If you want to live a godly life, taming your tongue is one of your top priorities. As Jesus noted, "By your words you will be acquitted, and by your words you will be condemned" (Matthew 12:37 NIV). The kindness of your speech may be the difference for others too—particularly unbelievers—in whether they see Christ in you.

Some people are naturally kind. For perhaps up to half the people you encounter, being courteous, respectful, and gentle in their speech and manner is wired into them to some degree. But for the other half of the population, kindness requires discipline. This is where the "law of kindness" comes in. The best way to acquaint yourself with its precepts is to look in God's Word.

David hit on a key concept: "May these words of my mouth and the meditation of my heart be pleasing in your sight, LORD" (Psalm 19:14 NIV). When you internalize God's Word, kindness will govern your tongue.

God, it's fun to be known as clever or funny or friendly.
But I'd really love to be known as kind. Help me to
speak kind words every day. Amen.

Day 2

THE KINDNESS OF FORGIVENESS

Be kind to one another, tenderhearted, forgiving one another, even as God in Christ forgave you.

EPHESIANS 4:32 NKJV

Forgiveness is one of humankind's greatest needs. When you recognize that you've wronged someone, the desire to make things right burns within you. However, when you ask someone to forgive you, you give them the power. The ball is now in their court and you can do nothing until they return your volley—if they choose to. It's nerve-racking but oh-so-necessary.

It's different than telling someone you're sorry; *I'm sorry* just means you regret that it happened, but it's not a full acknowledgment that you're responsible for hurting that person. But if that person grants your request to be forgiven, that load is lifted. You can then begin to do what you must to make things right, to restore that relationship.

God's very heart is forgiveness, because He loves you and wants to have a close relationship with you. God is patient and longsuffering, and wants to shower you with blessings. His kindness is one of a kind, and until you embrace your desperate need to be forgiven, you can't fully experience it. But once you have, your life changes, and forgiveness gradually becomes a habit—an extension of the great kindness God gave you.

Lord, help me to remember that it is a blessing both to forgive and to be forgiven. Let me never hesitate to say I'm sorry when I'm in the wrong. Amen.

FRIENDLY FILTERS

Do not forget to show hospitality to strangers, for by so doing some people have shown hospitality to angels without knowing it.

HEBREWS 13:2 NIV

It's mildly amusing to think of serving angels dinner: "You guys eat, right? How about some more angel-hair pasta? And you'll never guess what we've got for dessert!" The idea is that you would do a better job of hosting angels than you would someone you've never met, whom you might or might not like. However, even though angels are on a higher plane of existence than you are, they are not the pinnacle of God's creation—people are.

It's hard to think of that woman with the cardboard sign that you gave a bottle of water and five bucks to this morning as the pinnacle of anything, or your unemployed brother-in-law who sleeps on your couch and eats all your leftovers, for that matter. But that's because you're still learning to see them through God's lens.

God uses some pretty serious filters looking at you; the best ones show you washed white by Christ's blood. He sees all people as potential royalty—sons and daughters of the kingdom—and that's how He wants you to see them too.

God, help me to open my home to anyone in need, no matter what they look like, where they are from, what job they do, or how they behave. Amen.

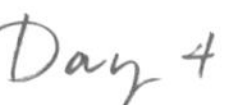

LOVE ONE ANOTHER

We must not just please ourselves. We should help others do what is right and build them up in the Lord.
ROMANS 15:1–2 NLT

There's no one like a fellow Christian to drive you completely nuts. It's funny how people labor under the assumption that a bunch of former sinners struggling daily with the battles of the flesh are supposed to have it together all the time. When they don't, it feels even worse than if an unbeliever had done the exact same thing. *I'd expect that from a pagan—they don't know any better! But you, brother, are supposed to be the spitting image of Christ at all times!* It's an unrealistic expectation.

Aside from the obvious need to extend forgiveness and grace, they need to recognize that different believers are at different points in their walk with Christ, with differing levels of spiritual maturity. Jesus told you to love one another (John 13:34), so that everyone would know that you are His. Quick, harsh, cynical judgment inside the church is unattractive to those outside. They can get that anywhere.

But if they see you building others up, gently correcting mistakes, offering support through hardships, patiently praying with and for others, and even enjoying others' company, that's going to look different, both inside the body of Christ and out.

What work goes into building others up? Kind words? Hugs? Acknowledgment of achievement? Training? Help me, Lord, to see how I can best support others. Amen.

Day 5

MINISTERS OF EMPATHY

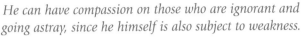

He can have compassion on those who are ignorant and going astray, since he himself is also subject to weakness.

HEBREWS 5:2 NKJV

In ancient Israel, the high priest was, ideally, an empathetic mediator between God and men. Now, however, because of the work of Jesus Christ, your Great High Priest, you no longer need that intermediary. You as a believer have been made a priest also (1 Peter 2:9), chosen by God to pray for others and to represent Christ to those who don't know Him.

One of the most important ways you can do that is by being kind. It was God's kindness, after all, that led you to repentance (Romans 2:4)—His desire to show you that He grasped your struggles and wanted to help. And He *could* help because Jesus was fully man and fully God.

In Christ's example, you see that great, life-changing kindness can come from understanding what it is to be tempted, to struggle, and to almost not make it, but it's not automatic. In fact, people often criticize most harshly those whose sins are most like their own. The scope of your ministry is different: when someone stumbles, you should "gently and humbly help that person back onto the right path. And be careful not to fall into the same temptation yourself" (Galatians 6:1 NLT). Forgiven sinners should be forgiving.

Lord, it is hard to forgive some people. But I know I have absolutely no right to withhold forgiveness forever. Help me to work on it, Lord. Amen.

Day 6

DEEP-HEARTED DECENCY

Never let loyalty and kindness leave you! Tie them around your neck as a reminder. Write them deep within your heart.
PROVERBS 3:3 NLT

Following ancient biblical tradition, observant Jewish men wear small boxes filled with Bible verses, called *tefillin,* strapped to their forehead and hand as they pray. The idea is that they keep God's Word on their minds and obey it in their deeds (Deuteronomy 11:18).

Of course, without internalizing such concepts, you run the risk of a superficial brand of service to Christ—the appearance of kindness without any deep concern for someone's spiritual health. But before you can truly invest in someone else's welfare, you have to spend time writing God's love deep within your own heart. Jesus said, "The mouth speaks what the heart is full of" (Luke 6:45 NIV). If God's words are in your heart, they will come out in your speech—discerning, life-giving, useful words "fitly spoken. . .like apples of gold in settings of silver" (Proverbs 25:11 NKJV).

Use sticky notes to post favorite verses around the house, where they can easily be seen. God wants to write His Word on your heart, and He will if you let Him. If you begin with loyalty and kindness, you'll be off to a good start, able to get along with both men and God.

Faithful Father, I want to be Your loyal servant. Help me to commit to studying Your Word so I can be trained in Your ways. Amen.

Day 7

CHANGE THE GAME

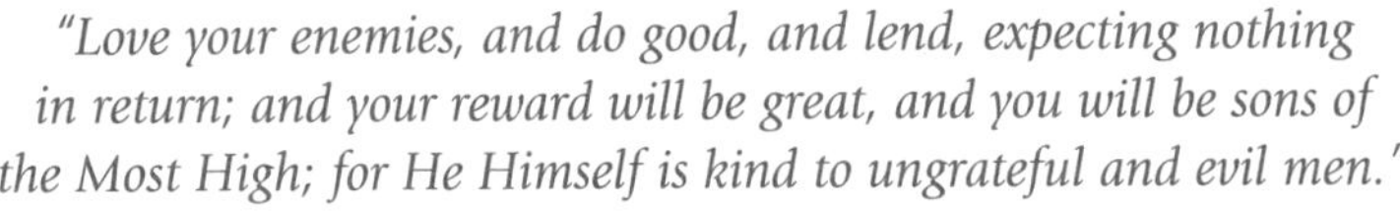

"Love your enemies, and do good, and lend, expecting nothing in return; and your reward will be great, and you will be sons of the Most High; for He Himself is kind to ungrateful and evil men."

LUKE 6:35 NASB

True kindness often comes with a cost—there's nothing simple or easy about loving your enemy or being decent to someone who has treated you badly. But that's what Jesus has called you to do. Talk about a tough task! Even if you aren't vengeful by nature, you wouldn't naturally want to have anything to do with someone who had stolen from you or lied about you.

But remember: even if you're the world's biggest sweetheart, you still need God's forgiveness. When Jesus said that God is kind to ungrateful, wicked people, He wasn't just talking about thieves and murderers; He meant everyone. Everyone needs forgiveness; everyone needs salvation.

Some of the greatest impacts you could ever have for God's glory could be in the way you treat those who have wronged you. That's how you show the difference Jesus has made in your life. When you love someone unlovable or give to someone who is insolvent, you're showing the kind of mercy God showed at the cross—and that's a game-changer.

God, I've seen that hating people does nothing except drain me of energy, peace, and joy. Help me to go the next step and love those who have wronged me. Amen.

HONEST AND TRUE

And in their mouth was found no deceit, for they are without fault before the throne of God.
REVELATION 14:5 NKJV

No deceit. Ponder those words for a moment. Have you ever known a human being incapable of deceit? Even the finest person occasionally fails. It's tough to be honest 100 percent of the time.

Don't think so? What do you say when your best friend asks your opinion of her new (over-the-top/crazy) hairdo? If you're like most, you fumble around for something kind (but wholly untrue) to say.

There's a fine line between kindness and sincerity, isn't there? Somehow, you have to find that place. God calls you to be sincere, which means you're called to honesty. That means you have to "speak the truth in love" (Ephesians 4:15 NLT). It's never easy, but honesty is always the best policy.

What does this have to do with your spiritual walk? God has called you to be genuine. You're a representative of Him, after all. When you walk in sincerity (free from hypocrisy) then you're the witness He has called you to be. Today, take some time to ask the Lord to shine His spotlight on areas of your heart that might be deceitful. Time to clean out those cobwebs!

Lord, little lies come so easily; it's easy to overlook them. But please burden me with guilt when I am dishonest. Point it out so I can stop it. Amen.

Day 2

A HOLY LONGING

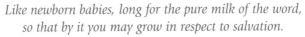

Like newborn babies, long for the pure milk of the word,
so that by it you may grow in respect to salvation.
1 Peter 2:2 NASB

You've likely heard the expression, "Fake it till you make it." Many times this flies in the face of what God expects from you. There's no "faking it" in His plan. He longs for your actions to be rooted in sincerity and honesty. He wants your trust in Him to be real, deep, and abiding.

Where does this type of sincerity come from? It begins with a genuine holy longing for the Lord. If you're going through the motions of reading your Bible and praying, if sincerity isn't the driving force, then you need to reexamine your core beliefs.

Have you made Jesus the Lord of your life? Does He sit on the throne of your heart? If not, then make things right today. When you come to Him with a sincere heart, genuinely longing for His presence, His touch, His Word, He's free to act on your behalf. His promises become more than possibilities; they are yours for the taking.

So, begin again. Like a babe, let your pure longing for the Lord drive you into His arms for a heart transformation you'll never forget.

God, when I focus on Your Word, I do want more of it.
But when I focus on other things, I forget my need to hear
from You. Help me to adjust my priorities. Amen.

Day 3

FROM THE HEART

For we are not, as so many, peddling the word of God; but as of sincerity, but as from God, we speak in the sight of God in Christ.
2 CORINTHIANS 2:17 NKJV

Likely you've come in contact with a con man or two over the years. These frauds often peddle religion in an attempt to snag your money. They have a clever scheme, one rooted in evil, but they spend most of their time pulling the wool over people's eyes. There's nothing sincere about them. Their acting skills are stellar, well-rehearsed, but time usually gives them away.

Contrast these not-to-be-trusted folks with a believer who would give his life for those he loves. He's the real deal, one who genuinely cares about others. That's what God is looking for. Either you're truly in—100 percent committed to the Lord and His call on your life—or you're not. God sees the heart and knows when you're not being genuine.

Today, take a little time to examine your *real deal* level. Are you putting on a show, hoping to convince others that you've got it all together? If so, draw near to God and do business with Him so that He can purify your heart and set you on a path of sincerity.

Father, in whatever I do, I want to be careful not to use Your Word or my beliefs for anything but Your glory. Help me to remember this. Amen.

Day 4

CHILDREN OF THE DAY

But let us, who are of the day, be sober, putting on the breastplate of faith and love; and for an helmet, the hope of salvation.
1 Thessalonians 5:8 KJV

Remember that old saying, "Nothing good happens after midnight"? While that may not be completely accurate, there is a nugget of truth at the core of the expression. Under the covering of darkness, in the depth of the shadows, bad things can be hidden away, out of view. The enemy gets away with his schemes in the dark. Thieves don't usually sneak into your home at noon, after all. They wait until midnight and slip in beneath the shadows.

Good things happen in the light—at least that's the perception. God has called you to be a child of the light (the day). Everything is out in the open. You're not hiding secrets. You're not covering up sin. You're an open book, one who is willing to deal with heart issues in a sincere way. How does a child of the day live? Honestly. Legitimately.

Take the time to analyze your faith walk today. Is anything hiding in the shadows? If so, let God sweep it away.

Father God, I want to be a child of the Light—to live my life out in the open, in the goodness and grace of Jesus Christ. Amen.

Day 5

A CLEAR CONSCIENCE

We can say with confidence and a clear conscience that we have lived with a God-given holiness and sincerity in all our dealings. We have depended on God's grace, not on our own human wisdom. That is how we have conducted ourselves before the world, and especially toward you.

2 Corinthians 1:12 NLT

Remember that feeling you would get as a child whenever you'd done something naughty? You couldn't control the feelings of guilt and shame. They swept over you. God created you to live in holiness and sincerity. It's in your spiritual DNA.

That's why conviction sweeps over you whenever you slip into illegitimate living. The Lord wants your life to be free from care, filled with His promises. A seared conscience isn't part of His plan. He wants your life to be peaceful and filled with joy. The path to such a life is rooted in complete truth. Where do you find truth? In relationship with your heavenly Father.

Sure, you can fool some of the people some of the time, but if you want true peace (freedom from guilt and shame) you have to *be* the person you *say* you are. Your conscience will be completely clear when you're living out your faith day by day, placing your sins at the feet of Jesus.

I've done things I'm not proud of, Lord. I want to confess everything to You so I can repent and receive Your forgiveness. Thank You, Lord. Amen.

....

....

....

....

....

....

....

....

A BLAMELESS LIFE

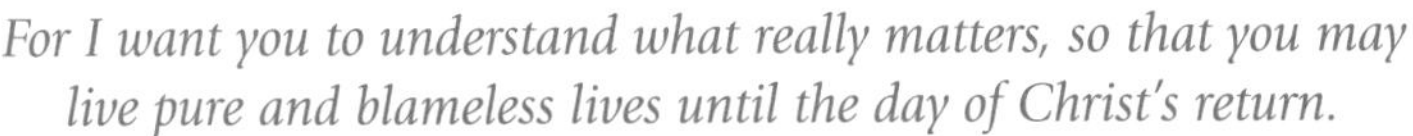

For I want you to understand what really matters, so that you may live pure and blameless lives until the day of Christ's return.

PHILIPPIANS 1:10 NLT

If someone asked you to make a top ten list of the things that really mattered in your life, what would you write down? Your family? Your friends? Your job? Your church? Your talents? Your material possessions?

It's good to take inventory of the things that matter the most so that you can check your heart's motivations to make sure they're pure and blameless. (Sometimes you do the right things, but for the wrong reasons.) God wants you to understand what really, truly matters. Sure, He's concerned about your job, your relationships, and your possessions, but He's mostly interested in making sure you're motivated to live for Him and to share His love with others.

Take that job, for instance. God wants you to work hard, but not just to bring home a paycheck. He longs for you to share His love with your coworkers.

Take another look at today's scripture. There's a promise buried within its words. If you understand what really matters, then you can live a pure and blameless life. Understanding what matters is key to seeing that amazing promise fulfilled.

Lord, living a blameless life seems impossible. But I know You will equip us to do impossible things for Your glory. Let me strive to live an excellent life. Amen.

GOD PLEASERS

For our exhortation was not of deceit, nor of uncleanness, nor in guile: But as we were allowed of God to be put in trust with the gospel, even so we speak; not as pleasing men, but God, which trieth our hearts. For neither at any time used we flattering words, as ye know, nor a cloke of covetousness; God is witness.
1 THESSALONIANS 2:3–5 KJV

You've tried so hard not to be a people pleaser. In fact, you've gone out of your way to make sure your motivations are pure. But here you are, struggling once again. You're tempted to do something, or say something, because you're feeling intimidated. You could kick yourself for feeling this way. You're guarded, fearful. If only you had the courage to speak God's words in the situation instead of stumbling your way through.

It's time to take inventory, friend. Make a list of people in your life who bring out the people pleaser in you. Give those names to the Lord. Ask for His help. He will show you how to redirect your focus so that your aim is to please Him, not them.

Sure, you want people to like you. That's important. But, at what cost? Put God in His rightful place and watch those relationships shift in a new, holy season.

Lord, You know I'm tempted to blend in and just go with the flow at times. Help me to remember that You are the only One I need to please. Amen.

Day 1

WHAT DO YOU NEED?

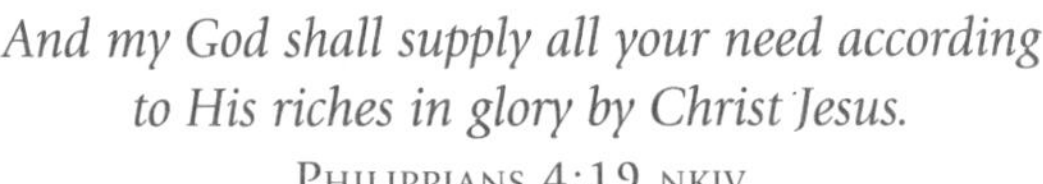

And my God shall supply all your need according to His riches in glory by Christ Jesus.

PHILIPPIANS 4:19 NKJV

What do you need? It's an important question. Some things on your list will be *needs* and some are *wants*. One can often be mistaken for the other, but you may assume that God should take care of both.

You may *need* a car, but may *want* a specific manufacture, model, and options package. You *need* food, but may *want* a specific type. You *need* water, but may *want* a brand that comes from exotic springs flowing from ancient mountains.

If God doesn't seem to be supplying your needs it's time to determine what your needs actually are. If you need food and water God can supply the need, but it may not be the brand or type you want. That doesn't mean God didn't supply. It might mean that what He supplied didn't match your want, even though it fully met your need.

Do you struggle with this? Everyone does. You could be convinced that when you pray God has to answer your prayers with a "yes" response. But more than anyone, God knows what you need. He knows better than you do. Giving you something you don't need fails to truly meet your need.

God, I know You can supply everything I need. Help me not to be consumed with wanting things that don't have real value. Amen.

Day 2

THE 20/20 BENEFIT

Once I was young, and now I am old. Yet I have never seen the godly abandoned or their children begging for bread.
Psalm 37:25 NLT

It's been said hindsight is 20/20. When you look back you have a clearer picture of what was true and what was false. You have greater insight, understanding, and wisdom.

The psalmist speaks from the perspective of one who's been there, done that. He makes two conclusions, powerful in their implications: (1) The godly have never been abandoned; (2) the children of the godly have never had to beg for bread.

These are the observations of a psalmist. The two lessons are from his experience over many years. The overarching conclusion is that *God provides*. He takes care of His family. His love is demonstrated repeatedly as He continues to meet your needs.

When you draw close to God you begin to learn His will (those things He wants you to do). You can be confident that when God gives you a task He also gives everything you need to complete the task. He doesn't ask you to do something without also making it possible to do what He asks.

He will supply your needs. He does have a plan. This is the part where you walk by faith.

I will never be left alone, for You are always with me.
That's a message I need to hear every
day, Lord. Thank You. Amen.

Day 3

BE GOD RICH

Charge them that are rich in this world, that they be not highminded, nor trust in uncertain riches, but in the living God, who giveth us richly all things to enjoy.
1 TIMOTHY 6:17 KJV

If God gives you everything you need but not everything you want, how could you possibly be considered rich? Doesn't most of what you want *cost* something? Wouldn't it make more sense to have *more* if you're to be considered rich?

Just as there's a difference in the mind of God between a need and a want, there's also a difference between rich and poor. Today's verse points out that those who are rich according to society's standards may place their trust in what they own and not in the God who provided everything.

No one could ever own more than God. No one but God could provide the majesty of a lightning storm in summer, the rush of a waterfall, the splendor of a canyon. These are riches you can enjoy due to God's generosity. But it doesn't end there. You might enjoy conversation with an aging relative, the laughter of a baby, or late-night conversations with your spouse. These too are incredible riches.

Do you trust in money, or the God who gives blessings money could never buy?

When everything is going well, God, I forget to depend on You. Break me of that habit. Let me never forget that I owe everything to You. Amen.

Day 4

GOD KNOWS—NO WORRIES

"Your heavenly Father knows that you need all these things.
But seek first His kingdom and His righteousness,
and all these things will be added to you."
MATTHEW 6:32–33 NASB

For Christians, worry can be described as a lack of faith. The verses that came right before today's passage talk about birds, flowers, and grass. They're all taken care of by God and are perfect examples demonstrating that He can be trusted to provide.

You worry about so many things and act as if worrying is the only logical answer to controlling whatever it is you worry about. God says worry can't add time to your life, and science says it may actually decrease your lifespan. God says life is more than what you wear and what you eat. When you throw out the leftovers and drop off last year's fashions to the secondhand shop, you should remember that God provided what you're getting rid of while you worry about what you *don't* have.

Because God knows what you need He asks you to seek Him first, above everything else. He puts His spotlight on relationship. If you seek Him above the worry, hoarding, and gathering, He will be free to take care of all the things you've tried to take care of alone.

Lord, You know my heart is full of many wants and worries.
Get rid of anything in me that keeps me
from getting closer to You. Amen.

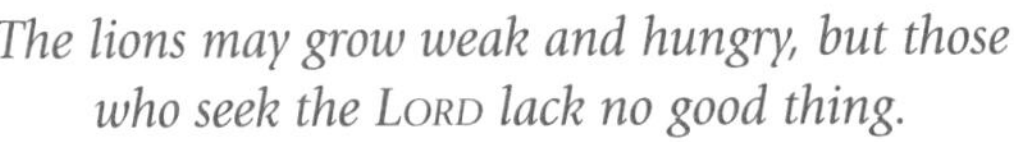

WHAT YOU SEEK

The lions may grow weak and hungry, but those who seek the LORD *lack no good thing.*
PSALM 34:10 NIV

God doesn't have to borrow from the bank, ask you to wait until He gets paid, or sell some of His Creation to take care of your need. He is lavish, needs no additional help, and only asks you to wait if it's in your best interest to wait.

The psalmist in this verse describes hungry lions. He's pointing out that lions who are predatory by nature can't always provide for themselves if there's no prey to be found. On the other hand, you get to go straight to the source of need fulfillment—God.

If your thinking can be transformed you can begin to see that in God's economy money is only a tool and His blessings often don't arrive in the form of cash.

He promises that if you seek Him you will lack *no good thing*. Is it possible the lions in this verse describe those who only rely on their personal strength, wisdom, and skill? Is it possible that the psalmist is saying actions that don't include dependence on God lead to spiritual hunger and weakness? If that's true, how should this change what you seek?

God, sometimes I'm not sure how to seek You. And sometimes I just don't make the time to figure that out. Forgive me, Lord. Amen.

Day 6

CONTENT AND SATISFIED

Keep your lives free from the love of money and be content with what you have, because God has said, "Never will I leave you; never will I forsake you."

Hebrews 13:5 NIV

God's provision works in cooperative partnership with your personal contentment. When you love money more than God you will *not* experience contentment and you *will* rely on yourself more than God.

It's ironic that when you're discontent you'll choose money over God's provision. You want what you don't have and sidestep God in an effort to crave more, get more, and take more. When you're chained to money you'll be dissatisfied in your bondage.

Contentment believes that when God promised He would never leave or forsake you, He meant it. You can be satisfied in knowing that God's gifts can't be bought, earned, sold, or transferred. You could offer God every dollar the world has ever known and it wouldn't be enough to buy a single gift from His hands. He would be offended if you tried to buy what He offers at no cost. His gifts are free, and His currency of choice has never been money.

If you can think of God's provision in terms of something *more* than money, you'll take enormous strides toward a contentment that's designed to satisfy.

Lord, day after day I'm amazed how You provide for me. I truly have everything I need to live and love and serve You. Amen.

Day 7

THE SHEPHERD PROVIDES

The Lord is my shepherd, I shall not want. He makes me lie down in green pastures; He leads me beside quiet waters. He restores my soul; He guides me in the paths of righteousness for His name's sake.

Psalm 23:1–3 NASB

Sheep often wander from their shepherd. One particular sheep was of a variety known for rich and thick wool. This sheep avoided capture many times over several years. He faced a self-imposed death sentence because his wool then grew so thick it created numerous health challenges that he couldn't overcome on his own. And the sheep couldn't shear himself. The shepherd ordered a drastic measure to save it. Once sheared, the sheep's health improved and, if he stays with the shepherd, he'll live happily ever after.

God compares believers to sheep and calls Himself the Shepherd. They're given the benefits of His leadership. He prepares the way, gives them confidence when facing opposition, and refreshes their innermost being. Oh, there's one more benefit—*they lack nothing*.

God takes care of His people's needs in the same way a shepherd cares for his sheep. He understands the fear in their hearts, questions in their minds, and pressing needs of each moment. That's where He meets them—and it's just where they need to be met.

God, You are such a good, good Shepherd. You give me rest. You refresh me. You guide me. Lead me forever, Lord. Amen.

Day 1

ABOUNDING IN FAITHFULNESS

The Lord passed in front of Moses, calling out, "Yahweh! The Lord! The God of compassion and mercy! I am slow to anger and filled with unfailing love and faithfulness."
Exodus 34:6 NLT

As the Lord passed before Moses, He introduced Himself in a way that revealed His very nature. This is such a beautiful declaration that it bears a closer look. The Lord said that He was "the God of compassion and mercy" and "slow to anger." These are very attractive attributes, because humans make frequent mistakes and require compassion, mercy, and patience.

The Lord is also "filled with unfailing love and faithfulness." Think of it: God is filled to overflowing with love. It colors and drives everything He thinks, says, and does. That's why 1 John 4:8 (KJV, emphasis added) says, "God *is* love." And He's also filled with faithfulness; He's the very essence of dependability and trustworthiness.

Do you sometimes question whether God actually is utterly loving in His attitude toward you? Do you wonder if you can always depend on God or whether He will zone out during your times of trouble? Not a chance. He's watching over you constantly and has your back.

Even when it *seems* as if God has failed, a deeper gaze into His eternal purposes will reveal that He never stopped loving you.

God, Moses had a temper, and yet You came to him. Help me to remember that You love me as I am. Amen.

GOD IS UTTERLY FAITHFUL

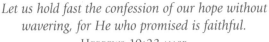

Let us hold fast the confession of our hope without wavering, for He who promised is faithful.

HEBREWS 10:23 NASB

This is one of the most powerful, beautiful promises in the Bible. In it, the unknown writer of Hebrews urges you to tightly grasp your Christian faith and refuse to let go, to cling to it without doubting or becoming anxious. The reason he can so confidently tell you to do this is because "He who promised is faithful." God, who made so many promises, can be counted on to do what He has said.

For example, God promised, "Whosoever shall call upon the name of the Lord shall be saved" (Romans 10:13 KJV), and since He's utterly faithful to stick to what He has sworn He would do, God will be certain to save you if you have sincerely cried out to Him.

In the same way, God will be sure to look after your financial needs. Philippians 4:19 (NKJV) promises that "God shall supply all your need according to His riches in glory." And in Philippians 4:13 (NKJV), Paul states, "I can do all things through Christ who strengthens me."

These are all promises that you can confidently lay hold of and claim that the Lord will fulfill. Why? Because He's faithful, unchanging, and constant.

Lord, when I am unfaithful, You are faithful. When I am fickle, You are constant. When I am indecisive, You hold the course. Thank You for being You! Amen.

Day 3

GOD CANNOT—DOES NOT—LIE

God is faithful, through whom you were called into fellowship with His Son, Jesus Christ our Lord.
1 Corinthians 1:9 nasb

This verse opens with the profound statement: "God is faithful." According to the dictionary, to be "faithful" is to be loyal, constant, steadfast, and unswerving. If there was any room for doubt, if God were capricious, you'd never be certain if you had firm footing to stand on. But God is the solid Rock that you can confidently base your life upon.

"God is faithful," and because He has called you into a spiritual relationship with His Son, Jesus, you can count on the fact that He will perfect the work He has begun in you and safely bring you into His heavenly kingdom. He "will also confirm you to the end, blameless" (v. 8 nasb).

Paul spoke "in the hope of eternal life, which God, who cannot lie, promised long ages ago" (Titus 1:2 nasb). The devil, who is the ultimate deceiver, often likes to try to get you to doubt that God is faithful. But remember, Satan "is a liar and the father of lies" (John 8:44 nasb), whereas "God. . .cannot lie."

God is not constantly changing His mind. He won't mislead you or pull the rug out from under your feet. Trust Him.

Father God, You know how hard it is for me to trust people sometimes. So few people keep their word. But You do, Lord. Every single word. Amen.

GOD WILL MAKE IT GOOD

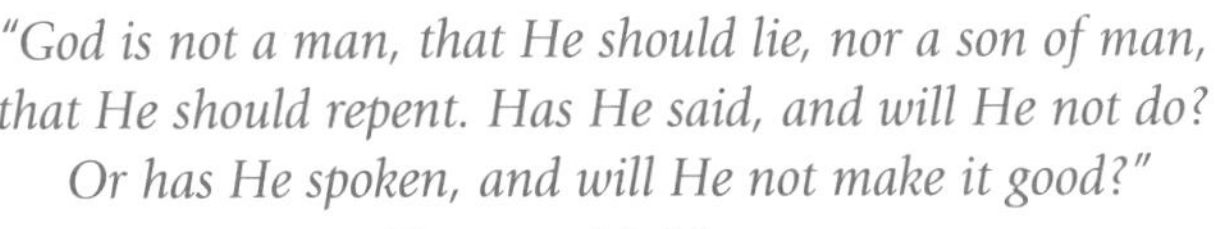

"God is not a man, that He should lie, nor a son of man, that He should repent. Has He said, and will He not do? Or has He spoken, and will He not make it good?"

Numbers 23:19 NKJV

Humans often *intend* to do good, but fall short. They lie, recant on good intentions, back out of commitments, and change their minds. They say they'll do something, but in the end often wind up *not* doing it. They make promises, but frequently fail to follow through on them.

The expression "make it good" means to fulfill a promise. It's not heard too much these days, but it has a clear, unchanging meaning. Once God says He'll do something, He follows through on His promise. That's because He's faithful. He doesn't have second thoughts or suddenly come across new information that forces Him to change His mind. God is all-knowing, and nothing surprises Him.

If God has *said* He will do something, He will *do* it. Of course, you have to be certain that He was actually saying what you thought He was, otherwise you're setting yourself up for a disappointment. But once you're convinced that God intends to do something for you, or do a miracle in your life, don't let go of your faith.

God, I love Your perfection. I love that You are complete and whole in every way. There is no one like You, Lord. Holy, holy, holy is our God! Amen.

Day 5

GOD'S UNNULLIFIABLE FAITHFULNESS

What if some were unfaithful? Will their unfaithfulness nullify God's faithfulness? Not at all! Let God be true, and every human being a liar.

ROMANS 3:3–4 NIV

Paul was discussing how God had chosen Israel to be His special people and planned to save them, and this led to a discussion of the fact that the majority of Jews down through history had been unfaithful. So Paul asked if their disobedience ruined God's plans. Did God give up and cease to uphold *His* end of the covenant because His people had failed to live up to their part?

Paul responded, "Not at all! Let God be true, and every human being a liar." God was still faithful to do what He *said* He would do, human failings notwithstanding. God still brought His stated purpose about. "All Israel will be saved" as God had promised (Romans 11:26 NIV), but He clarified that "not all who are descended from Israel are Israel" (Romans 9:6 NIV).

God is faithful. He has clear, unalterable purposes for the nation of Israel—and for you as well—and He's determined to bring those plans to fruition. But how much *you* enjoy the fulfilment of God's plans depends on your own faithfulness.

Every human being can lie and mess up, but God will still be true.

Why is it so hard for us to hold to the truth, Lord?
Sometimes I don't even know what the truth is.
I look to You. Show me the truth. Amen.

UNFAILING LOVE AND FAITHFULNESS

"I am not worthy of all the unfailing love and faithfulness you have shown to me, your servant."
GENESIS 32:10 NLT

As Jacob was returning from Haran to Canaan, he told God, "I am not worthy of all the unfailing love and faithfulness you have shown to me." He reminded God that twenty years earlier, he had left Canaan with only his staff in his hand, but while in Haran, God had blessed him as He had promised and made Jacob fabulously rich.

Despite declaring that he wasn't worthy of God's faithfulness, Jacob was desperate for the Lord to help him now. So he reminded God that He'd told him to return to Canaan—where he now faced imminent danger—and prayed, "You promised me, 'I will surely treat you kindly, and I will multiply your descendants' " (v. 12 NLT). For that promise to be fulfilled, Jacob and his family had to survive. So Jacob asked God to *remain* faithful and keep *this* promise too.

God was faithful to Jacob, and He still shows His unfailing love and faithfulness to you today. Like Jacob, you may feel utterly unworthy, but your desperate need overrides all else, and so you cry out to God for Him to love and be faithful to you as well. Trust Him and He will.

God, when I read the stories of Your faithfulness to Your children, I am so inspired and filled with gratitude for who You are. I love You, Lord! Amen.

Day 7

A TRULY FAITHFUL GOD

"He is the Rock; his deeds are perfect. Everything he does is just and fair. He is a faithful God who does no wrong; how just and upright he is!"
DEUTERONOMY 32:4 NLT

The verse above makes several strong, positive statements about God's nature, but perhaps in a discouraged moment you might feel like disputing them. For example, the phrase: "He is a faithful God who does no wrong." Sometimes when you've desperately prayed for finances—claiming Philippians 4:19 (NIV), "My God will meet all your needs"—and the money doesn't arrive, you may feel like God *hasn't* been faithful.

It takes great faith in times when it appears that God has fallen down on the job to continue to say, "His deeds are perfect. Everything he does is just and fair." But while it looks from your limited viewpoint that God *hasn't* been faithful, remember that He's looking down on things from a much higher vantage point.

With your limited understanding, all you're able to understand are simple equations like 2 + 2 = 4, but when things don't work out that simply, you protest that they "don't add up." But God, by comparison, is working with quantum equations that you can never comprehend, with far more complex factors to consider. . .and He's not finished yet.

Lord, if You even did one tiny thing wrong, You could not be righteous. You wouldn't be our standard of goodness. But You are perfect, Lord. Thank You. Amen.

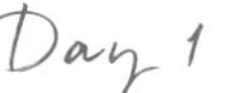

THINK THE TRUTH, SPEAK THE TRUTH

Who may dwell in Your holy hill? He who walks uprightly, and works righteousness, and speaks the truth in his heart.

Psalm 15:1–2 NKJV

Honesty is a habit, and like most habits, it begins in the mind. Thought determines action, which sounds simple enough until you have to do it. Each day brings opportunities for dishonesty—not because you're a malicious fraud but simply because you're human. As a human, you fall under Paul's blanket statement: "All have sinned and fall short of the glory of God" (Romans 3:23 NKJV).

You're prone to putting your own interests above what you know is right. Whether it's fudging your taxes or filtering your social media posts, you want to give the impression that you have it all together. But you know you don't. And God knows that.

He knows everything about you, including those paper clips you "borrowed" and those "accomplishments" on your résumé that aren't actually yours. An upright walk and righteous works begin with speaking truth in your heart. God wants you to walk and talk the holiness He purchased for you. Keep doing what you're doing—spending time in His Word, learning it, and speaking its truth in your heart—and His truth will become a habit in all you think, say, and do.

God, I know if I don't walk with integrity, I'll never be able to lead anyone. Help me to bear that in mind in everything I do. Amen.

Day 2

SELF-PROTECTION THROUGH GROUP INTERVENTION

Pray for us; for we are confident that we have a good conscience, in all things desiring to live honorably.
HEBREWS 13:18 NKJV

Sometimes, accountability gets a bad rap, reduced to the level of a trend or eye-rolling Christianese, when really, it's a crucial tool in an honest life. When you spend too much time trapped in your own head, it becomes frighteningly easy to stumble. Either your own concerns overwhelm you to the detriment of losing perspective or the weeds of sin grow unfettered by concerned eyes and hearts.

God will honor your desire to serve Him with honesty and integrity, but one of the reasons you are to stay in fellowship with other believers (Hebrews 10:25) is to be encouraged to honor God with an honest assessment of your conscience and behavior.

Without someone to pray for you—an individual or small group—you're susceptible to your heart's own brand of honesty, which, frankly, is subject to decay. "The human heart is the most deceitful of all things, and desperately wicked. Who really knows how bad it is?" (Jeremiah 17:9 NLT).

When you bring someone into your life, letting them know your desires and troubles and habits, you're safeguarding your honesty in an effort to live honorably.

God, bring me people who will speak truth to me.
People who love me enough to want me to be my best.
Thank You for friends who love like You. Amen.

Day 3

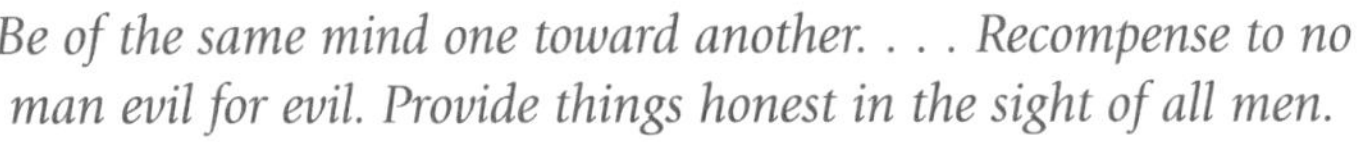

LACK OF COMMUNICATION

Be of the same mind one toward another. . . . Recompense to no man evil for evil. Provide things honest in the sight of all men.

ROMANS 12:16–17 KJV

One of the most challenging things for a Christian is being open and honest with other Christians. People in the church are quick on the draw when it comes to any sense of unbiblical behavior among the brethren. On the one hand, the Bible tells disciples to be vigilant when it comes to false teaching and false teachers and to hold one another accountable to the truth.

At the same time, Christians put on a good front on Sundays, if only because they don't want to get kicked out of the club. The downside of that is they lack honesty in simple things, like the struggles they're facing in their marriages, with their kids, at work, or with old ghosts from their pre-Christian days that have resurfaced.

God's children need less fear of excommunication and more fear of the separation that comes from lack of communication. The battle between the Spirit and the flesh is hard. When they encourage and strengthen a fellow believer, they respect the entire body of Christ, caring for that particular representation of it that God has placed in their path.

God, help me to be a voice of unity and kindness in my family of believers. I don't want to be judgmental or self-righteous. I want people to know You. Amen.

Day 4

ATTAINING INTEGRITY

For we are taking pains to do what is right, not only in the eyes of the Lord but also in the eyes of man.
2 CORINTHIANS 8:21 NIV

Ben Franklin said, "Honesty is the best policy," but Paul would tell you it's not necessarily the easiest. However, he did suggest it's the most worthwhile, because honest habits and words carry weight with both God and men. Above all else, he strove to be God's man in every situation, whether he was teaching in the synagogue or making tents.

It didn't matter to Paul whether he was speaking with dignitaries or ditch-diggers, the message was on-point: "I resolved to know nothing while I was with you except Jesus Christ and him crucified" (1 Corinthians 2:2 NIV). You may think, *Okay, that's Paul; he was pretty radical*—and you'd be right. But what made him that way was his unwavering commitment to know Christ and to represent Him in all that he did.

Paul probably didn't miss many chances to share the Gospel, but he earned a ready audience because he was also a good tentmaker and a good neighbor, and a leader who challenged and supported his fellow believers. Those things aren't uncomplicated, but they are necessary in living a day-in-day-out commitment to Jesus.

Lord, I want to be a good example. I want to be a good ambassador for You. Clean out anything in my life that keeps me from doing that. Amen.

HONEST IN EVERY WAY

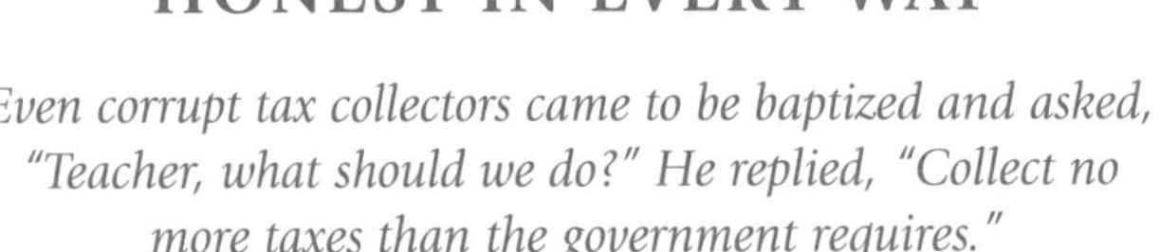

Even corrupt tax collectors came to be baptized and asked, "Teacher, what should we do?" He replied, "Collect no more taxes than the government requires."

LUKE 3:12–13 NLT

John the Baptist shot straight with the crowds who came to be baptized: "Prove by the way you live that you have repented of your sins and turned to God" (Luke 3:8 NLT). John's no-nonsense, no-holds-barred message presaged the deep honesty of Christ's coming—the undeniable truth of what God was willing to do in order to make you a way home to Him.

Our response to that great salvation is to live honorable lives with the added bonus of doing kingdom work: sharing with others about Jesus, His great love and work, and how He has changed you.

It's a message that resonates in the most unexpected ways with the unlikeliest of people—much as John's call to repentance struck a chord with tax collectors. Jews in Rome's employ, they were hated for their corrupt ways, increasing burdens to fatten their own wallets. But John called them to do their work honestly as a reflection of God's call to be holy—set apart, different—from the world around them. More than anything, honesty sets you apart and gives you the chance to tell others why it matters.

God, does my life show that I've repented? Does it show that I belong to You? If it doesn't, tell me, Lord. I want to do better. Amen.

Day 6

CLEAN HEART, CLEAN HANDS

He that hath clean hands, and a pure heart; who hath not lifted up his soul unto vanity, nor sworn deceitfully.

PSALM 24:4 KJV

When Jesus taught, He went straight to the heart of a matter. Looking lustfully at someone is the same as committing adultery with them, and wishing evil on someone is the same as killing them. While legally there's a big difference between a thought and an act, with God, there's none.

That shouldn't surprise you; after all, as far back as David, God made it clear that, while people look at appearances, He looks at the heart (1 Samuel 16:7). What is in the heart influences behavior. Regarding bad deeds, Jesus said, "But those things which proceed out of the mouth come from the heart, and they defile a man" (Matthew 15:18 NKJV).

Literal dirt on your hands isn't a source of spiritual uncleanness, but the dirt in you hearts is fertile ground for the worst things imaginable. Fortunately, the heart can also be a fount of good behavior. With Christ as the source, supported by prayer and time in the Word, living water can fill your heart, flowing through you, cleansing the bad habits, and replacing them with godly wisdom, perspectives, and action.

Lord, I want to be able to open up my life to You, and not be ashamed. Help me to clean my thoughts, control my feelings, and correct my actions. Amen.

KEEP YOUR EYE ON THE BALL

"My righteousness I hold fast, and will not let it go;
my heart shall not reproach me as long as I live."
JOB 27:6 NKJV

If, in a moment of decision, you have to decide whether to be honest, you've already got two strikes against you: one, that you know the truth and are still considering a lie, and two, that you fear men more than God. One of the reasons God singled out Job as a man of integrity (Job 2:3) is that when he stepped up to the plate, he already knew what pitches he was going to swing at. He understood that God was the source of his blessings and character, not himself.

Anything that looked like temptation, Job was ready to back off and let it pass without a second look—affairs, self-righteousness, hardships. He wasn't disconnected from life, just prepared. His honesty came from a place of preparation and obedient practice of what God said was right.

He "maintained his righteousness" the way a ballplayer works the batting cage: learning from opponents' tendencies, perfecting technique, and trusting in preparation come game time. Job's statement wasn't a brag but a declaration: he followed God in every way he could think of, and God gave him peace and comfort in the trials of life.

Lord, let me make a practice of righteousness. In the same way I stretch my body every day, let me stretch my heart and mind to be like You. Amen.

MOTIVATING LOVE

Let us think of ways to motivate one another to acts of love and good works. And let us not neglect our meeting together, as some people do, but encourage one another, especially now that the day of his return is drawing near.

HEBREWS 10:24–25 NLT

You can encourage others who are in a season of need; that's an obvious way to show love. Sometimes overlooked is the fact that you can encourage others, especially those who are in a season of plenty, to join you in acts of love and good works.

Christians should constantly be thinking of ways to motivate themselves and fellow believers to help others. One of the best ways to do so is to be a dedicated member of a solid Christian fellowship. If your church is truly Bible-believing, it cannot help but be actively meeting needs of people in its community and encouraging its members to work hand-in-hand in loving service.

The author of Hebrews urges believers to not give up meeting together. Gathering for church each week is immensely important and not to be neglected or done just when the mood strikes you or there's nothing better to do. Hearing the Word preached, worshipping, and serving others together are excellent ways to show encouragement and love.

God, people gain so much through serving one another. Let me lead always with a servant's heart. Amen.

Day 2

LAVISH LOVE

"Can a mother forget the baby at her breast
and have no compassion on the child she has borne?
Though she may forget, I will not forget you!"
ISAIAH 49:15 NIV

Early one morning over breakfast, a four-year-old girl said sincerely to her mom, "I don't like it when my sister gets in trouble. I love her." The mother smiled and asked, "Then why do you tattle on her sometimes, trying to get her in trouble?" The little girl replied tearfully, "Sometimes I forget my love."

You will forget your love for others at times too. Everyone does. Thankfully your heavenly Father never forgets His love for you! And because His love for you—and mindfulness of you—never fails, He reminds you of His love constantly, calls you to it, and urges you to share it with others.

First John 3:1 (NIV) says, "See what great love the Father has lavished on us, that we should be called children of God! And that is what we are!" Though Christians still might act like selfish children at times, first and foremost they are children of a heavenly Father who lavishes His love on His people. That cannot help but fill up your life and overflow to the people He has placed around you.

God, no one here on earth is perfect. Even the best mothers
and fathers get it wrong sometimes. But You,
Lord—Your love is perfect. Amen.

Day 3

FREE TO LOVE

Be careful so that your freedom does not cause others with a weaker conscience to stumble. For if others see you—with your "superior knowledge"—eating in the temple of an idol, won't they be encouraged to violate their conscience by eating food that has been offered to an idol? So because of your superior knowledge, a weak believer for whom Christ died will be destroyed. And when you sin against other believers by encouraging them to do something they believe is wrong, you are sinning against Christ. So if what I eat causes another believer to sin, I will never eat meat again as long as I live—for I don't want to cause another believer to stumble.

1 Corinthians 8:9–13 NLT

Tripping someone to make them fall definitely isn't a loving thing to do. At best, it's a thoughtless prank; at worst, it can cause injury. One important way Christians can love others is by not causing them to stumble spiritually, as that can cause harm to their soul and even destruction. You are called to freedom and you are covered in God's grace, yet as Galatians 5:13 (NLT) says, "For you have been called to live in freedom, my brothers and sisters. But don't use your freedom to satisfy your sinful nature. Instead, use your freedom to serve one another in love."

Lord, I know that sometimes I let my pride and my idea of my rights and freedoms get in the way of others who are seeking You. Forgive me. Amen.

Day 4

LOVING ENEMIES

"You have heard that it was said, 'You shall love your neighbor and hate your enemy.' But I say to you, love your enemies, bless those who curse you, do good to those who hate you, and pray for those who spitefully use you and persecute you, that you may be sons of your Father in heaven; for He makes His sun rise on the evil and on the good, and sends rain on the just and on the unjust."

MATTHEW 5:43–45 NKJV

Does anyone actually *like* this passage of scripture? The Bible surely isn't a feel-good self-help book but is "sharper than any two-edged sword, piercing even to the division of soul and spirit, and of joints and marrow, and is a discerner of the thoughts and intents of the heart" (Hebrews 4:12 NKJV).

God's holy Word will convict and make you uncomfortable. It's hard to think of anything more uncomfortable than showing love to, blessing, doing good to, and praying for those who curse and hate you. Yet that's exactly what Jesus Himself instructs in this passage.

You might wonder how on earth to even *start* showing love to your enemies. Begin by asking for God's help and by sincerely praying for them. Then read Proverbs 25:21–22 and do likewise.

God, help me to love my enemies. Help me to love those who would seek to hurt me. This is hard to do, Lord. Help me. Amen.

Day 5

LOVE LETS GO

Thou shalt not avenge, nor bear any grudge against the children of thy people, but thou shalt love thy neighbour as thyself: I am the LORD.

LEVITICUS 19:18 KJV

Have you ever been guilty of offending someone, sincerely apologized, but then had that mistake held against you despite your repentance? It's disheartening to say the least. Thankfully, your heavenly Father never acts that way toward you. First John 1:9 (NKJV) promises, "If we confess our sins, He is faithful and just to forgive us our sins and to cleanse us from all unrighteousness."

Now, have *you* ever been the one to hold a grudge against someone? If your holy God forgives you so fully, how can you hold anything against someone who comes to you in repentance? No, you are to love like 1 Corinthians 13:4–5 (NIV) describes: "Love is patient, love is kind. It does not envy, it does not boast, it is not proud. It does not dishonor others, it is not self-seeking, it is not easily angered, it keeps no record of wrongs."

Did you catch that last part? It keeps *no record* of wrongs.

Let the God who sees all and knows all and loves all be the one to judge each person according to their actions. *You* are called to forgive and love and leave justice in God's hands.

God, I confess that I do keep a record of wrongs, even though I know it does nothing good for my heart! Help me to stop it! Amen.

Day 6

FERVENT LOVE

Since you have in obedience to the truth purified your souls for a sincere love of the brethren, fervently love one another from the heart.

1 Peter 1:22 NASB

To "fervently love" means to do so intensely, zealously, with very strong feelings. That's how Peter states Christians should love one another. In a later chapter he says, "Finally, all of you be of one mind, having compassion for one another; love as brothers, be tenderhearted, be courteous" (1 Peter 3:8 NKJV). And in 1 Peter 4:8 (NIV, emphasis added), he concludes, "Above all, love each other *deeply* because love covers over a multitude of sins."

Peter isn't describing a surface-level kind of love for one another; he's talking about profound, rich, and abiding love among believers. How do you experience this? Pray for more love! Be a student of the believers God has placed around you and ask Him to help you know how best to love them. Listen earnestly to others when they need someone to talk to. Truly care about others, "rejoice with those who rejoice; mourn with those who mourn" (Romans 12:15 NIV). And "bear one another's burdens, and so fulfill the law of Christ" (Galatians 6:2 NKJV).

God, sometimes the gathering of believers feels more like a business than a family. Help me to do my part to love others faithfully and fervently. Amen.

Day 7

LET LOVE GROW

And this I pray, that your love may abound still more and more in knowledge and all discernment.

PHILIPPIANS 1:9 NKJV

The longer you walk with God and mature in your relationship with Him through Christ and the work of the Holy Spirit, the greater and better your love will grow. Your obedience to the Great Commandment will increase.

When asked what was the greatest commandment in the Law, Jesus replied, " 'Love the Lord your God with all your heart and with all your soul and with all your mind.' This is the first and greatest commandment. And the second is like it: 'Love your neighbor as yourself.' All the Law and the Prophets hang on these two commandments" (Matthew 22:37–40 NIV).

You will have more knowledge of love and more wisdom to determine God's will for you in sharing His love.

So let love grow. Don't let anything hinder your walk with God. When temptation comes your way, reject it and draw closer to your Savior. Fill your mind up with scripture and then, "Do not merely listen to the word, and so deceive yourselves. Do what it says" (James 1:22 NIV).

God, every sin in me takes up space that could be loving You. I don't want that. I want Your wisdom and love and truth to fill me up. Amen.

Day 1

A MIGHTY PROTECTOR

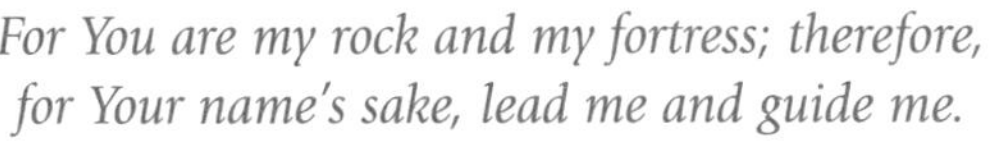

*For You are my rock and my fortress; therefore,
for Your name's sake, lead me and guide me.*

PSALM 31:3 NKJV

When you need protection from life's storms, you can *always* find safety in the One who is the Rock and Fortress. Throughout the scriptures you'll find several references to God as "my rock," "my fortress," "my deliverer," "my shield," "my stronghold," and "my salvation." God is a mighty protector. For starters, check out these verses:

Psalm 18:2 (NLT)—"The LORD is my rock, my fortress, and my savior; my God is my rock, in whom I find protection. He is my shield, the power that saves me, and my place of safety."

Psalm 62:2 (NLT)—"He alone is my rock and my salvation, my fortress where I will never be shaken."

Psalm 94:22 (NLT)—"But the LORD is my fortress; my God is the mighty rock where I hide."

Second Samuel 22:2 (NKJV)—"The LORD is my rock and my fortress and my deliverer."

Reach out to God. Seek refuge in the One who waits, ready to rescue you. No matter how strong, how confident, how secure in faith you are, you can never do any better than to give yourself over to God, who will help you to safely navigate through life's storms—today and for all time.

*God, my Rock! I know I can lean on You, stand on You,
trust You, count on You. You will never change! Amen.*

Day 2

WHEN TROUBLES COME

God is our refuge and strength,
an ever-present help in trouble.
PSALM 46:1 NIV

You don't need to invite trouble into your life. If you've lived any number of years, you understand and know with 100 percent certainty that hard times will come whether you want them to or not. John 16:33 (NIV) states, "In this world you will have trouble." Not *might* have trouble. . .but *will*.

No matter how hard you push or pull, your will is no match against unsettling life events. You can't close your eyes and make them disappear. And, quite unfortunately, there's no avoiding them.

Sickness. Job loss. Infertility. Divorce. Death of a loved one. Just to name a few hard things. You've likely experienced at least one—maybe even all—of these difficult life circumstances. So where do you choose to run when troubles come and you're deep in the mire of despair?

Jesus says, "Take heart! I have overcome the world" (John 16:33 NIV). With a power like that on your side, you need to fear nothing in this world. Your Savior is powerful. He is sovereign. There isn't one hardship—no matter how insurmountable it may seem—that He can't help you to overcome. You can rest secure in your heavenly Father, who's *always* present (Psalm 139:7–10).

God, I feel so weak and helpless. When bad things
happen, it's like all the air gets sucked out of me.
Protect me, Lord. Strengthen me. Amen.

....

....

....

....

....

....

....

Day 3

YOUR BURDEN-BEARER

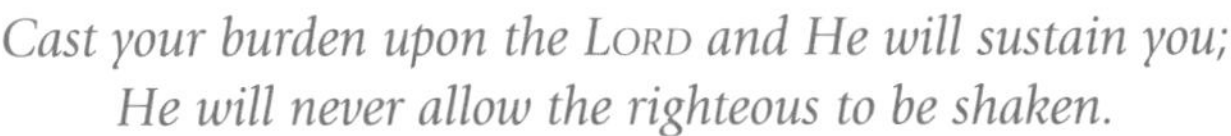

Cast your burden upon the Lord and He will sustain you;
He will never allow the righteous to be shaken.
Psalm 55:22 NASB

Worry is an overwhelming, often suffocating, cumbersome companion. If you allow worry to seep into your soul, it's difficult to break free from its strong grasp.

What burdens you most? The unknown? A persistent barrage of "what ifs" that plagues your thoughts? Whatever it is, there's hope. You don't need to carry it alone. In fact, Jesus promises to give you rest from the afflictions that weigh you down: "Come to me, all you who are weary and burdened, and I will give you rest" (Matthew 11:28 NIV). You can flee to Him when your thoughts become too much to handle, when life becomes oppressive. . .because He cares for you: "Cast all your anxiety on him because he cares for you" (1 Peter 5:7 NIV).

Whatever burden you're carrying today, give it to the ultimate Burden-Bearer. He will carry the load for you. If you feel weighted down with worries and cares, scripture has a beautiful promise. Read this verse aloud and commit it to memory: "And my God will meet all your needs according to the riches of his glory in Christ Jesus" (Philippians 4:19 NIV). You won't be disappointed!

Lord Jesus, my burdens are so heavy. But You've told me
You will carry them. Help me to hand them over to You. Amen.

CONFIDENT GUARANTEE

In the fear of the LORD there is strong confidence,
and his children will have refuge.
PROVERBS 14:26 NASB

Has insecurity ever threatened to rip away your very last shred of confidence? Doubt is a crippling enemy that can leave you feeling uncertain, weak, and fearful.

If you've ever, for even a moment, doubted your heavenly Father's promises, spend time bolstering your faith—right now. Begin fortifying your heart with the hopeful promise of Proverbs 14:26. If you trust and obey the Lord, He'll provide all the confidence you'll ever need. You will always find a safe haven with Him. "God is our refuge and strength, a very present help in trouble" (Psalm 46:1 KJV).

The benefits to those who fear the Lord are many: "Blessed be the Lord, who daily loadeth us with benefits, even the God of our salvation" (Psalm 68:19 KJV). He offers peace, guidance, grace, love, salvation, and so much more! Just one of the benefits He provides to His children is this confident guarantee: the heavenly Protector will equip your spirit with courage while providing a peaceful refuge.

Today set your soul free to soar with the assurance of God's promises. . .even if you're feeling insecure. For when you're weak, there you will find strength (2 Corinthians 12:10). Praise the Lord for His faithfulness!

God, whenever I doubt that You are with me, I read Your Word.
I see You standing by Your people. And I know You
are standing by me too. Amen.

Day 5

HEAVENLY ARSENAL

Above all, taking the shield of faith, wherewith ye shall be able to quench all the fiery darts of the wicked.
EPHESIANS 6:16 KJV

When evil threatens your soul, God wants you to know that you have a heavenly arsenal at your disposal: "Put on the full armor of God, so that you can take your stand against the devil's schemes" (Ephesians 6:11 NIV). According to Ephesians 6, you can stand firm against evil and arm yourself with protection like:

The belt of truth (v. 14)
The breastplate of righteousness (v. 14)
Feet fitted with the readiness that comes from the Gospel of peace (v. 15)
The shield of faith (v. 16)
The helmet of salvation (v. 17)
The sword of the Spirit (v. 17)
Prayer—on all occasions (v. 18)

Ask God to give you the courage and the weapons you need to win against the enemy. When you arm yourself with His spiritual protection, you'll be living according to His best plan for you, and your faith will be resolute.

There's no need to cower in fear and weakness when the devil comes knocking. Stand tall. Stand confident. Stand strong. "Be strong in the Lord and in his mighty power" (Ephesians 6:10 NIV). The protection of almighty God is there for you; He has your back.

God, You have designed our hearts and minds in the perfect way to trust You and to be able to stand against Satan. Thank You! Amen.

Day 6

EVERY STEP OF THE WAY

"When you pass through the waters, I will be with you; and when you pass through the rivers, they will not sweep over you. When you walk through the fire, you will not be burned; the flames will not set you ablaze."

Isaiah 43:2 NIV

Can you imagine stepping into a raging river and not getting swept away by its current? Or walking through a blazing inferno and suffering not even one minor burn? Impossible, right? However, that's exactly the kind of protection your heavenly Father offers His children.

Think back to the story of Shadrach, Meshach, and Abednego in Daniel 3. King Nebuchadnezzar had the trio thrown into the fiery furnace when they refused to bow down to his image. When he looked into the blazing furnace, the king saw a fourth man walking around with Shadrach, Meshach, and Abednego—and all appeared alive and well! "Look!" Nebuchadnezzar shouted. "I see four men, unbound, walking around in the fire unharmed! And the fourth looks like a god!" (Daniel 3:25 NLT).

Remember, God is with you through every challenge you'll ever face. He always has your best in mind. And although He doesn't promise you won't have to deal with hard things, He does promise to be with you *every single step* of the way.

Lord, I'm pretty sure I don't have the kind of courage that could walk through fire. But I want to stand strong for You. Grow my faith, Lord. Amen.

Day 7

A FIRM FOUNDATION

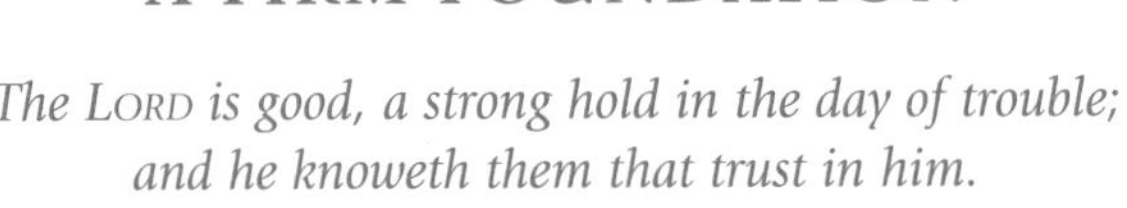

The Lord is good, a strong hold in the day of trouble;
and he knoweth them that trust in him.

Nahum 1:7 kjv

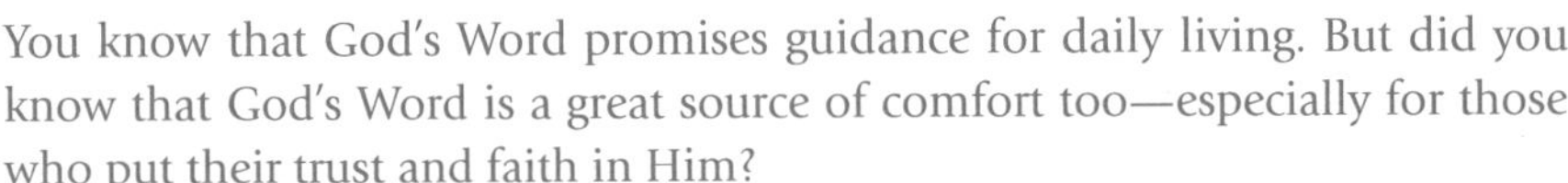

You know that God's Word promises guidance for daily living. But did you know that God's Word is a great source of comfort too—especially for those who put their trust and faith in Him?

No doubt about it, it's human nature to attempt to escape life's troubles. Whether your escape hatch leads to outright denial or drowning your worries and cares in some kind of addiction (alcohol, drugs, overwork) or other unhealthy habits, when you choose to take matters into your own hands rather than handing them over to Jesus, the outcome is always the same. *You really can't fix anything on your own.* However, you do tend to create more of a jumbled mess out of your life.

When troubles come—and they will—seek the comfort your soul craves in the above verse from the book of Nahum. Meditate on the promise of God's goodness and protection. Rest your troubled soul in the peace that can only come from your heavenly Father. He *alone* is the firm foundation you need.

Instead of running away from your troubles, run into the open arms of Jesus. There you will find safety and protection.

You hold tight to me, Lord, when I am weak and wavering.
Thank You for reminding me that I can do what
You have designed me to do. Amen.

Day 1

SEEKING WISE COUNSEL

A wise man will hear and increase in learning, and a man of understanding will acquire wise counsel.
PROVERBS 1:5 NASB

If you're an understanding person, you value other people's opinions. As a result, you make a concerted effort to seek out their counsel, and generally *get* the information you're looking for. And when you get it, you listen to it carefully. That's precisely why the Bible says that a wise man "will acquire wise counsel" and "will hear and increase in learning."

It's all so easy and the benefits so enormous, you wonder why anybody would *not* seek out good counsel. The problem sometimes is pride: you're ashamed to admit that you don't know something, and rather than humble yourself and learn, you try to muddle through on your own.

Or you may be too impatient. You want to get going immediately and don't want to take the time to sift through people's varying opinions and decide on the best course of action.

Often, you avoid seeking advice because you already know others will caution you that your plan won't work—and you don't want to hear any opposing views. But that isn't wise. Take the time to seek out godly, informed counsel and you'll make decisions that are safer and more likely to succeed.

Lord, open my ears. May I never ever turn away a word of wise counsel. Amen.

....

....

....

....

....

....

....

....

Day 2

THE ULTIMATE COUNSELOR

For a child will be born to us, a son will be given to us;
and the government will rest on His shoulders;
and His name will be called Wonderful Counselor,
Mighty God, Eternal Father, Prince of Peace.
ISAIAH 9:6 NASB

We so often think of Jesus as the helpless baby born in a stable in Bethlehem, or as the flesh-and-blood man who went to the cross at Golgotha to die for your sins. But Jesus' many exalted titles—"Mighty God, Eternal Father, Prince of Peace"—reveal that although He was a mortal man, He is also the divine, eternal Son of God. As the Nicene Creed states, He is "very God of very God. . .being of one substance with the Father."

Among Jesus' magnificent titles is this one: "Wonderful Counselor." Kings and rulers in ancient times habitually sought the advice of the very wisest counselors when making important decisions. Jesus is the best possible counselor. Because He is one with God the Father, "His understanding is infinite" (Psalm 147:5 NKJV). He is "perfect in knowledge" (Job 37:16 NKJV).

When you need divine wisdom and supernatural insight, look to "Christ, in whom are hidden all the treasures of wisdom and knowledge" (Colossians 2:2–3 NKJV). He has the answers you so desperately need for every situation.

Lord, I think it's amazing that the God who created the
universe and conquered death is willing to give me advice.
Crazy but amazing! Thank You, Lord! Amen.

A DIVINE COUNSELOR

When he, the Spirit of truth, is come, he will guide you into all truth: for he shall not speak of himself; but whatsoever he shall hear, that shall he speak: and he will shew you things to come.

JOHN 16:13 KJV

The Holy Spirit, the Spirit of Truth, is also called "the Spirit of Christ" (Romans 8:9 KJV), so since Jesus Christ is the Wonderful Counselor, the Spirit is also. In fact, it's through His Spirit living in your heart that God speaks to you. How does He counsel you? He "[guides] you into *all* truth." Whatever you need to know about, literally *everything,* the Spirit can reveal truth to you about it.

Sometimes He will whisper the precise answer into your heart in a supernatural revelation, speaking to you in "a still small voice" (1 Kings 19:12 KJV) that only you can hear. Other times He will guide you through a set of seemingly natural circumstances that gradually lead you to the right conclusion.

The Bible describes the Spirit in John 14:16 (KJV) as the "Comforter," but while the Greek word certainly means "Comforter," it also means "Advocate, Encourager, or Counselor." Allow the Spirit of Christ to counsel you. He longs to speak to you, to show you the truth. Listen to His voice today.

God, I know full well that I could never find truth without You. Remind me to come to You first when I am trying to gain understanding. Amen.

LISTENING TO COUNSEL

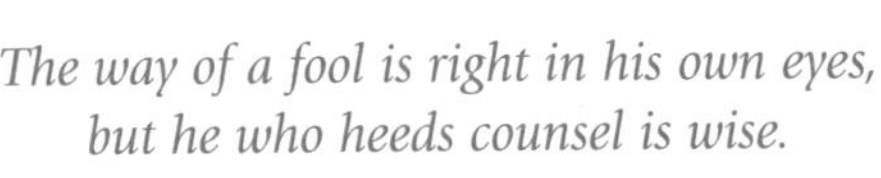

The way of a fool is right in his own eyes,
but he who heeds counsel is wise.
PROVERBS 12:15 NKJV

Everyone gets into headstrong moods at times and becomes so convinced that they're right that they refuse to listen to counsel from others. It's understandable if this happens once or twice, but when it's a recurring attitude this is very foolish. It's what the Bible is talking about when it says, "The way of a fool is right in his own eyes."

If you want to be wise and spare yourself a great deal of trouble, heed the counsel that mature Christians give you. They truly care for you and have your best interests at heart. "Get all the advice and instruction you can, so you will be wise the rest of your life" (Proverbs 19:20 NLT).

God will often give you wise advice through ordinary people, but if you're fired up about an idea, you may ignore them and ride roughshod over them—and this is especially true if you have a dominant or persuasive personality and are used to getting your way.

Remember, as a disciple of Jesus, you are to love the Lord, yield your plans to Him, and be willing to change them if He counsels a better course of action.

Lord, how many times have I relied on my own wisdom—
and then fallen flat on my face! Help me, Lord.
I don't want to be a fool. Amen.

Day 5

INSTRUCTION AND LEARNING

Give instruction to a wise man and he will be still wiser,
teach a righteous man and he will increase his learning.
PROVERBS 9:9 NASB

It's frustrating to give advice to someone who gets irritated when you try to point things out, who constantly cuts you off with, "Yeah, yeah, I already know. You don't need to tell me." Then you watch them continue blithely on their way, run into the very problem you tried to warn them about, and suffer the consequences.

And even more frustrating is when they refuse to learn their lesson from that. They *continue* to refuse to listen, and run into similar trouble *again*.

It's much more rewarding to give instructions to a wise-hearted individual who isn't too stubborn or proud or impatient to listen. It pays big dividends to be humble enough to admit that you don't know everything, and to listen. If you give instruction to such a man, he will become wiser. If you teach a righteous man—a man who isn't proud and full of himself—he will increase his learning.

Does this describe you? You may not think of yourself as wise in the sense of being highly educated and knowledgeable, but true wisdom is often simply having a humble spirit and being patient enough to listen to others.

Lord, get rid of any pride in me that keeps me
from learning more. I have so, so much to learn. Amen.

Day 6

HEARTFELT COUNSEL

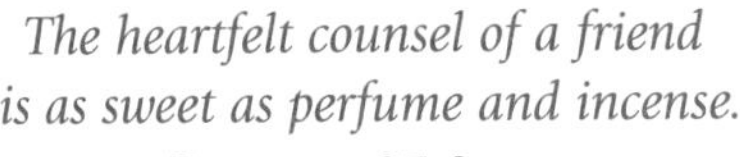

The heartfelt counsel of a friend
is as sweet as perfume and incense.
PROVERBS 27:9 NLT

Wisdom is more than simply being able to quote applicable information, refer to pertinent facts and figures, or pass on valuable life lessons. While all these are essential elements of imparting wisdom, there's another facet to it: you must *love* the person you're reaching out to. In the best scenario, it's genuine love—not a critical attitude or a know-it-all spirit—that motivates you to communicate advice to others.

Having a genuine concern for people's welfare is what motivates you to make yourself vulnerable and share from your heart. Love inspires you to humble yourself and disclose your own past mistakes for the benefit of others. It's what makes sharing heartfelt counsel so sweet.

When others sense that you truly care for them, they're far more apt to take what you say and put it into practice. And long after that incident has passed, they'll remember the loving way you shared and the compassion in your face and voice.

That's why the Bible says, "The heartfelt counsel of a *friend* is as sweet as perfume and incense." A true friend gives you advice and counsel because they genuinely care for you. And love is what motivates you to do the same for others.

Jesus my Friend, sometimes my desire to guide someone
to right living jumps ahead of my caring for them.
Help me to always lead with love. Amen.

COUNSELING WITH MANY PEOPLE

Where no counsel is, the people fall: but in the multitude of counsellors there is safety.
PROVERBS 11:14 KJV

When you insist on doing detective work and trying to figure out problems all by yourself, you frequently arrive at a skewed conclusion. That's because, being human, you often start with a mistaken presumption, and so screen out certain facts. But it can be very insightful to ask others their opinion. They might just be in possession of key pieces of information, details that will make all the difference in what you plan to do or say.

An autocrat is convinced that he knows everything and thinks he needn't run his decisions past any other person, and while some people *are* naturally good at decision-making, this management style often leads to collapses—and rather spectacular ones at that: "Where no counsel is, the people fall."

You've heard the expression, "Get a second opinion." But in the Bible, that's the bare minimum. God's Word advises you to get as many opinions as possible, stating that "in the *multitude* of counsellors there is safety." Do you *really* want to play it safe? Talk with as many counselors as you can. It pays to carefully research and base important decisions on a broad range of life experiences and perspectives.

Lord, help me to slow down and not make any decisions in haste. I need to hear what You have to say through wise counselors and through Your Word. Amen.

Day 1

YOU KNOW HIM

The world cannot accept [the Spirit of truth],
because it neither sees him nor knows him.
But you know him, for he lives with you
and will be in you.
JOHN 14:17 NIV

The unconverted look for truth in science, experience, and sometimes even gut feelings. The problem with all of these is that they're not necessarily objective or comprehensive. You've listened to a friend, coworker, or even a foe dance around the topic when you brought it up. Maybe that person even studied religion in college, but they never actually met the Truth, so it remained elusive.

Bible commentator Albert Barnes said it this way in *Notes on the Bible*: "The men of the world are under the influence of the senses. They walk by sight, and not by faith. Hence, what they cannot perceive by their senses, what does not gratify their sight, or taste, or feeling, makes no impression on them."

Christians, on the other hand, acknowledge their senses, but are not governed by them. For you know that Truth is found in the person of the Holy Spirit, who lives in you. He is the promised Comforter who offers guidance and direction as you submit yourself to the reading and preaching of the Word.

God, if I had to rely on my senses to lead me through life,
I'd never get anywhere. What's important is often invisible.
Help me to see You everywhere I go. Amen.

GOD, THE ROCK

"The Rock! His work is perfect, for all His ways are just; a God of faithfulness and without injustice, righteous and upright is He."
DEUTERONOMY 32:4 NASB

Rodney King. O. J. Simpson. Ferguson. Charlotte.

Regardless of where you stand on those issues, nothing incites anger and unrest more than injustice, or sometimes even just a perceived injustice, due to skin color, social status, gender, or belief system.

You grew up with the expectation, or at least the hope, of being treated fairly. You wanted the same size piece of pie as your sister. You anticipated receiving a fair wage for your first job as well as after your most recent promotion. And you have every expectation of being treated fairly under the law. But injustice often wins the day in this world. Thanks be to God, that won't always be the case.

God is a rock. In John Wesley's commentary, he referred to God as being stable, invincible, and immutable "in his counsels and promises and ways." So take heart. God is faithful and just, righteous and upright in all His ways. He will administer ultimate justice in due time. In fact, He's in the process even now through the redeeming power of Christ.

Work for truth and justice in the here and now, but count on *God's* righteousness and justice.

My Judge, I am often disheartened by injustice and corruption in this world. Help me to support leaders who care about truth and goodness. Amen.

Day 3

LOVELY THOUGHTS

Finally, brothers and sisters, whatever is true, whatever is noble, whatever is right, whatever is pure, whatever is lovely, whatever is admirable—if anything is excellent or praiseworthy—think about such things.

PHILIPPIANS 4:8 NIV

Whatever you think about, you eventually act on. If you're thinking about the promises of God and about whatever is pure and lovely, then you'll feel peace, security, and hope. You'll want to be the hands and feet of Christ to those who are hurting and lonely.

If you're thinking about the falsehoods that Satan whispers into your ear and about whatever is impure and unlovely, then you'll feel anxious, insecure, and hopeless. You'll want to withdraw from everybody, where you'll remain ineffective for the kingdom of God.

You won't always be able to control your thoughts. Satan is on the prowl, seeking those whom he can kill and destroy, so he won't give up while you still have breath in your lungs. But you can reject him and his ways in favor of truth and love.

Do a quick inventory of your actions this past week. Which category do they most closely align with? Did you actively seek to minister to others or were you withdrawn? How can you change your thought pattern this week by focusing on truth?

God, I want my thoughts to lead me closer to You,
not further away. Help me to take charge of them. Amen.

SPEAK THE TRUTH

"These are the things you are to do: Speak the truth to each other, and render true and sound judgment in your courts."
ZECHARIAH 8:16 NIV

After a period of judgment, God wanted His remnant to know that they shouldn't fear because He had "determined to do good again to Jerusalem and Judah" (Zechariah 8:15 NIV). Following His promise, He told them how they were to treat one another: speaking truth to one another and rendering true and sound judgments in court.

You might bristle at the idea of fellow Christians speaking truth to you because you had a bad experience with believers who were harsh or jumped to conclusions about your actions in the past. But just as God tells His people to issue sound judgment in court, He wants the same for His people when they are in fellowship. Believers are to stir up one another in truth.

Are you engaging in deep conversations with fellow believers weekly? Are you speaking truth to others? Are you growing as a result? While it's not always easy to find a safe place to have such conversations, never stop looking.

Invite somebody from church to dinner this week. Be honest about your faith walk. And be willing to give and receive truth.

God, sometimes the truth really does hurt. But help me to grow from whatever stings I take in hearing where I've gone wrong. Amen.

Day 5

TRUTH PERSONIFIED

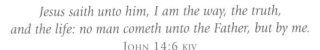

Jesus saith unto him, I am the way, the truth,
and the life: no man cometh unto the Father, but by me.

JOHN 14:6 KJV

After Jesus promised His disciples that He was going to prepare a place for them in heaven and then return for them, Thomas queried, "Lord, we know not whither thou goest; and how can we know the way?" (John 14:5 KJV). Jesus explained that He was the way, the truth, and the life; He was and is *the* way to the Father.

Two thousand years later, in an age in which the very notion of truth is questioned, Jesus is still truth personified. His ways, His words, and His thoughts are truth. He revealed characteristics of the Father for you so you would know how to live. He loved His enemies. He cared for the poor. He healed the sick. He taught the spiritually ignorant. And He spent time alone with the Father.

Does your life look like this? Or do you spend more time arguing about the truth? If you really want to see truth advance, then love your enemies, help the poor, nurse the sick back to health, disciple new converts, and spend ample time in prayer with the Father each day. For these are the acts of truth.

Lord, I'm so glad You are the way! I'm so glad You chose
to show us! What a loving God You are! Amen.

Day 6

BUY THE TRUTH

Buy the truth, and do not sell it,
also wisdom and instruction and understanding.
PROVERBS 23:23 NKJV

Your grandparents or great-grandparents probably never dreamed of buying a car on credit. Instead, they scrimped and saved until they had enough to pay cash for it. Then they carefully selected the vehicle that would best serve their needs for the long haul, since they wouldn't be buying one again anytime soon. Once they brought the vehicle home, they valued it—maintaining it to the best of their ability.

This is the word-picture that the writer of today's verse paints for readers regarding truth. When you work hard to save for a significant purchase, you value the product once you get it home. You would never consider abandoning it.

Are you putting in the effort to "buy the truth" from God's Word? Are you scrimping and saving truth as you find it? Are you investing time and energy to dig into commentaries? Are you listening to sermons? Are you taking notes about your truth findings? Or are you simply taking free samples?

Christianity isn't a religion for the reluctant. While your salvation is established and secure through Christ's efforts, your sanctification only comes as you learn and submit to the truth, at the leading of the Holy Spirit.

Lord, I see how important it is to keep growing in understanding.
The more I read and study Your Word, the more I see You. Amen.

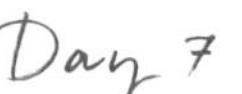

FROM GENERATION TO GENERATION

For the Lord *is good. His unfailing love continues forever, and his faithfulness continues to each generation.*
Psalm 100:5 NLT

God has been at work in your bloodline since long before you were born, no matter how far previous generations in your family strayed from Him.

King Josiah's family is a great example. His father, King Amon, "did what was evil in the Lord's sight, just as his father, Manasseh, had done" (2 Kings 21:20 NLT). Manasseh worshipped idols, abandoned the Lord, and refused to follow Him (see verses 21–22), and his son did likewise. But King Josiah's *great-*grandfather, Hezekiah, "did what was pleasing in the Lord's sight, just as his ancestor David had done. He removed the pagan shrines, smashed the sacred pillars, and cut down the Asherah poles" (2 Kings 18:3–4 NLT).

Each generation in Josiah's family had a chance to serve the Lord. Some chose to do so and others turned their backs on Him. But the Lord was still faithful, and Josiah's own reforms rank him as one of the greatest kings in Judah's history.

Regardless of how wayward previous generations in your family may have been, you can decide today, this moment, to serve the Lord. His unfailing love continues forever. Lean into that promise today.

God, to stand up in a world of wrongdoers and commit to righteousness—there may be nothing harder. I want to support people who are willing to do that. Amen.

Day 1

KEEPING WORDS IN CHECK

We all stumble in many ways. Anyone who is never at fault in what they say is perfect, able to keep their whole body in check.
JAMES 3:2 NIV

People speak to communicate, but too often share things from a skewed perspective, or don't have all the facts, or say things in an insensitive tone. Misunderstandings and offenses are the blight of relationships. In their efforts to share their thoughts, everyone makes mistakes. But if anyone consistently avoids offending others because he or she is considerate and speaks carefully, that person has great self-control.

There's a valuable promise in this verse also. It states that anyone who habitually refrains from foolish speech is *also* able to refrain from impulsive, thoughtless actions, and thus spare themselves much trouble in life.

Proverbs 31:26 (KJV) describes the ideal woman and gives the key to how to always speak wisely: "She openeth her mouth with wisdom; and in her tongue is the law of kindness." Because she determines in her heart to say only kind and loving words, her actions display the same gentle consideration and make her greatly loved.

Pray and ask God to help your tongue be ruled by the law of kindness. Then, whether you're highly intelligent and educated or not, your speech will display profound wisdom.

Well, Lord, You will certainly never hear me claim to be perfect. I stumble on my words every day! But I do want to get better. Will You help? Amen.

DANGERS OF IDLE CHATTER

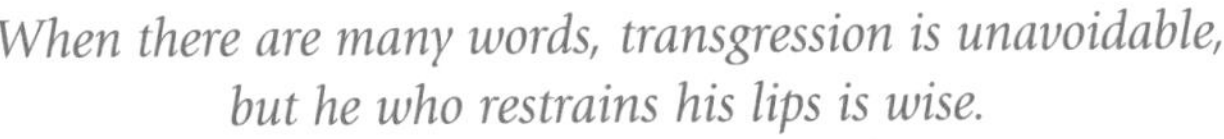

When there are many words, transgression is unavoidable, but he who restrains his lips is wise.

PROVERBS 10:19 NASB

People who incessantly indulge in small talk often say things they shouldn't. They try to fill the void, so they end up doing a lot of idle chatter and outright gossip. Others constantly try to be amusing, but when they run out of things worth saying, they keep talking, getting more and more foolish. "The beginning of the words of his mouth is foolishness: and the end of his talk is mischievous madness" (Ecclesiastes 10:13 KJV).

They end up chattering like a bird, making a great deal of noise, but not saying much that's intelligent. Hezekiah described this racket when he said, "Like a crane or a swallow, so did I chatter" (Isaiah 38:14 KJV).

Much of the time, the saying is true: "Silence is golden," and a person who refrains from speaking is wise. Solomon observed, "Even fools are thought wise when they keep silent; with their mouths shut, they seem intelligent" (Proverbs 17:28 NLT). Now, it's true that it can be frequently helpful to have the gift of gab. . .but more often it pays to be the strong, silent type.

If you're a chatterbox, ask God to help you to understand the wisdom in restraining your speech.

Hmmm. "Restraint" and "lips" are two words that don't go together automatically in my mind. Lord, help me not to say everything I think. Amen.

Day 3

HEALING WORDS

Gracious words are a honeycomb,
sweet to the soul and healing to the bones.
PROVERBS 16:24 NIV

Hearing considerate, gracious words is as pleasing to your ear as eating a honeycomb is to your tongue. And kind words are very healing to your spirit. The power of loving words can warm and release deep hurts of the past, like an expert masseur's probing fingers unlocking the stiffness and pain buried deep within cramped muscles.

Contrast this with careless, hate-filled words: "There is one who speaks rashly like the thrusts of a sword, but the tongue of the wise brings healing" (Proverbs 12:18 NASB). When people make cutting remarks intended to inflict pain, they are very much like the thrusts of a sword.

Since God has promised that gentle, Spirit-filled words can bring healing, you ought to strive for your words to relieve pain in people's lives—not add to it. Many people struggle through life, unable to deal with the baggage and hurts of their past, but loving words can bring life to their inner person and cause them to bloom.

God's Word is even more life-giving and healing. As Jesus said, "The words that I speak unto you, they are spirit, and they are life" (John 6:63 KJV). So speak encouraging promises into people's lives today.

God, I don't want to sting people with my words.
I want to comfort, and encourage, and cheer up,
and teach, and love. Help me, Lord. Amen.

EMOTIONAL OUTBURSTS

A fool vents all his feelings,
but a wise man holds them back.
PROVERBS 29:11 NKJV

Many people are very emotional, and this has both benefits and drawbacks. When they're *up* and happy, they can be a sheer pleasure to be around. But when they're *down* and moping around, they spread dark clouds of misery. Such people often freely vent their emotions. But they need to be aware that such venting can be very discouraging to others.

This verse is talking about self-absorbed people who don't *care* how they drag others down, but who rage, sulk, and complain loudly when things aren't going their way. They only think about themselves and don't attempt to restrain themselves.

In fact, they *knowingly* engage in angry outbursts to manipulate others. They find it much more effective than reasoned arguments. But these kinds of tactics destroy respect and love, and drive friends away, so though they often help people get what they want, they're also very foolish.

All believers, at one time or another, speak emotionally-charged words and need to consider the effect their speech is having on others. May God's children cease being guilty of wheedling, whining, manipulating others, and using guilt trips to get their way. There are more honest, mature ways of communicating needs to others.

Lord, what I say and how I say it has a big effect on those around me. Help me to keep my emotions in check so I don't hurt others. Amen.

SPEAKING ENCOURAGING WORDS

"The Lord God has given Me the tongue of the learned,
that I should know how to speak a word in
season to him who is weary."
Isaiah 50:4 NKJV

This is a good promise to claim, because the ability to encourage others is a valuable gift. Barnabas had it. He "was a good man, full of the Holy Spirit" and he "encouraged them all that with purpose of heart they should continue with the Lord" (Acts 11:23–24 NKJV).

When you love others, you become aware of their needs and are more eager to reach out to them when they're going through difficult times. Isaiah said, "Strengthen the weak hands, and make firm the feeble knees. Say to those who are fearful-hearted, 'Be strong, do not fear! Behold, your God will. . .come and save you' " (Isaiah 35:3–4 NKJV). Often people just need to be reminded to get their eyes on the Lord and trust Him.

Job had the gift of encouraging speech as well. One of his friends remarked, "Your words have supported those who were falling; you encouraged those with shaky knees" (Job 4:4 NLT). Ask God to give you a wise tongue as well, and to teach you to speak the right words at the right time to those who are weary and worn out.

Lord, help me never to be moving so fast through life that
I miss the chance to care for someone nearby.
Let me be an encourager. Amen.

Day 6

SPEAKING WITH GRACE

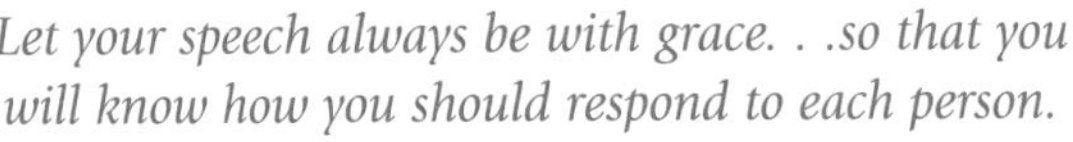

Let your speech always be with grace. . .so that you will know how you should respond to each person.
COLOSSIANS 4:6 NASB

It's important to study your Bible and know basic information about the faith to share with others. "You must worship Christ as Lord of your life. And if someone asks about your hope as a believer, always be ready to explain it" (1 Peter 3:15 NLT). But this doesn't mean just having pat, memorized explanations. You need to be able to respond in a nuanced manner to people to meet their individual needs.

For that, you have to allow the Holy Spirit to give you wisdom, because only He knows people's hearts and is aware of exactly what will touch them in a profound way. If you're constantly striving to walk in God's Spirit and be in tune with Him, He will give you the wisdom to know what to say (see Matthew 10:19–20).

This doesn't necessarily mean you'll have a perfect batting score and always know precisely what to answer, but "the love of God has been poured out in our hearts by the Holy Spirit who was given to us" (Romans 5:5 NKJV), so if your heart is filled with Him, you'll automatically speak in love, and that's the *most* important thing.

Lord, I don't want to stomp on anyone with my words. Help me to handle people with the same gentleness that You offer to me. Amen.

AVOID FOUL LANGUAGE

But now is the time to get rid of. . .malicious behavior, slander, and dirty language.
COLOSSIANS 3:8 NLT

As a believer, you are to avoid foul language, not because it's "not nice," but because it's abusive and demeaning. It's understandable when new believers slip up once in a while, because they're still in the process of leaving their old life behind. The problem comes, however, when someone who has been a disciple for many years habitually uses coarse language.

Some believers like to shock fellow Christians by swearing. They believe that using gutter talk proves that they're more genuine and in touch with reality than "sanctimonious Christians who are too polite to swear."

The New Testament is clear, however, saying: "Don't use foul or abusive language. Let everything you say be good and helpful" (Ephesians 4:29 NLT). A few verses later, Paul adds: "Obscene stories, foolish talk, and coarse jokes—these are not for you" (Ephesians 5:4 NLT). *These are not for you.* God's Word couldn't be much plainer.

By saying, "Now is the time to get rid of. . .dirty language," God makes it clear that you *can* control your tongue. If you determine to obey God and make a conscious effort to refrain from swearing, He will help you.

God, I know careless words can create pain and division. Help me to be thoughtful and aware always of the impact of my words. Amen.

....

....

....

....

....

....

....

Day 1

THE POWER OF HIS MIGHT

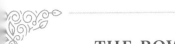

Finally, my brethren, be strong in the Lord,
and in the power of his might.
EPHESIANS 6:10 KJV

How many times have you felt so weak that you wondered if you could go on? There really are days when pulling the covers over your head seems like a better plan than getting out of bed. But people depend on you, so you put your feet on the floor and get going, even when you don't feel like it. On days like this your inner man might need a shot of vitamin B-12, but your outer man has to keep moving, one foot in front of the other. Time to get going.

Oh, but there's good news! You don't have to square your shoulders and pretend to be strong when your knees are wobbly. It's not up to you, anyway. God wants you to be strong in the power of His might. *His,* not yours. Isn't that a relief?

So, go ahead and kick back those covers. Get out of bed. But tell your inner man to get ready, because God is going to do a supernatural, invigorating work to give you the strength you need to face the day. He's going to load you up with holy vitamins to complete the tasks ahead of you.

God, sometimes the strength to get up and get through
the day seems impossible to obtain. Keep me
moving, Lord. Push me. Amen.

Day 2

ON BEHALF OF THOSE HE LOVES

"For the eyes of the Lord run to and fro throughout the whole earth, to show Himself strong on behalf of those whose heart is loyal to Him. In this you have done foolishly; therefore, from now on you shall have wars."

2 Chronicles 16:9 NKJV

Don't you love the image of God's eyes running to and fro throughout the earth? What a wonderful thought, that He's ready and willing to show Himself strong on your behalf. The very moment His eyes land on you, the work begins. In your moment of greatest weakness, He's there, eyes fixed on you, His child. He springs into action, bringing strength.

What a wonderful promise! There's a role you have to play in this promise, though. Did you catch it? Your heart must remain loyal to Him. In other words, you can't be swayed by other things, however tempting.

If you want His strength, you have to stay in His presence. If you foolishly turn away from Him, however, you'll lose His strength. The internal and external wars will be devastating. But God promises to give strength to those who remain loyal because of His great love.

Lord, what a comfort it is to know that You are constantly watching over me. I'm thankful that I don't have to go through this world on my own. Amen.

TRADING WEAKNESS FOR STRENGTH

He gives strength to the weary
and increases the power of the weak.
Isaiah 40:29 NIV

Have you ever watched a thermometer inch its way up, up, up? If so, then you've witnessed a genuine transformation. That thermometer is being changed from the inside out as an external force (the heat) serves as trigger. The mercury deep inside the thermometer responds to the external trigger and is nudged upward.

This is similar to what happens when you give God control of your heart. He longs to change you from the inside out. When you're at your weakest (picture that thermometer at its lowest point), the Lord steps in. He gives strength. Your internal/spiritual temperature begins to rise. Your perspective changes. Your desire to do His will kicks in.

Eventually, you're loaded with energy, ready to go. Why? Because God is always in the "increasing" business. The words *weak* and *powerless* don't exist in His vocabulary.

So, brace yourself. He's in "Let's get going!" mode today. Give Him what you have—your exhaustion, your crazy schedule, your pain—and watch as the Lord invigorates you, transforming you from the inside out. Whew! It's getting hot in here!

God, when I am close to You—reading Your Word,
singing Your praise, listening for Your voice—
I feel stronger. I can do anything with You. Amen.

Day 4

ALL THINGS

I know how to get along with humble means, and I also know how to live in prosperity; in any and every circumstance I have learned the secret of being filled and going hungry, both of having abundance and suffering need. I can do all things through Him who strengthens me.

PHILIPPIANS 4:12–13 NASB

Oh, how hard you try to do things in your strength. You muster the courage to put one foot in front of the other, even when you don't feel like it. You press forward, though you're beaten down. But you can't do it. Not in your own strength. So, defeat sets in.

But there's good news today. What you can't do in your own power, God *can* do. He can bolster you from the inside out and make it possible for you to accomplish not just a few things, but all things. Ponder that word: *all*. You can do *all* things through Christ Jesus who gives you strength.

Those things you fear most? You can conquer them in Jesus' name. That person who intimidates you the most? You can face him with courage. You can get through any situation, good or bad. That's a promise you can take to the bank.

God, in lean times, You've been with me, providing for me. And in times of fullness and growth, You've also been with me. I know I can depend on You. Amen.

Day 5

WINGS LIKE EAGLES

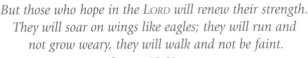

But those who hope in the LORD will renew their strength. They will soar on wings like eagles; they will run and not grow weary, they will walk and not be faint.

ISAIAH 40:31 NIV

Have you ever renewed something? Your insurance policy, for instance? Your contract with the electric company? Your driver's license? It's impossible to renew something you haven't already taken possession of in the first place. To keep it, you have to acknowledge that you already have it.

That's how it is with God's strength too. No matter where you are now, no matter how low you might feel, it's possible to once again take hold of what is already yours. But first you have to acknowledge that He's already done the work. God has given you a promise that if you put your hope in Him, then He will renew your strength. All He asks is one thing: actually put your trust in Him, not in your own accomplishments. He will do the rest.

Oh, what an amazing, over-the-top God you serve! His strength will send you soaring above your circumstances. You'll be a witness to others that a daily renewal policy is a terrific idea—one with amazing benefits.

God, I love that I can keep coming back to You, over and over again, and You never run out of love and strength and peace and joy. You are so amazing! Amen.

Day 6

AN ETERNAL PORTION

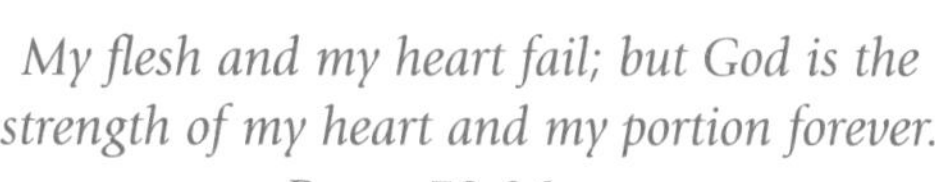

My flesh and my heart fail; but God is the strength of my heart and my portion forever.

PSALM 73:26 NKJV

When you think about the word *portion*, what comes to mind? Perhaps you think about your dinner plate, filled with carefully portioned selections—a healthy balance of proteins, vegetables, and grains. A little of this, a little of that.

Even a carefully-portioned meal is just temporary, though. Once you eat it, it's gone. God's idea of portioning is just the opposite. His Word says that He is your portion forever. In other words, He's all you'll ever need, not just for today, but for tomorrow and all eternity. He really gives a generous portion.

No matter what you're walking through today, no matter how close you are to giving up, God's promise hasn't changed. He's got an eternal portion of strength for you. He won't give it and then take it away. So, lift your eyes to Him. Remind yourself—by speaking it aloud—that He's enough, not just for the problems you're facing today, but for all eternity. Next time someone remarks that you have a full plate, point to heaven and say, "Yes, I do."

God, the idea that You have set aside part of You just for me is astounding. I am in awe of Your generous love for me. Amen.

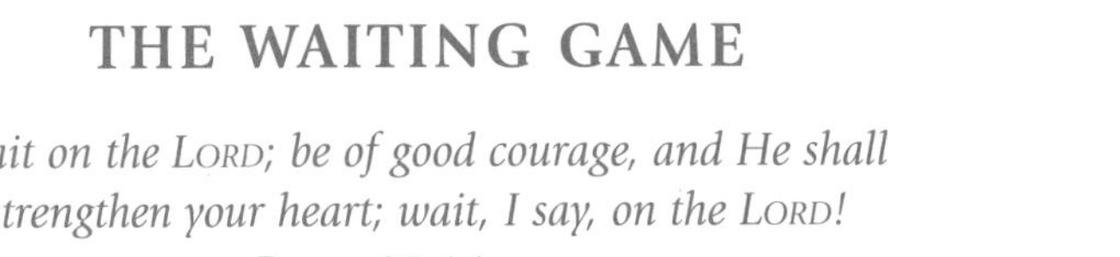

THE WAITING GAME

Wait on the LORD; be of good courage, and He shall strengthen your heart; wait, I say, on the LORD!
PSALM 27:14 NKJV

Patient people have the supernatural ability to accept delays without panicking. They go through struggles without knee-jerking or letting anger get the best of them. Impatient people are often frustrated. They want what they want and they want it now. (Sound like anyone you know?)

Isn't it interesting that the Lord commands His kids to wait on Him? He doesn't want you to get out ahead of Him and mess things up. He asks you to wait to see His promises fulfilled. He also wants you to trust His timetable. If you're waiting for your dreams to come true, you have to recognize the truth: His calendar is perfect. God also wants you to be of good courage while you're waiting.

Talk about a tough request. It's hard enough to wait, but to keep an uplifted heart? Oh, but the payoff is sweet! God will strengthen your heart if you follow His "wait it out" plan. So, where do you stand today? Patient. . .or impatient? The right choice can change the outcome of your situation in a hurry.

You know, my Lord, how I struggle with waiting for some things. Calm my anxiety. Bring peace to my fearful heart. Wait with me, Lord. Amen.

Day 1

FINDING WISDOM

Joyful is the person who finds wisdom, the one who gains understanding. For wisdom is more profitable than silver, and her wages are better than gold. Wisdom is more precious than rubies; nothing you desire can compare with her.

PROVERBS 3:13–15 NLT

How different might your life look if you hadn't made bad choices out of ignorance?

Maybe you quit college, not realizing how much a lack of education would hinder your career choices, and you've struggled ever since. Or maybe you entered a romantic relationship for the wrong reasons and it turned into a disaster. Whatever it was, finding wisdom wasn't as high of a priority as your immediate wants. . .and you paid a price.

Most people spend large portions of their lives chasing the temporal. They seek a bigger nest egg, an attractive spouse, nice possessions, and, if they're honest, power and prestige—with little regard for finding true wisdom.

Today's verse says wisdom is more profitable than silver and her wages are better than gold. Nothing you desire can compare with her. And it says wisdom brings joy. Do you believe this? If so, how, specifically are you seeking wisdom? Proverbs 9:10 (NLT) is a great starting place: "Fear of the LORD is the foundation of wisdom. Knowledge of the Holy One results in good judgment."

God, forgive me for the many times when I've started down a path without ever consulting You first. I'm looking for You now. Show me the way. Amen.

....

....

....

....

....

....

....

Day 2

A FLOOD OF KNOWLEDGE

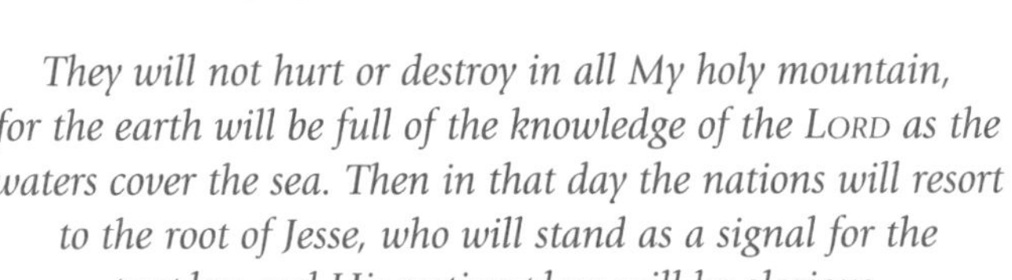

They will not hurt or destroy in all My holy mountain, for the earth will be full of the knowledge of the Lord *as the waters cover the sea. Then in that day the nations will resort to the root of Jesse, who will stand as a signal for the peoples; and His resting place will be glorious.*

Isaiah 11:9–10 nasb

According to the United States Geographical Survey website (www.usgs.gov), about 71 percent of the earth's surface is water-covered. So, even if you live in a landlocked part of the country, it's still hard to avoid water. Drive a few miles one way or another, and you're bound to encounter a stream, river, lake, or pond.

A day is coming, promises the prophet Isaiah, in which the earth will be full of the knowledge of the Lord, just as the waters cover the sea. The nations will turn to Jesus, as the root of Jesse, who will stand as the symbol of righteousness for all the people.

If you're discouraged by political events, court decisions, moral downturns, corruption, or just an overall lack of biblical understanding around you, take heart. A day is coming when the knowledge of the Lord will flood this earth and nobody will be able to miss it.

God, I long for the day when you will make all things new and perfect and holy. Come, Lord Jesus! Amen.

Day 3

FORSAKE EVIL

"And this is what he says to all humanity: 'The fear of the Lord is true wisdom; to forsake evil is real understanding.' "

Job 28:28 NLT

The world offers all sorts of wisdom. In many ways, it has turned knowledge and wisdom into gods, sitting in judgment of God and His Word. It says God's principles, as found in scripture, are archaic, outdated, out of touch—or, at the very least, not really meant to be taken literally.

Job, on the other hand, said something very different: the fear of the Lord is true wisdom. He had complete faith in what God said and feared Him in the healthiest of ways, knowing that if he forsook God, then he'd pay the price. But his next sentiment in today's verse is most intriguing: "To forsake evil is real understanding."

Doesn't the world today say the exact opposite when it embraces, promotes, and even legislates practices that God calls evil? In so doing, it reveals a lack of real godly understanding.

With that said, are there areas in your life in which you are failing to forsake evil, offering excuses instead of taking action? Be honest with God and in your own heart. Return to the Lord and He will have abundant mercy. You can make things right today.

God, help me to never mistake evil for good. Help me to always start any new plan with the purpose of honoring You. Amen.

Day 4

WISDOM OF THE ANCIENT

"With the ancient is wisdom; and in length of days understanding. With him is wisdom and strength, he hath counsel and understanding."
JOB 12:12–13 KJV

In 2014, there were 45.2 million people in the United States who were sixty-five years of age and older, according to the Administration on Aging. And, amazingly, there were 72,197 people who were at least 100 years of age.

Many of these senior citizens lived through the Great Depression, a world war, and the changing dynamics of family and society in general. They know a lot about hardship, sacrifice, honor, and adapting to change. And yet, too many of them will die with that knowledge and wisdom inside them because not enough people cared to ask them about it.

Today's verse says that with the ancient is wisdom, understanding, and strength. Have you tapped into this reservoir of wisdom? Or is your first call generally to a peer? What can you do to begin intentionally availing yourself of the wisdom of the ancient?

How about asking a grandparent for specific advice about a situation you face? Or visit a senior citizen and steer the conversation toward current events so you can hear him or her put events into a larger historical context. Reach out and be willing to listen.

Lord, too often I discount or forget the wisdom of my elders. Help me to learn from those saints who have traveled so many of life's roads with You. Amen.

Day 5

BIBLICAL MEDITATION

Make me understand the way of Your precepts;
so shall I meditate on Your wonderful works.
PSALM 119:27 NKJV

In Amos 8:11, God warned His people about a day coming when they would experience a famine of hearing from Him. "They shall wander from sea to sea, and from north to east; they shall run to and fro, seeking the word of the LORD, but shall not find it," said the Lord (Amos 8:12 NKJV).

As dire as that situation was in Amos's day, it's even worse today. You probably aren't noticing many people wandering from sea to sea seeking a word from the Lord. Instead, the Bible sits on bookshelves, coffee tables, and nightstands without being opened for weeks or months on end.

Many churches and small groups are encouraging Bible reading plans as a way to get people back into God's Word, but today's verse talks about going even deeper. The psalmist asks God to make him *understand* His precepts so he can *meditate* on His wonderful works.

What are you doing to digest and meditate on God's precepts? Some jot down Bible verses on index cards and then refer to them throughout the day. Others text Bible verses back and forth for discussion. And others journal through the scriptures. If you want a solid foundation, meditate on the Word.

God, let me soak in Your Word. Let me steep my mind in Your ways. Let me savor every bit of wisdom You offer me. Amen.

Day 6

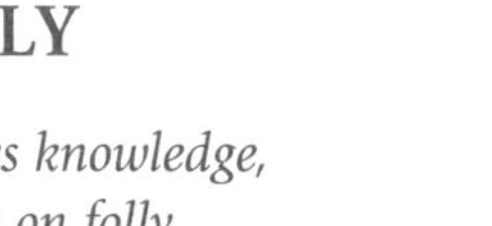

FADING FOLLY

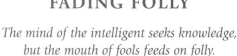

The mind of the intelligent seeks knowledge,
but the mouth of fools feeds on folly.
Proverbs 15:14 NASB

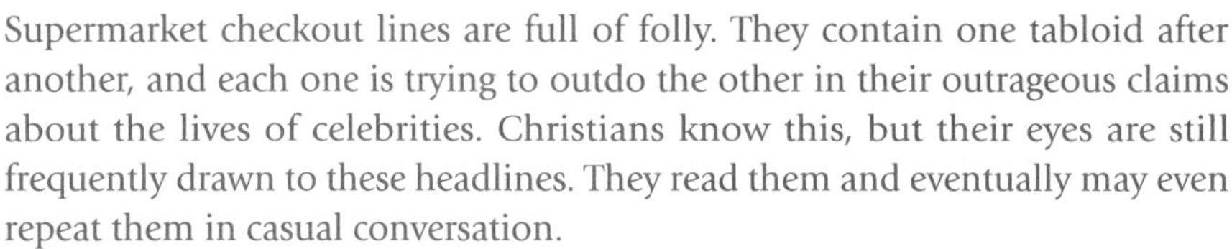

Supermarket checkout lines are full of folly. They contain one tabloid after another, and each one is trying to outdo the other in their outrageous claims about the lives of celebrities. Christians know this, but their eyes are still frequently drawn to these headlines. They read them and eventually may even repeat them in casual conversation.

"Wickedness is meat and drink to them [those who feed on folly]," wrote John Wesley in his commentary about this verse.

The human mind, when it's not in a constant state of renewal by the Word of God, feeds on folly. This is a by-product of the Fall. But there's good news: you can choose to seek knowledge instead. And today's verse indicates that those who have knowledge crave even more.

How are you currently seeking biblical knowledge? Do you have a Bible reading plan in place? Are you keeping up with it? Are you in a Bible study, taking classes at church, or in a small group that reads and discusses the Bible? If not, jump in. You'll find that once you get a taste of the truth, you'll want even more. And the folly of this world will begin to fade.

God, my mind is full of such useless stuff. Empty it of anything that is wicked or unwise. Help me to fill it with the knowledge You teach me. Amen.

Day 7

FEAR THE LORD

Then shalt thou understand the fear of the Lord,
and find the knowledge of God. For the Lord giveth wisdom:
out of his mouth cometh knowledge and understanding.
Proverbs 2:5–6 KJV

If you respect the fast-moving current of a river you plan to navigate, then you learn how to properly operate a canoe. If you respect the height of a mountain you plan to climb, then you learn everything you can about how the harness system works. If you respect the inherent hardships of a hiking trail, then you learn which provisions you need to take.

Respect, even fear, leads to knowledge—at least it should. In Proverbs 2, the writer begins by saying that if people are going to receive wisdom from God, then they will hide God's commandments in their hearts so they can incline their ears to wisdom and apply their hearts to understanding. Their fear of the Lord leads to understanding. They wouldn't dream of navigating a spiritual river, or climbing a spiritual mountain, or hiking a spiritual trail apart from such fear because they know that a lack of respect often leads to injury, or even death.

How about you? Do you approach difficult circumstances without being spiritually prepared? If so, begin this day by hiding God's commandments in your heart.

Awesome God, I see Your greatness, and I understand
how much I don't understand. Teach me,
Lord. I am listening. Amen.

Day 1

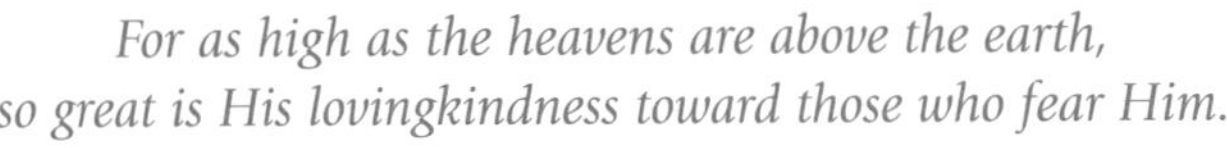

THE SCOPE OF GOD'S LOVE

For as high as the heavens are above the earth,
so great is His lovingkindness toward those who fear Him.
PSALM 103:11 NASB

God's love is deeper than the roots of your despair, higher than the pinnacle of your best moments, longer than the number of your days, and wider than the sum total of what you see and understand. God's love exceeds your expectations, surpasses your greatest dreams, and informs your response to those around you.

God is love, and His love is kind. His kindness leads you to Him, and when He issues the invitation to be part of His family the only barriers to accepting His gift are the barriers you erect. God's love pursues, envelops, and offers a better-than-lifetime guarantee. His love outlasts everything you know, outshines the brightest sun, and outgives the most generous philanthropists.

You can break God's heart with your choice to sin, but you can't stop His love. You can reject rescue, but you can't stop Him from offering. You might be better off trying to empty the ocean with a thimble or moving a mountain using a teaspoon than trying to stop God from loving you. *It can't be done.*

God is love—and love is God's gift to you. Go ahead, discover it.

God, I love the bigness, the enormity, of Your love.
I feel confident that You could never ever
run out of love for me. Amen.

Day 2

SACRIFICIAL LOVE

"For this is how God loved the world: He gave his one and only Son, so that everyone who believes in him will not perish but have eternal life."
JOHN 3:16 NLT

The people of Israel were in the wilderness between the lands of slavery and promise. It had become common for them to break God's law, and as a result, deadly snakes were sent slithering through camp and began biting people. Then the Lord told Moses, "Make a snake and put it up on a pole; anyone who is bitten can look at it and live" (Numbers 21:8 NIV).

God was foreshadowing what it would be like when Jesus was offered as the only way to recover from the deadly bite of sin. God loves all humanity. He sent His only Son to be the healing agent by dying on a cross. The gift of forgiveness was offered and people need to be intentional about accepting it.

God didn't love you a little and tell you that you had to do some of the work yourself. He loved you completely and Jesus paid the price completely. God hates sin, but His love is never fickle. He can love you wholly because Jesus sacrificed everything. The sacrifice of One brought grace, forgiveness, and life to *all* who believe.

Father God, the gift of Your Son is beyond comprehension. I cannot thank You enough for Jesus' life, death, and resurrection. Help me to live to honor that gift. Amen.

Day 3

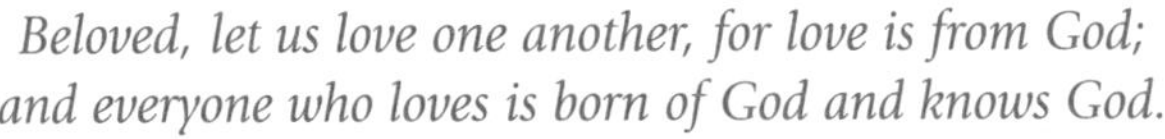

FILLED UP—SPILLED OUT

Beloved, let us love one another, for love is from God;
and everyone who loves is born of God and knows God.
1 JOHN 4:7 NASB

Water features are the focus of many gardens, backyards, and interior living spaces. In many of these features a pool fills and then spills onto smaller pools or rocks below. The water continues to fill and overflow. Just so, God's love fills you to overflowing. This is why you should overflow with joy on others.

You've already learned that you can authentically love others because He loved you first. His love teaches you how to love. Love is an intentional choice that proves your family resemblance to God.

The love you share needs to be shown to those who love God and those who aren't quite there yet. No exclusions, conditions, or disclaimers apply. You don't ignore sin, but you also don't ignore the very thing that God said would help identify those who belong to His family—*love*. People who aren't sure about God don't need your condemnation. They need a love and kindness that points to an aspect of God that can redeem anyone from the pawnshop of peddled futures.

God pours His love into your life every day. Are you pouring out to others?

Loving one another seems easy—until I actually try it.
But I know that You've made it possible for every one
of us to do. Help me to keep trying! Amen.

Day 4

NOT JUST A GOOD IDEA

"This is My commandment, that you love one another as I have loved you."
JOHN 15:12 NKJV

A command is something that tells your computer what to do. A command is something children are to follow when it's issued by a parent. Likewise, when God does the commanding, you are to obey Him.

God isn't a self-help guru. He doesn't offer an optional five-step plan for believers who desire a happy life. He's less interested in your preferences than He is in transforming your life into what He planned. When you follow His commands you're agreeing that He's in control. You don't usually follow the command of someone who doesn't have authority. God *does.*

God's command? "Love one another." He didn't say, "You might want to have a few warm, fuzzy thoughts about others" or "It's helpful to let people think you care." His command requires you to do the hard work of actually loving people, and if you need a reason you're reminded that God loved you first.

Love isn't just a good idea or something you should work toward. God commands you to love. God has loved you freely and commands you to share what He has given to you. Even if it *weren't* a command, it would still be a great idea—but remember: it *is* a command.

God, I want to obey You. Help me to be persistent in my efforts to love others. Amen.

A FAITHFUL AND STEADFAST LOVE

Thy lovingkindness is before mine eyes:
and I have walked in thy truth.
Psalm 26:3 kjv

The sun rises and sets. Flowers grow and send forth fragrance. Pets become friends. The stars invite you to gaze their way. Birds sing and you notice. Each of these moments are sponsored by God's love for you.

God's love is unshakable, steadfast, and unmovable. It's something you notice in the beauty of nature and the innocence of children, and that you appreciate seeing in the lives of others. Your journey with Jesus is assured. The God who's given what the world needs to support life is absolutely faithful in His promise to love you.

Today's verse encourages you to keep God's love fixed in your mind by simply noticing the everyday things around you. God's love comes in both the unexpected and common. He cares for you through the lives of others. He shares with you in every breath you take and in everything that takes your breath away.

God's love is never a one-time gift. It's absolutely complete and without equal. It bends the core of your being in His direction. It inspires you to see people the way God sees them. It opens a whole new world that's built on seeking the best for those you love.

God, Your love comes to me in so many surprising little ways.
I receive love letters from You through friends, through family,
and through everyday blessings. Thank You. Amen.

EVERY DAY

The Lord's lovingkindnesses indeed never cease,
for His compassions never fail. They are new
every morning; great is Your faithfulness.
Lamentations 3:22–23 NASB

This verse picks up where yesterday's thoughts ended. Yes, God's love is an immovable rock. It can be counted on, trusted, and shared. Yet this verse creates a sense of anticipation. You can almost visualize the author perpetually looking forward to Christmas morning—every day.

Mercy is described as lovingkindness that's given when it's least deserved. It's personal, intentional, and desperately needed. Mercy is unexpected in a world of justice, yet it's described as a gift from God that has no end.

Faithfulness is always doing what you say you'll do, being absolutely trustworthy and willing to prove the truth of your promise. God's love is like that.

Every morning, without fail, you must make a quick assessment of where you stand with God, and every morning identify God's steadfast love, never-ending mercy, and rock-solid faithfulness.

God doesn't skip a day, take vacations, or change His mind. He loves you, always has, and will never stop. This is observable, assured, but undeserved. And that's the point: God does what you can't. He is love. He is mercy. He is faithful. And He shows you how to do the same. Every day.

God, some days just don't go so well. I get impatient.
I get irritated. I get ugly. Help me to start again every
day, knowing You are faithful to me. Amen.

PART OF THE FAMILY

"Are not five sparrows sold for two cents? Yet not one of them is forgotten before God. Indeed, the very hairs of your head are all numbered. Do not fear; you are more valuable than many sparrows."

LUKE 12:6–7 NASB

You may not pay much attention to sparrows. They flit from one place to the next with few people pausing to pay attention. They're rarely complimented for their looks and even fewer people keep sparrows for pets, yet Jesus says they never classify as forgettable to God.

You probably haven't taken the time to catalog, number, and track the hairs on your head. You may notice if it seems some hair is changing color or falling out more than usual, but you probably don't obsess over numbering your hair. You likely don't give it much thought.

This is where the contrast to God's love shines bright. If God cares for the well-being of sparrows and hair, do you have any real idea how much He cares for *you*?

Nothing escapes God's notice, and it extends to your entire life. If God were to be interviewed and asked to talk about you, He could describe every moment. And in sharing all the things He loves about you He could say, "You know, they're part of My family."

Father God, when I am out in nature I see Your care and craftsmanship and creativity in every little piece of the world. That shows me how much You care for me. Amen.

HATE IS SUCH A STRONG WORD

All who fear the LORD will hate evil. Therefore, I hate pride and arrogance, corruption and perverse speech.

PROVERBS 8:13 NLT

No question about it: God uses some strong words against pride. It's easy to wonder: Does God hate it when I feel proud of a job well done? Does God hate it when I feel proud of my children's accomplishments? Does God hate it when I feel proud of my church for the way they have served our community and spread Jesus' love?

No, that feeling of pleased satisfaction is *not* what the Bible is referring to when it talks about the pride that God hates. God hates the kind of pride that keeps people from realizing their need for Him. He hates it because of how much He wants to give salvation through Jesus Christ to everyone. But if people won't acknowledge and accept Him, He can't save them. So when you read scriptures saying that God hates pride, think of what a loving God He is that He hates what keeps people from receiving His gift of eternal life.

This week, let's gain some perspective on the issue of pride and what God's Word says about it.

Lord of all, help me to remember that I can't do anything apart from You. Don't ever let my arrogance get in the way of Your message. Amen.

Day 2

DON'T PLAY WITH PRIDE

Pride goes before destruction, and a haughty spirit before stumbling. It is better to be humble in spirit with the lowly than to divide the spoil with the proud.
PROVERBS 16:18–19 NASB

Scripture warns you that pride is dangerous and not a trifling matter. So you are to strive for humility, which is the opposite of pride. James 4:6 (NIV) says, "God opposes the proud but shows favor to the humble." True humility recognizes the importance of God above all and others above self. If everyone lived in true humility, think of what a wonderful world it would be!

Pride is often an overassurance about status and plans and goals, and it's foolish since you can't even guarantee your next breath, let alone guarantee what you'll do next year or even tomorrow. Consider 1 Corinthians 10:12 (NIV) which says, "So, if you think you are standing firm, be careful that you don't fall!"

Of course, you can make wise plans and goals. It would be silly not to. But believers should always be asking for God's direction in those plans and goals and recognize that "in their hearts humans plan their course, but the LORD establishes their steps" (Proverbs 16:9 NIV).

I want to submit my steps to You, Lord. I acknowledge that what little knowledge I have is nothing compared to Your wisdom. I ask You to guide me today. Amen.

Day 3

IN YOUR OWN EYES

Do not be wise in your own eyes;
fear the L*ORD and shun evil.*
PROVERBS 3:7 NIV

It's certainly no fun to feel like a fool, so who honestly doesn't want to seem wise in their own eyes? Of *course* you want to sound and seem like you have your wits about you. So, does scripture promote kids shirking their schoolwork or adults never learning something new? Should Christians be ignorant and uneducated in the world so that they never feel satisfaction in what they've learned? No, not at all. There's a big difference between worldly wisdom and knowledge, and there's a healthy balance in fearing the Lord first and letting true knowledge and wisdom result from that.

The Bible says in Proverbs 9:10 (NASB), "The fear of the LORD is the beginning of wisdom, and the knowledge of the Holy One is understanding." God is the very beginning of all wisdom and knowledge. Respecting Him first is the only way to really know anything at all. It makes perfect sense that the source of learning about the world around you is the One who created it all in the first place!

So don't be proud in what you've learned. Be proud of God for giving you the ability to learn, and for who He is, what He has done, and what He reveals to you.

Father, help this child of Yours to be cautious
and examine all things in the light of Your truth. Amen.

....

....

....

....

....

....

....

....

Day 4

FIGHTING PRIDE AND SELF-PRESERVATION

"If anyone desires to be first, he shall be last of all and servant of all."
MARK 9:35 NKJV

Perhaps the hardest part of the Christian life and the most countercultural aspect is the issue of pride and self-preservation. Believers have to fight for a good perspective because you constantly hear the likes of: "Do what feels right for *you*." "Look out for Number One." "You can't help others if you don't help yourself first."

Yet many scriptures contradict these statements. Consider these:

"Don't be selfish; don't try to impress others. Be humble, thinking of others as better than yourselves" (Philippians 2:3 NLT).

"Jesus said to his disciples, 'If any of you wants to be my follower, you must give up your own way, take up your cross, and follow me. If you try to hang on to your life, you will lose it. But if you give up your life for my sake, you will save it' " (Matthew 16:24–25 NLT).

"If you want to be my disciple, you must, by comparison, hate everyone else—your father and mother, wife and children, brothers and sisters—yes, even your own life" (Luke 14:26 NLT).

Of course, it's a balance that takes wisdom. Give your life fully to God then constantly pray for His perfect guidance on how He wants you to use it for His glory.

God, help me not to hide behind others. Help me to actively work for others, submitting my will and leading in service and humility. Amen.

Day 5

LET YOUR WORDS BE HUMBLE

"Talk no more so very proudly; let no arrogance come from your mouth, for the LORD is the God of knowledge; and by Him actions are weighed."

1 SAMUEL 2:3 NKJV

Do you struggle to guard your tongue? Is there a human on the planet who doesn't? All believers spout off with pride at times. James chapter 3 talks about how boastful the tongue is and how hard it is to control it. It's a bittersweet, comforting passage of scripture that lets you know the struggle is real for absolutely everyone.

Striving to eliminate pride in your life and focusing on humility before God and others will help you with your communication and relationships. For good reason, the Bible instructs you to keep your words humble. "A gentle answer deflects anger, but harsh words make tempers flare. The tongue of the wise makes knowledge appealing, but the mouth of a fool belches out foolishness" (Proverbs 15:1–2 NLT).

So what's the best thing you can do to control your tongue and guard it from pride? Keep it so busy with prayer and praise that it can't do much else. If you feel like boasting, get pumped up about God. "As the Scriptures say, 'If you want to boast, boast only about the LORD' " (2 Corinthians 10:17 NLT).

God, sometimes I act like I know things when I really know nothing. Help me not to use prideful or boastful language. Amen.

HEALTHY PERSPECTIVE

For by the grace given me I say to every one of you: Do not think of yourself more highly than you ought, but rather think of yourself with sober judgment, in accordance with the faith God has distributed to each of you.

Romans 12:3 niv

Scriptures on pride and humility can be misused. God doesn't ever want you to think you're worthless. He thinks you're so valuable that He sent His Son to die to save you, so obviously you have great worth. But a healthy perspective on pride and humility is to realize that *real* and *lasting* self-worth comes from your identity in Christ.

In this world, yes, it's possible to go it alone without Jesus as Lord of your life, but no one can ever be truly fulfilled that way. They can make it look good from the outside, of course, but they'll always be hollow and aimless inside without Jesus. Ultimately, this world will amount to as much as the briefest blink of an eye compared to eternity. So remember that your value and status for eternity is based wholly on Jesus.

How you humbly follow Jesus determines what your eternal future looks like. To sacrificially put others first in the here and now earns unimaginable rewards for you in heaven forever! (Luke 12:33–34; Luke 18:22; 2 Corinthians 5:10; 1 Timothy 6:17–19.)

King of heaven, I want to live each day with the knowledge of eternity set deep in my heart. Help me to make choices that lead me closer to You. Amen.

Day 7

HE CARES

"But it is wrong to say God doesn't listen,
to say the Almighty isn't concerned."
JOB 35:13 NLT

Do you believe God cares about you and listens to you? Don't let worldly circumstances ever make you doubt that. Job 35:13 says it's wrong to say He's not listening or concerned about you. Acting like God doesn't care about you can be a form of pride.

Some people use the excuse that "God doesn't care about little old me" to simply fuel their desire for self-dependence and pride in their own abilities because "no one *else* is looking out for me anyway." Not true. Acting like you're not worthy of God's concern or that you've fallen off His radar contradicts His Word. God promises that He never leaves or forsakes you and that nothing can ever separate you from His love.

If you ever feel tempted by false humility in the attitude of "I'm not worthy so God must not care," read and remember this scripture: "What is the price of five sparrows—two copper coins? Yet God does not forget a single one of them. And the very hairs on your head are all numbered. So don't be afraid; you are more valuable to God than a whole flock of sparrows" (Luke 12:6–7 NLT).

I know I've thought before, Lord, that You weren't listening.
I thought in my pride that the answer I wanted was
the only right one. Forgive me, Lord. Amen.

KEEPING THINGS IN PERSPECTIVE

For I reckon that the sufferings of this present time are not worthy to be compared with the glory which shall be revealed in us.
ROMANS 8:18 KJV

As a Christian, you're destined to suffer for your faith at one time or another, and though you know it's for a truly noble cause, it can still hurt. It can be humiliating, cause you financial loss, or seem downright unjust. And as a result, it can be discouraging.

Contrary to what you may wonder at times, God doesn't enjoy seeing you suffer. "He does not afflict willingly, nor grieve the children of men" (Lamentations 3:33 NKJV). Why then does He allow such unwanted trouble? Why does he permit adversaries to do awful things to His children? Well, believe it or not, God is able to get much good out of what men intend as evil.

And the best news is, the Lord has promised to reward—*greatly* reward—you for suffering for His name. Jesus advised that when people persecute you, "Rejoice in that day and leap for joy! For indeed your reward is great in heaven" (Luke 6:23 NKJV).

Leap for joy? Yes, that's what Jesus said. This tells you heaven must be wonderful beyond your wildest dreams. You may be suffering now, but one day you'll be overjoyed.

Loving God, some people's troubles here on earth are pretty easy to get over. But some people have an overwhelming mountain of suffering. Help us all, Lord. Amen.

Day 2

GOD'S SPIRIT UPON YOU

If you are reviled for the name of Christ, you are blessed, because the Spirit of glory and of God rests on you.
1 PETER 4:14 NASB

When opponents attack you because of your Christian beliefs or lifestyle, and their anger and scorn are directed against you, it can be intimidating. It's something you'd normally try to avoid. But although they're uttering vitriolic curses against you, you're blessed instead.

This is because when you obey Christ and identify with Him to the point of suffering for His name, you're clearly walking in His Spirit. Jesus said, "Abide in me, and I in you" (John 15:4 KJV). His Spirit abides (dwells) in your heart, but you in turn must seek to walk so close to Him that you're in the center of the cloud of His presence (Exodus 13:21), surrounded by Him.

His presence then envelops you and rests upon you. "You are blessed, because the Spirit of glory and of God rests on you." In Psalm 90:17 (KJV) the Israelites prayed, "Let the beauty of the LORD our God be upon us," and one of the surest ways for you to have God's beauty is for you to walk close to Him, in the midst of His presence, so that His Spirit rests upon you.

God, taking a stand for You is going to cost me. But I know nothing I suffer can compare to what You went through to save me. Thank You. Amen.

Day 3

OVERCOMING THE WORLD

"These things I have spoken to you, that in Me you may have peace. In the world you will have tribulation; but be of good cheer, I have overcome the world."
JOHN 16:33 NKJV

This is a beautiful promise, and one you can constantly take to the bank. Perhaps low finances are wearing you down; perhaps you're struggling with illness; perhaps friends are badmouthing you; perhaps family members look at you as some kind of "religious weirdo"; or perhaps people are maligning your character in the workplace.

As Jesus promised, "In the world you *will* have tribulation" (emphasis added). And Paul added, "All that will live godly in Christ Jesus shall suffer persecution" (2 Timothy 3:12 KJV). It's guaranteed.

But Jesus *also* guarantees that you can have marvelous peace. Despite difficult circumstances, you can be cheerful, knowing that Jesus has overcome the world. All that the world had to throw at your Savior couldn't take Him down. And His Word then promises in turn that *you* "have overcome them: because greater is he that is in you, than he that is in the world" (1 John 4:4 KJV).

What is the secret to having peace in the midst of such trials? Trusting God. "You will keep him in perfect peace. . .because he trusts in You" (Isaiah 26:3 NKJV).

Jesus, thank You for telling me that You have overcome this world. I can live each day, whatever trouble comes, knowing You are in control of it all. Amen.

ESTABLISHED BY GOD

After you have suffered for a little while, the God of all grace, who called you to His eternal glory in Christ, will Himself perfect, confirm, strengthen and establish you.

1 Peter 5:10 nasb

As much as you would like to, you can't always avoid trouble. Problems relentlessly assault you, and a number of them will find a way through your defenses. In fact, you will experience *many* troubles. But just as relentlessly, God comes to your aid. The Psalms promise, "The righteous person faces many troubles, but the Lord comes to the rescue each time" (Psalm 34:19 nlt).

However, you often have to suffer from life's problems for a while before God delivers you from them. Like Jesus, you may at times be "a man of sorrows, and acquainted with grief" (Isaiah 53:3 kjv). You can forget that little Sunday school song about being "happy all the time." Life doesn't work that way, and the Bible makes no such promises.

But one thing the Bible *does* promise is that after you have suffered for a while, God will deliver you. He will personally come alongside you to confirm, strengthen, and establish you. Yes, He allows you to be tested by the refiner's fire, but His end goal is not to destroy you, but to purify you and to strengthen you.

God, I long for Your deliverance. But even so, I want to do Your work here on this earth well. Show me what You want me to do. Amen.

SHARING IN CHRIST'S SUFFERINGS

Dear friends, do not be surprised at the fiery ordeal that has come on you to test you, as though something strange were happening to you. But rejoice inasmuch as you participate in the sufferings of Christ, so that you may be overjoyed when his glory is revealed.

1 Peter 4:12–13 NIV

You willingly participate in the sufferings of Christ when you go out of your way to help the less fortunate. Such sacrifices cost you time and effort, and may even bring hardship and discomfort upon you. You may give to the needy when you already have many bills to pay. Or you may do good to your enemies, only to be mocked and rebuffed for your efforts.

If you're new at following Christ in self-sacrificial ways, you may be surprised that He allows you to suffer for doing good. (Perhaps you expected to be rewarded instantly instead.) But what's happening should *not* strike you as strange. You're following in Jesus' footprints, being rejected as He was rejected and suffering as He suffered.

Of course this will hurt, but God promises that when Jesus returns in all His glory, He will amply reward you. So don't be afraid to take on a little trouble as you reach out to others. God *will* reward you. . .in the end!

Lord, it is so good to know that You understand every part of our experience. Thank You for reminding me of the glory that is to come. Amen.

Day 6

REIGNING IN ETERNITY

If we suffer, we shall also reign with him.
2 Timothy 2:12 KJV

You know God will reward you for suffering for His sake, because Jesus said that when you're persecuted, "great is your reward in heaven" (Matthew 5:12 KJV). Exactly *how* magnificent is your reward? Very great indeed. Paul said, "If we suffer, we shall also reign with him."

When Jesus' kingdom comes upon the earth, you who have followed and obeyed Him and suffered for His name will literally rule the earth with Him. Jesus personally promised, "To the one who is victorious and does my will to the end, I will give authority over the nations—that one 'will rule them with an iron scepter' " (Revelation 2:26–27 NIV). It also says, "They. . .reigned with Christ a thousand years" (Revelation 20:4 NIV).

You may suffer scorn now, but in that day you'll be highly exalted. God will enjoy rewarding you with tremendous authority and blazing glory, causing all people to greatly honor you.

It's no fun suffering, and sometimes you wonder, "Is it worth it?" It's definitely worth it! God will delight to lavish wonderful things on you in heaven and give you tremendous happiness. So remain faithful to Him now, even during difficult times. You'll be glad that you did.

Living with You in heaven, God, will be more beautiful
and exciting than I can even remotely imagine.
When hard times come, let me glimpse Your glory. Amen.

Day 7

WALKING AS JESUS WALKED

For to this you were called, because Christ also suffered for us, leaving us an example, that you should follow His steps.
1 PETER 2:21 NKJV

One of the less appreciated truths of Christianity is that God frequently calls you to suffer. In the Gospels you see Jesus suffering, and this wasn't just something that He experienced because it was His unique destiny. Jesus was doing it because He was setting an example for His followers. He intended for you to follow His example.

Here's another little-loved truth. Paul declared, "I now rejoice in my sufferings for you, and fill up in my flesh what is lacking in the afflictions of Christ, for . . .the church" (Colossians 1:24 NKJV). Christ's suffering on the cross is all you need to obtain salvation, but preaching the Gospel and living a godly life frequently involve self-sacrifice and privation.

This may not be the comfort zone you were seeking, but remember, Jesus calls you to a self-sacrificial lifestyle. It's wonderful to be blessed and prosperous and lacking nothing, but that isn't always the path to becoming more Christlike. Nor is it usually the path to reaching the world with the Gospel.

God uses adversity to test your faith, teach you patience and perseverance, and to refine you and make you pure.

Lord, let my life be a witness of the love and joy I have found in You. Give me more and more chances to tell others about Your grace. Amen.

Day 1

HOLD FIRMLY

We have come to share in Christ, if indeed we hold our original conviction firmly to the very end.
HEBREWS 3:14 NIV

This scripture describes what perseverance in the Christian faith is about—holding firmly to the trust you had when you first accepted Jesus as your Lord and Savior. Do you remember that day? Take a moment to think back to the moment when you surrendered your life to the only One worthy.

Maybe it was years ago, maybe you were very young, or maybe it was more recent. You realized your need for a Savior. You confessed your sin and asked His forgiveness. You believed in His death on the cross as the sacrifice for your sin, and you trusted in His resurrection, His victory over death, and His promise for eternal life. And now you have the Holy Spirit dwelling in you.

Hold fast to all that, friend. Hold tight and don't let go. This world will constantly try to steal your faith. Your enemy the devil relentlessly tries to devour you. Don't let him. Persevere. Actively maintain your faith and live it out even though the world is constantly hostile toward you because of it. Don't let that discourage you. Let the devotions this week encourage you to hold firmly to the confidence you had at the beginning.

Lord, when I first came to You, I didn't know much. I still don't! But You are teaching me. Let me never forget the joy of accepting Your grace. Amen.

Day 2

EYES ON JESUS

Therefore, since we are surrounded by such a huge crowd of witnesses to the life of faith, let us strip off every weight that slows us down, especially the sin that so easily trips us up. And let us run with endurance the race God has set before us. We do this by keeping our eyes on Jesus, the champion who initiates and perfects our faith. Because of the joy awaiting him, he endured the cross, disregarding its shame. Now he is seated in the place of honor beside God's throne.

HEBREWS 12:1–2 NLT

To persevere in the Christian faith you must keep your eyes on Jesus. As the old hymn says, "Turn your eyes upon Jesus. Look full in His wonderful face. And the things of earth will grow strangely dim, in the light of His glory and grace." Both the triumphs and the troubles of this world pale in comparison to the glory and grace of Jesus. He sustains you through any difficult and trying periods.

Today's scripture reminds you that Jesus "endured the cross, disregarding its shame" because He had joy waiting for Him just beyond this life, in heaven. Your life may be full of trouble, but take heart. You too have eternal joy awaiting you in heaven. Don't give up!

God, when I think of all the faithful ones who lived fully for You, I am encouraged. I know I can finish this race of life with You by my side. Amen.

ACTION REQUIRED

[They strengthened] the souls of the disciples, encouraging them to continue in the faith, and saying, "Through many tribulations we must enter the kingdom of God."
ACTS 14:22 NASB

To persevere in your faith, you can't just sit back and relax. Real faith is active. If you let it stagnate, you won't confidently continue in it. If you don't actively work on building your relationship with Jesus Christ, you will falter.

Acts 14:22 says that we will enter the kingdom of God "through many tribulations." That sure doesn't sound like rest and relaxation, but God strengthens you and increases your ability to persevere through many difficulties.

How do you keep your relationship with Jesus thriving in the midst of hardship? By daily personal time in God's Word. By regular fellowship and worship in a Bible-teaching church. By service to others. By discipling someone less mature than you. God uses all these things to increase your perseverance. He strengthens your relationship with Him as He helps you connect with people and encourage one another.

Colossians 1:10 (NLT) says, "Then the way you live will always honor and please the Lord, and your lives will produce every kind of good fruit. All the while, you will grow as you learn to know God better and better." That's the kind of perseverance to strive for.

God, everything that is worthwhile involves hard work. Help me to be ready for whatever trials I must go through to get to eternal life with You. Amen.

Day 4

TRIED AND TRUE

These trials will show that your faith is genuine. It is being tested as fire tests and purifies gold—though your faith is far more precious than mere gold. So when your faith remains strong through many trials, it will bring you much praise and glory and honor on the day when Jesus Christ is revealed to the whole world.

1 PETER 1:7 NLT

Keeping the faith through adversity is never easy, but it shows God and others that you're for real. No one escapes hard times in this world, but a person's faith in Christ, or lack of it, will determine how he handles them. You have to be willing to go through the heat of the fires to make your faith strong and pure. Then see what happens, as God develops your character to be more like Jesus.

Romans 5:3–5 (NLT) says, "We can rejoice, too, when we run into problems and trials, for we know that they help us develop endurance. And endurance develops strength of character, and character strengthens our confident hope of salvation. And this hope will not lead to disappointment. For we know how dearly God loves us, because he has given us the Holy Spirit to fill our hearts with his love."

Lord, the people who have made the biggest impact on my life are those who have struggled and remained faithful. Help me to live like that. Amen.

Day 5

CONSTANT PRAYER IS KEY

With all prayer and petition pray at all times in the Spirit, and with this in view, be on the alert with all perseverance and petition for all the saints.

Ephesians 6:18 NASB

You absolutely cannot persevere in faith in Jesus Christ all on your own. It's just not possible. So how, then? Through constant, endless, diverse prayer. Notice how many times Ephesians 6:18 uses the word *all*. And reread this powerful phrase: "With *all* prayer and petition pray at *all* times. . ." Paul put a lot of emphasis on that word *all*, and it shows the kinds of prayer and times for prayer—all kinds and at all times! There is no bad topic or request to pray about and no bad time to do it.

Do like 1 Thessalonians 5:16–18 (NLT) instructs: "Always be joyful. Never stop praying. Be thankful in all circumstances, for this is God's will for you who belong to Christ Jesus."

Many people are looking for God's will in their lives, and this scripture spells it out clearly. It's God's will that you be joyful, that you never stop praying, and that you be thankful in all circumstances. Do these things and you'll be able to persevere until Christ's return.

Lord, in the morning I come to You. In my day, let me pause and think of You. And before sleep comes, let me remember You. Amen.

SOMETIMES SAY NO

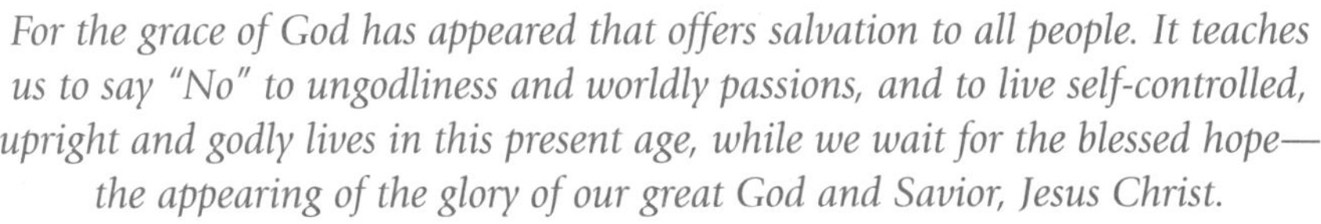

For the grace of God has appeared that offers salvation to all people. It teaches us to say "No" to ungodliness and worldly passions, and to live self-controlled, upright and godly lives in this present age, while we wait for the blessed hope—the appearing of the glory of our great God and Savior, Jesus Christ.

Titus 2:11–13 niv

If you've ever overcommitted yourself, you've learned the importance of saying no. In a fallen world, there sure are a lot of bad things to get involved in. But there are also a lot of wonderful things to do, especially in the church. But too many people get the idea that they should commit to *everything* they're asked to do, or be a part of *every* ministry going on, and so on. That can be overwhelming.

Titus 2 talks about saying no to ungodliness and worldly passions. For sure, you must avoid such things. But it's wise to be aware that even the best ministries in your church might be ungodly (in that they're not God's will for you) if you're doing them for the wrong reasons or they're stealing your time from what God *really* wants you to do.

Ask God to help you persevere in the good works He has planned for you. Nothing more, nothing less.

Lord of my life, help me to fiercely and firmly reject the desires and feelings and thoughts that would draw me away from You. Every day! Amen.

Day 7

THOUGH YOU FALL. . .

Though he fall, he shall not be utterly cast down;
for the Lord upholds him with His hand.
Psalm 37:24 NKJV

Psalm 37:24 encourages you to persevere, knowing that God never abandons you no matter how bad your circumstances are. "Nothing can ever separate us from God's love. Neither death nor life, neither angels nor demons, neither our fears for today nor our worries about tomorrow—not even the powers of hell can separate us from God's love. No power in the sky above or in the earth below—indeed, nothing in all creation will ever be able to separate us from the love of God that is revealed in Christ Jesus our Lord" (Romans 8:38–39 NLT).

Consider a heroine of the faith, Corrie ten Boom, who persevered through absolute horror in Hitler's Europe. She learned firsthand that "we are hard pressed on every side, but not crushed; perplexed, but not in despair; persecuted, but not abandoned; struck down, but not destroyed. We always carry around in our body the death of Jesus, so that the life of Jesus may also be revealed in our body" (2 Corinthians 4:8–10 NIV).

Knowing that God's love will never leave you and that faithful ones have preceded you, choose to persevere each new day, confidently hoping in Jesus Christ.

How beautiful to know that when I fail, You will not leave me.
Instead, You will pick me up and hold me close. Thank You, Lord. Amen.

Day 1

THE PROOF IS IN THE PUTTING (OTHERS FIRST)

For this is the love of God, that we keep His commandments. And His commandments are not burdensome.

1 John 5:3 NKJV

Love is hugely misunderstood in the world. It gets characterized as warm, fuzzy feelings that are strong enough to make two people promise undying loyalty to each other but not strong enough to last a lifetime. Marriages wither and drop when one or both spouses can no longer muster whatever it was they felt when they first dated and fell for each other. Parents harshly criticize children, children disrespect and disobey parents, friends fall out over miscommunication, and grace is nowhere to be found. It gets worse when you love God that way.

That was John's concern, so he cleared up a few misconceptions and laid out love's parameters: As Christians, you know you love God if you obey His commandments, which means loving His children (1 John 5:1–3). When you sacrifice your comfort and self-interest for the welfare of others, you're showing them the kind of love that Jesus showed you.

When you love like that, you're loving God, and you're relieved of the burden of this world's weakened affections. "Every child of God defeats this evil world, and we achieve this victory through our faith" (1 John 5:4 NLT).

God, obedience isn't glamorous. It doesn't even seem attractive. But obeying You is how I get to know You and love You. I do love You, Lord. Help me to obey. Amen.

Day 2

WAITING ON LOVE

But as it is written, Eye hath not seen, nor ear heard, neither have entered into the heart of man, the things which God hath prepared for them that love him.

1 Corinthians 2:9 KJV

Waiting, as they say, is the hardest part. But for the Christian, it's the best part. Paul quoted the prophet Isaiah, who instead of *love* used the word *wait*: "what [God] hath prepared for him that waiteth for him" (Isaiah 64:4 KJV). Paul's switch indicates that there is something in waiting on God that relates closely to loving Him.

On one hand, waiting on God shows your love for Him, your trust that He has shown you in His Word and by His Spirit all the amazing and wonderful things He has planned for you. And yet, His best gifts are not hidden from you—abundant life, peace, and salvation—things that no one on the earth could give or teach you.

The world can't fathom the wonder of God's Holy Spirit living in you, guiding and directing you into His truth, and drawing out good fruit: love, joy, peace, longsuffering, kindness, goodness, faithfulness, gentleness, and self-control (Galatians 5:22–23). The gifts that God's people awaited in Isaiah's day became available through Jesus—and people who love Him are part of His work in spreading that good news.

God, if Noah and Abraham and the Israelites and Joseph and Mary could all wait for the gift You promised, then surely I can too. Grow my faith, Lord. Amen.

Day 3

WHO'S YOUR DADDY?

Jesus told them, "If God were your Father, you would love me, because I have come to you from God. I am not here on my own, but he sent me."
JOHN 8:42 NLT

Human instinct picks and chooses what version of truth and knowledge best serves its own advantage. It's not natural to be others-oriented; in fact, even believers tend to "orient" others for their own purposes, cultivating those relationships that best suit their agenda. They can only break from this propensity by the blood of Christ.

If that sounds harsh, consider the context of the verse. Jesus was engaged in another showdown with the Pharisees, who had gone from just hating His guts to wanting Him dead. They thought they were doing God's work in dealing with this uneducated carpenter and His "blasphemous" claims, but Jesus took a different view, telling them: "You belong to your father, the devil, and you want to carry out your father's desires" (John 8:44 NIV).

His point was that loving God is not just a matter of knowledge but of understanding God's heart—which matches His holiness with grace and His justice with reconciliation. When God is your Father, you will take Him at His word—loving Him first and foremost, but also loving others and seeking to win them to His kingdom.

Lord, help me to know the difference between knowing a lot about You and really knowing Your heart. I want to live fully for You. Amen.

Day 4

DESIRE RESTRAINED BY DELIGHT

Take delight in the Lord, and he will give you your heart's desires.
Psalm 37:4 NLT

Imagine the damage you would do using only the second half of that verse—if God were, in fact, some type of cosmic genie whose sole purpose was to please your heart. Some would take the easy path and turn their lives into pleasure gardens, indulging whims, lusts, and momentary feelings.

Then, there would be those who determined that they knew what was best for everyone else and set about creating a world in their image—from the family all the way up to government, with society, culture, and knowledge all reflecting the maxim: *Do what you want; you know best.*

Both scenarios sound a lot like Satan-approved dystopias, as well as reflections of the world you actually live in. Thankfully, though, God is there, not as a wish-machine but as a loving King. When Jesus returns, He will set the world to rights, exercising iron-hard justice against those who have refused to delight in Him.

Until then, you can be thankful that you have a heavenly Father in whom you rejoice, and that the more you seek Him, the more your heart's desires will align with His and you'll have a fighting chance to bring His light into your corner of this dark world.

God, You shaped my heart. You've created me to do good. Help my desires to be purely for Your purposes. Amen.

LOVE FEARLESSLY

God is love, and all who live in love live in God, and God lives in them. And as we live in God, our love grows more perfect. . . . Such love has no fear, because perfect love expels all fear. If we are afraid, it is for fear of punishment, and this shows that we have not fully experienced his perfect love. We love each other because he loved us first.

1 John 4:16–19 NLT

Have you ever loved someone so completely, so joyfully, that there is no sacrifice you wouldn't make, no humiliation you wouldn't endure, no length to which you wouldn't go in order to ensure that person's best and highest good?

That kind of love is truly remarkable, rare and special in a selfish world—but even so, your love isn't perfect. You know what you want to do and why, but your imperfections keep you from always doing it.

Only God loves perfectly, because only God is perfect. You can rest in His love, knowing He has done everything in Christ to forgive your past, provide for your present, and secure your future. Let His love fill you and flow through you, so that you can also love others fearlessly—loving like Jesus loves you, His special one for whom He gave all.

God, I know the difference in my life between living in You and living in fear. Thank You for the freedom I have as I live in Your kingdom. Amen.

Day 6

A SANCTIFIED SPONGE

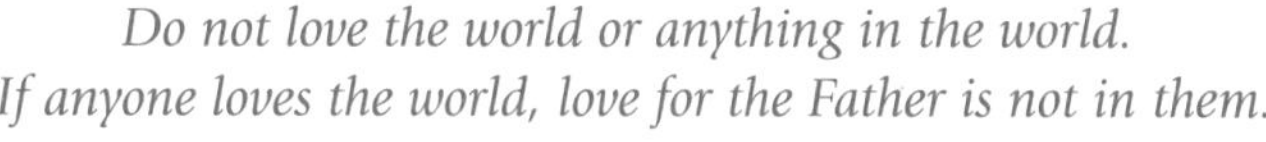

Do not love the world or anything in the world.
If anyone loves the world, love for the Father is not in them.
1 John 2:15 NIV

You are like a sponge, probably far more than you'd care to admit. You absorb everything that happens, taking in the bad with the good—learning, experiencing, and growing as you go. While sponges are impressively expansive, however, they are not unlimited in capacity. You have to be careful what you take in, because there's only so much room. And if you absorb the wrong things, the good gets squeezed out.

The world pressures you to conform, squeezing you with materialism and relativism, hoping to push God out and fill you with fleeting pleasures and convenient truths that never fully satisfy. The reason Jesus prayed that God would protect you in the world but not take you out of it (John 17:15–16) was so that you might have a godly influence.

Fortunately, you can squeeze out the world and absorb God's love and truth instead. Staying regularly in prayer, Bible study, and Christian fellowship all keep you filled with living water, steeped in God's Spirit and presence. Those practices sanctify you, helping you to love God more and be conduits of His love to others.

Father God, it's way too easy for me to get caught up in
the things of this world—things that will not last.
Help me to focus totally on You. Amen.

STRAIGHT LINES FROM CROOKED STICKS

We know that all things work together for good to them that love God, to them who are the called according to his purpose.
ROMANS 8:28 KJV

A medieval saying observed that God makes straight lines with crooked sticks. All of life's mysteries, disappointments, successes, and failures fall under that purview. Romans 8:28 is famous for covering similar territory, but because it's so well-known, it's worth noting a few things this promise is *not*.

For starters, it's not a promise for all people, but just for those who love God, who understand what the Bible says about love—that God *is* love and those who love Him show it by obeying Him and turning their best in life to His service and glory.

Furthermore, it's not because you deserve it, but because He called you. You seldom love God well or enough, and yet He loves you, saving you, adopting you as His child, and making you part of His work on the earth.

Finally, it's not about some things, or most things, but *all* things. You can commit with confidence to whatever work He is doing—even if it's one by which you and others are allowed to suffer or fail—because God has given us the victory, and you can know "that your labor is not in vain in the Lord" (1 Corinthians 15:58 NKJV).

God, it's amazing to me to see the way You weave all the parts of our lives together to create a beautiful picture of Your love. Thank You! Amen.

NO MORE SORROW

The Lamb which is in the midst of the throne shall feed them, and shall lead them unto living fountains of waters: and God shall wipe away all tears from their eyes.
REVELATION 7:17 KJV

Sometimes life is so difficult that you don't know how you're going to make it another day. Financial pressures, health issues, and family problems can cause tremendous strain on you—physically, mentally, and spiritually. You cry out to God for relief, but He doesn't seem to answer, at least not immediately, nor in the way you wish. And so you cry bitter tears.

You wonder if God has abandoned you. You ask yourself if He even cares about your pain. Yes, He does. The Bible tells you, "In all their affliction he was afflicted" (Isaiah 63:9 KJV). Your God was there feeling your pain every time you suffered. Jesus was "a man of sorrows, and acquainted with grief" (Isaiah 53:3 KJV). He knows every tear that you've cried (see Psalm 56:8).

One day Jesus will personally lead you into the transcendently beautiful gardens of heaven, with the fountains of the water of life cascading close by, and God, your Father, will hold you in His loving arms and wipe away all the tears from your eyes. Even now He seeks to comfort you in your sorrows.

God, I cry out for Your peace to come. Lead me in the way that leads to eternal life in You. Amen.

TAKING THE LONG VIEW

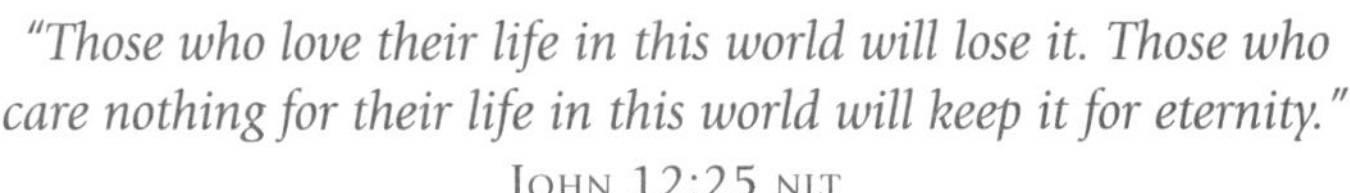

"Those who love their life in this world will lose it. Those who care nothing for their life in this world will keep it for eternity."
JOHN 12:25 NLT

Many people seek primarily to enjoy the things and the pleasures of this world. They want to live "the abundant life," to have a comfortable, affluent Christianity; and to enjoy continually the best this world has to offer. They're generally not that interested in sacrificing or suffering for the sake of the Gospel.

It's not a sin to be wealthy, but possessing riches does present constant challenges. Jesus warned, "Take heed and beware of covetousness, for one's life does not consist in the abundance of the things he possesses" (Luke 12:15 NKJV). He also stated that "the deceitfulness of riches, and the desires for other things entering in choke the word" (Mark 4:19 NKJV).

On the other hand, if you live modestly and are willing to share with those in need, you avoid many temptations and snares. Your *true* rewards are in heaven, not on the earth. You have to take the long view, the eternal view, to have this mind-set. You must know that you won't receive all your compensations in this life, but trust God to reward you in the next life.

Lord, I realize I need to lose my hold on short-term wants to gain eternal life in You. Help me to see how to do this in my everyday decisions. Amen.

THE CITY OF LIGHT

There will no longer be any night; and they will not have need of the light of a lamp nor the light of the sun, because the Lord God will illumine them.
Revelation 22:5 NASB

This passage says "they will not have need of the. . .light of the sun," so some Christians conclude that when God creates the new heavens and the new earth there will no longer be a sun. With no star to orbit, Earth will wander aimlessly through space. But that's missing what the verse is saying.

There will still be a sun, and its light will continue to shine on the earth, but those who live in God's magnificent city won't *need* its light. God Himself will dwell in the heart of the new Jerusalem and fill it with intense glory. But the regions at the far side of this planet will still need sunlight.

John noted that "the city was pure gold, like clear glass" (Revelation 21:18 NASB). The nature of this material will allow God's light to glow throughout the entire city unimpeded. God's glory will fill every nook and cranny of the new Jerusalem, including the saints who dwell there.

God, I love the way light fills my world on a bright, warm, sunny day. I can only imagine how much better, warmer, and brighter Your light will be! Amen.

Day 4

ETERNAL LIFE IN JESUS

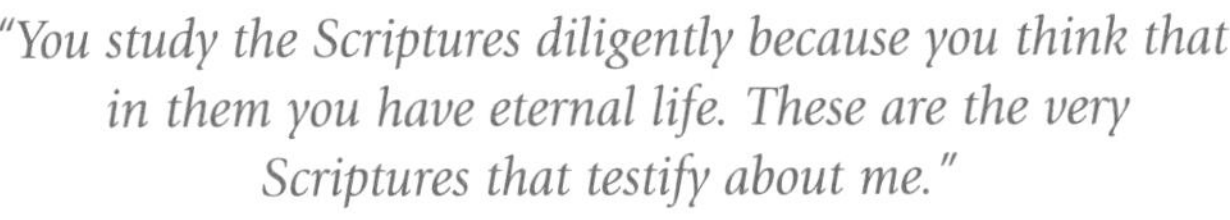

"You study the Scriptures diligently because you think that in them you have eternal life. These are the very Scriptures that testify about me."
JOHN 5:39 NIV

The Jews in Jesus' day read, studied, discussed, and memorized the Hebrew scriptures from childhood, seeking to encounter everlasting life. But frequently, despite their in-depth studies, they were still left wondering, "What good thing shall I do, that I may have eternal life?" (Matthew 19:16 KJV).

When Jesus told some Jews to work "for the food which endures to eternal life" (John 6:27 NASB), they asked, "What shall we do, so that we may work the works of God?" Jesus answered, "This is the work of God, that you believe in Him whom He has sent" (vv. 28–29 NASB). Jesus was plainly declaring that the only "work" necessary to acquire endless life was to put their faith in Him.

From the mention of the Prophet whom the people were required to hear and obey (see Deuteronomy 18:15–19), to the Suffering Servant who would take on the sins of humankind (Isaiah 53:4–8), to the resurrected Son of God (Psalm 16:8–11), the scriptures gave witness to the coming Savior.

Jesus is the only way God has provided for people to encounter eternal life. Have you received the Spirit of Jesus into your heart?

Lord, every time I look in Your Word,
let me meet You there. Amen.

Day 5

A NEW, ETERNAL EARTH

But in keeping with his promise we are looking forward to a new heaven and a new earth, where righteousness dwells.
2 Peter 3:13 NIV

God promised in 600 BC, "Behold, I create new heavens and a new earth; and the former things will not be remembered" (Isaiah 65:17 NASB).

Right now your mortal body only lives about eighty years, but during the Rapture when it's transformed, it will become indestructible and immortal. This physical planet is now temporal as well, but it will go through a transformation also. One day, "the heavens shall pass away with a great noise, and the elements shall melt with fervent heat, the earth. . .shall be burned up" (2 Peter 3:10 KJV).

John declared, "Then I saw a new heaven and a new earth; for the first heaven and the first earth passed away" (Revelation 21:1 NASB). The original earth was dissolved (2 Peter 3:11–12), but God promised "the new heavens and the new earth which I make will endure before Me" (Isaiah 66:22 NASB). They will literally last for all eternity.

Earth will become a global paradise, full of wonderful exotic flora and fauna, lovelier than the Garden of Eden. But best of all, from its iron core to its basaltic crust, it will be transformed into eternal materials.

Lord, I look forward to the day when the world will be made new, and I will be made new with it. New heart, new mind, new body, new life! Amen.

Day 6

WITH THE LAMB FOREVER

Therefore are they before the throne of God, and serve him day and night in his temple: and he that sitteth on the throne shall dwell among them.

REVELATION 7:15 KJV

One day you'll be personally with Jesus and spend the rest of eternity in His presence. You'll no longer need to try to imagine what God is like, because you'll gaze on Him with your own eyes and have direct access to His throne. And you'll see His Son, Jesus, sitting at His right hand.

You'll spend a great deal of time in His heavenly temple—in His presence, in the area immediately surrounding His throne. "One thing I ask from the LORD. . .to gaze on the beauty of the LORD and to seek him in his temple" (Psalm 27:4 NIV).

And God who sits on the throne will live with you. Think of it! God Himself will hold you and comfort you.

Even now, before that day, you have a High Priest—Jesus Christ—who can sympathize with your sins, shortcomings, and weaknesses, because He was tempted on the earth just as you are. "Let us therefore come boldly to the throne of grace, that we may obtain mercy and find grace to help in time of need" (Hebrews 4:16 NKJV).

My King, my God, my Savior—I come to Your throne, confident that I will find a friend. I cannot wait until the day You live right with me. Amen.

Day 7

ABIDING ETERNALLY

And the world is passing away, and the lust of it;
but he who does the will of God abides forever.
1 John 2:17 NKJV

This decrepit world with all its flagrant lust and anti-God agendas seems to be in its heyday, going strong and glorying in its pride and exaltation, but if you know the signs to look for, you can see that it's even now cracking at the seams and teetering off the rails into the deep ditches to join the wreckage of other doomed ideologies and failed philosophies.

The Lord is constantly "casting down. . .every high thing that exalteth itself against the knowledge of God" (2 Corinthians 10:5 KJV), and one day He will bring man's entire corrupt world system to its knees. Then "the meek shall inherit the earth; and shall delight themselves in the abundance of peace" (Psalm 37:11 KJV).

Yes, in that day the righteous shall truly enjoy peace! They'll no longer be a despised minority, persecuted by the immoral majority.

It can be very difficult at times to remain faithful to God's Word when most of the world is aggressively fighting to go in the opposite direction, but take cheer! You'll still be around in the everlasting Kingdom of Christ, utterly unopposed, when the wicked have fallen and are no more.

Jesus, my Lord, I rejoice in the knowledge that the day is coming when love and life will reign, and everything destructive will fall away. Amen.

Contributors

Quentin Guy writes from the high desert of New Mexico, to encourage and equip people to know and serve God. He currently works in publishing for Calvary Albuquerque and has cowritten such books as *Weird and Gross Bible Stuff* and *The 2:52 Boys Bible*, both of which are stuck in future classic status. A former middle school teacher, he serves with his wife as marriage prep mentors and trusts God that his children will survive their teenage years. Quentin's devotions appear in weeks 4, 13, 22, 26, 29, 35, 39, and 51.

Glenn A. Hascall is an accomplished writer with credits in more than a hundred books. He is a broadcast veteran and voice actor and is actively involved in writing and producing audio drama. Glenn's devotions appear in weeks 3, 7, 12, 19, 24, 30, 37, and 47.

Kelly McIntosh is a wife, mother of twins, and editor from Ohio. She loves books, the beach, and everything about autumn (but mostly pumpkin spice lattes). Kelly's devotions appear in weeks 6, 11, 32, and 41.

JoAnne Simmons is a writer and editor who's in awe of God's love and the ways He guides and provides. Her favorite things include coffee shops, libraries, the Bible, good grammar, being a wife and mom, dogs, music, Disney World, punctuation, church, the beach, and many dear family and friends—but not in that order. If her family weren't so loving and flexible, she'd be in big trouble; and if God's mercies weren't new every morning, she'd never get out of bed. JoAnne's devotions appear in weeks 8, 14, 18, 23, 31, 40, 48, and 50.

Ed Strauss was a freelance writer living in British Columbia, Canada, who passed into heaven in 2018. He authored or coauthored more than fifty books for children, tweens, and adults. Ed had a passion for biblical apologetics and besides writing for Barbour, was published by Zondervan, Tyndale, Moody, and Focus on the Family. Ed has three children: Sharon, Daniel, and Michelle Strauss. Ed's devotions appear in weeks 1, 9, 15, 21, 25, 28, 33, 38, 42, 44, 49, and 52.

Janice Thompson, who lives in the Houston area, writes novels, nonfiction, magazine articles, and musical comedies for the stage. The mother of four married daughters, she is quickly adding grandchildren to the family mix. Janice's devotions appear in weeks 16, 20, 36, and 45.

Lee Warren is published in such varied venues as *Discipleship Journal, Sports Spectrum*, Yahoo! Sports, Crosswalk.com, and ChristianityToday.com. He is also the author of the book *Finishing Well: Living with the End in Mind (A Devotional)*, and he writes regular features for *The Pathway* newspaper and *Living Light News*. Lee makes his home in Omaha, Nebraska. Lee's devotions appear in weeks, 2, 5, 10, 17, 27, 34, 43, and 46.

Scripture Index

Old Testament

Proverbs

New Testament

MORE EDITIONS OF *THE BIBLE PROMISE BOOK*—JUST FOR WOMEN!

Everyday Bible Promises for Women

Here's more scriptural encouragement, featuring Bible promises for every day of the year. Covering topics like Wisdom, Faith, Prayer, Encouragement, Love, Joy, and more—each scripture, devotional thought, and prayer speak directly to the heart, drawing you ever closer to the heavenly Father.

DiCarta / 978-1-63409-531-0 / $14.99

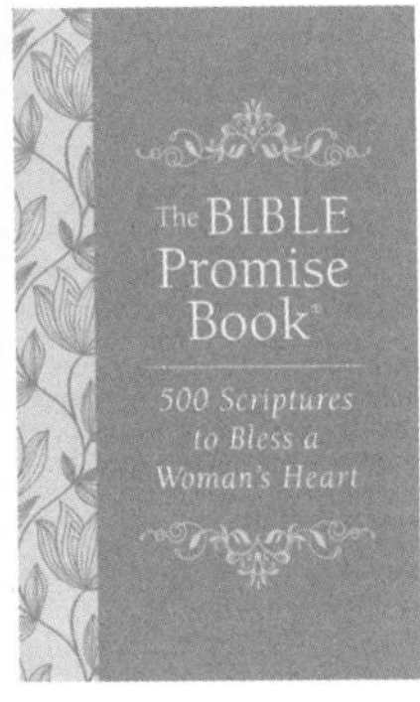

The Bible Promise Book: 500 Scriptures to Bless a Woman's Heart

Barbour's *Bible Promise Books* are perennial bestsellers, with millions of copies in print. This *Bible Promise Book* is available in a lovely paperback edition featuring 500 scripture selections plus encouraging prayer starters to bless your heart. With 50 topics that matter most to you—including Comfort, Love, Faith, Worry, Worship, Courage, Joy, and Contentment—you can quickly and easily locate a topic that will speak to your needs.

Paperback / 978-1-68322-729-8 / $5.99

Find These and More from Barbour Books at Your Favorite Bookstore
www.barbourbooks.com